DOUGLAS GILL was born in 1941. After studying philosophy, politics and economics at Oxford, he did research on military and diplomatic history at the universities of Ohio State and Warsaw. In 1969, he became editor of *The Black Dwarf*. A year later, he co-founded and published *L'Idiot International* in Paris. In the 1970s he worked as a businessman in London, where he now lives with his two daughters. He has been a contributor to the *New Statesman*, *New Society*, *New Left Review* and *Past and Present*.

GLODEN DALLAS read history at Lady Margaret Hall, Oxford. After university her interests turned from eighteenth century Whig politics to the socialist and feminist movements of the early twentieth century. She pioneered the study of women's history in the North of England, having moved from London to West Yorkshire in the 1970s. Herself a mother of three children, she wrote the introduction to the Virago edition of Margaret Llewelyn Davies's *Maternity Letters from Working Women*. She died in 1983, aged 40.

Douglas Gill and
Gloden Dallas

Verso

The Unknown Army

British Library
Cataloguing in Publication Data

Dallas, Gloden
   The unknown army.
   1. Great Britain. *Army* — Military life
   2. World War, 1914–1918 — Great Britain
   I. Title   II. Gill, Douglas
   306'.27'0941   U767

First published 1985
© Douglas Gill

Verso
15 Greek Street, London W1

Filmset in Sabon by
PRG Graphics, Redhill, Surrey

Printed in Great Britain by
The Thetford Press, Thetford, Norfolk

ISBN 0 86091 106 3
    0 86091 814 9 pbk

Contents

Acknowledgement 7
Introduction 9
1. Of Soldiering They Learn Little 13
2. A Unique Family 22
3. The Real Business of War 26
4. The Manufacturing Hands 35
5. Not Irishmen But English Soldiers 46
6. Unrest and Discontent 63
7. Shootings Out of Hand 77
8. This Irregular Method 89
9. It's Us That's Going to Talk to You 100
10. The Power to Enforce Their Will 113
11. A Dangerous and Growing Unrest 122
12. Agitators and Discontented Men 134
Notes 141
Index 168

Acknowledgement

The letters cited in the present work, unless indication is given to the contrary, were addressed to one or other of the authors: the majority in response to notices placed in the British and the Irish press. For the liberality of the editors concerned and the kindness of those who made reply, the authors must express their thanks.

Chapter six is a revised version of our article 'Mutiny at Etaples Base in 1917', which first appeared in *Past and Present: A Journal of Historical Studies*, in November 1975 (Copyright: The Past and Present Society, Oxford).

Acknowledgement is due, in addition, to the Controller, Her Majesty's Stationery Office, for permission to reproduce Crown copyright material in the Public Record Office.

Introduction

In the year 1813 when a British army faced the soldiers of a revolution, the resources of a continent, and the strategems of an acknowledged prince of war, 194 of its regimental officers were dignified by courtesy or hereditary title. Whether titled or untitled, its officers were drawn in vast majority from among the 'sons and grandsons of the lesser or greater landed gentry', and had earned commissions by buying them outright.[1] Eighty-six years later, at the time of the South African rebellion, 195 of the British army's regimental officers were dignified by title;[2] and, though the system of purchasing commissions had long been swept away, to be replaced by one of simple competition, the workings of the new system had done nothing to encourage candidates who were socially unfit. The officers entering the service under open competition 'are of the same stamp as those who entered before it came into force. The same classes furnish them . . . '[3]

The corps of officers was not alone in social isolation. During the Napoleonic Wars it was to the rural population that the British army looked for its recruits, and the dependence on the countryside in replenishing the rank and file continued until well into the nineteenth century. Despite the growth of industry and the urban working class, the attentions of recruiters remained centred on 'respectable, docile country lads';[4] even in mid-century, the proportion of recruits from rural areas was practically two-thirds.[5] And though the decline of agriculture as the century drew on compelled the army to look towards the towns, the Queen's shilling attracted only destitute and unemployable young men. In 1899 less than 15 per cent of the men undergoing the army's medical inspection, prior to attestation, were drawn from the kingdom's 'manufacturing artisans', the overwhelming majority being classed as from rural, menial and casual occupations.[6]

A gulf existed between the army and the decent working class. To the skilled and the unskilled in regular employment, the remuneration offered by the army could not match what they might earn otherwise themselves; and even in bad times when work was scarce and hardship often to be found, the prospects of service in the army could rarely overcome the antipathies which were everywhere expressed. As Sir John Fortescue confessed, there were respectable families of wage-earners which wept and thought it a disgrace if one of their's 'went for a soldier'.[7] Equally, the army preferred the country lads for service in its ranks. It adjudged them more robust than the casual labourers recruited in the towns,[8] and more likely to accept the 'long contracts of engagement, and submission to discipline' which army life entailed.[9]

In August 1914 the isolation of the Old Army was effectively destroyed. The German march through Belgium brought Great Britain into war — a war absorbing more divisions than the army could provide. The need for soldiers, the recruiting, not of thousands, but eventually, of millions, brought face to face two quite separate institutions: the army and the working class. Among the territorial forces embodied at the outset, among those who volunteered, and among the conscripts later gathered in, men were to be found whose outlook was far removed from that of the youths and casual workmen who had made the soldier's life their own. For some, older years had left them less malleable of view. For others, experience in industry, in trade unions perhaps, had left them unsympathetic or indifferent to the Old Army and its ways — to its 'traditions of duty and long-suffering', to its system which set the regimental honour above all else.[10]

This book describes certain incidents involving some of the new soldiers. It concerns not the thousands, even millions, who saw loyal service throughout their passage through the ranks, but that fraction — a dozen here, a hundred there, and ultimately many, many thousands — who, at one time or another, laid some challenge to authority, upsetting the traditions on which the Old Army was built. It describes events in France, the Near and Middle East, and in the English depots during World War One — a multiplicity of riots, strikes and other conflagrations.

These incidents have not been properly recorded. Historians, whether military or social, have from time to time addressed them; but the very notion of 'mutiny' has encouraged bold strokes of the pen. Based on memories and hearsay, often without benefit of archival research, accounts of mutinies have been vivid or didactic, rich in clashes between officers and men. Of course, a mutiny is drama, where rebels hold the stage, but too great an emphasis on drama has led to the neglect of elements common to both mutinies and other forms of social and industrial unrest. Equally, the emphasis on conflict, the clash between officers and men, has made for too simplistic a picture of quite complex events.

And thus the burden of this book. The forgotten details from the archives, supported by the recollections of those present at the time, provide more than day-by-day description of what happened when the various mutinies took place. They throw light on the inner workings of the army: on the relationship, that is, between officers and men, between the men of one unit and those drawn from another, between officers at a lower level and those at GHQ. They outline the impact of an influx of labourers and artificers, of colliers and clerks, on the Old Army, on its traditions and its ways. They illuminate the policies of Haig and Allenby, of the governments of Asquith and Lloyd George. Finally, they furnish a small chapter in the history of the army, and in the story of a fateful era for this country's working men.

1
Of Soldiering They Learn Little

Between the close of the Napoleonic Wars and the opening of those fought to contain the power of the Germans, the social background of British army officers remained essentially unchanged. Despite the growth of industry, the decline of gentility and land, despite military disasters and the depredations of reform, the officers continued to be drawn from the gently born and those of good family connection. Their corps was undiluted by men of humbler birth, by those whose families had prospered through industry and trade.

The corps remained socially exclusive, in particular, despite the reform of the army in 1871. This reform, introduced by Edward Cardwell, Gladstone's Secretary of State for War, comprised one element in the programme adopted by the Liberal ministry of 1868. Entry to and advancement in the country's leading institutions would be regulated by questions of competence alone. The standards of the advancing middle classes were stamped upon the universities, the Foreign Office and the church, and the prerogatives of landowners correspondingly reduced. In the army, the government introduced some change, but its reforms were either unrelated to the social basis of the officer corps or, if so related, failed to take significant effect.

The abolition of the purchase system formed one measure which Cardwell introduced. Under that system, commissioned ranks in the infantry and cavalry had been freely bought and sold. Entry by purchase, which had been so widespread in its application that nearly 80 per cent of the four thousand first appointments between 1860 and 1867 were thus obtained, was limited to those with wealth, social connections and influence with the commanding officer of the regiment concerned. Of the other means of entry, those from the militia and the universities were just as socially exclusive.[1] The purchase system applied, of course, to more than first appointments. When a vacancy occurred in the higher ranks of a regiment, through the retirement of an officer by sale of his commission, every officer had a claim according to his seniority to purchase the next rank in the regiment; always providing that no objection were lodged against him by the commanding officer or the

Commander-in-Chief. If no qualified officer in the regiment applied to buy the promotion, an officer was brought in from another regiment or from the half-pay list.

The arguments against the purchase system need no rehearsing here. Gladstone's government saw its abolition as a necessary step in improving the quality of officers, in restoring merit to the place which wealth and social influence usurped. Of greater interest were the arguments adduced in its defence: for these, rather than any Prussian notions of efficiency, more nearly express the social and political realities which the British officer embraced. In the first place, it was said, the landed aristocracy and gentry had for centuries been invested with a range of military duties. They were expected to officer, at times to actually provide bodies of soldiers when called upon to do so. Naturally, such an army had to be commanded by men 'of high social position, holding large possessions'; the Civil War, according to this view, having shown the danger of giving propertyless adventurers the power to command.[2] Purchase was the safeguard. It procured, in the words of the Duke of Wellington, officers 'of fortune and education; men who have some connexion with the interests and fortunes of the Country'.[3] And more than political stability was thought to be at stake. Purchase procured the gentlemen whom good discipline required.

> No one is quicker than Tommy Atkins at spotting the 'gentleman'; it may sound snobbish, I daresay it is snobbish to say so, but the fact remains that men will follow a 'gentleman' much more readily than they will an officer whose social position is not so well assured.
> That this is the case no one who knows our soldiers will dispute for a moment . . .[4]

Purchase had survived all major efforts to reduce it, it had survived both the reform of the Civil Service and the blunders of Crimea; and so strongly entrenched was its support that it might have survived the death of Gladstone had it not been abolished through a royal warrant, by-passing parliament itself.[5]

The purchase system was abolished, then, in 1871. Between that year and the outbreak of world war, two avenues were presented to candidates seeking a commission in the infantry or cavalry. They might pass either through the Royal Military College at Sandhurst or by way of the commissioned ranks of the militia.[6] Entry to Sandhurst came via an examination whose setting and marking were independently assessed.[7] Two years at the college were followed by gazetting as an officer. If entrance via the militia were preferred, a method, incidentally, yet more socially exclusive in its operation, the actual period of training was very short, a regiment of militia only drilling for twenty-seven days each year. Even then, gazetting only came after examinations had been successfully completed.

Did the reform have that harmful effect upon the quality of officers which the defenders of the purchase system had foreseen? Writing in 1889, nearly twenty years after the new measures had been introduced, Lt-Gen. Sir William Bellairs was able to reassure those who had originally opposed the change. He wrote of the methods of entry by examination and declared: 'The officers who have come into the service under that system are of the same stamp as those who entered before it came into force. The same classes furnish them . . . '[8] This verdict he reinforced with the following 'classification of the parentage of gentlemen cadets studying at the great military schools':

	Sandhurst
Peers	1
Baronets	3
Members of Parliament	1
Officers of the Army	138
Officers of the Navy	9
Clergymen	23
Judges, Barristers and Solicitors	15
Medical Profession	9
Civil Service	—
Indian Civil Service,	11
Private Gentlemen, Merchants, etc.[9]	95

Again, thirty years after the decline of purchase, Sir John Fortescue assessed the number of regimental officers (excluding Colonels-in-Chief) bearing hereditary or courtesy titles as being not greatly different to that obtaining in the year 1850, and as being practically the same as it had been in 1813; at which date, as Fortescue explains, Wellington's army was officered by the sons and grandsons of the gentry, 'descended in many cases immediately from younger sons of various professions, but deriving at the distance of a generation or two from the old stock'.[10] Or, as another historian describes it, taking in the century in a sweep: 'Between 1830 and 1912 the landed gentry achieved a remarkable stability in supplying recruits to the army'.[11]

During the decades which followed the decline of purchase and the opening of Sandhurst to simple competition, the middle classes found small representation in the college or, of course, in the army as a whole. What bars to entry, then, served to keep their sons and grandsons from obtaining a commission? In the first place, whatever the examinations, all but the least important regiments required a degree of influence and recommendation if a young man was to get in. In the second place, a position in the army was expensive to maintain. In the early 1900s, a young officer would have found it out of the question to support himself on his pay of £95 a year, rising at the end of two or three years — when the rank of lieutenant was gained — to £125. In the average regiment of the line, he might have kept out of debt on an allowance of £60 a year, while an extra £200 a year would permit of no extravagance and provide no access to the sports and customs of his fellows.[12] In the cavalry his needs were even greater. 'Officers have lived in the 10th [Hussars] with an allowance of only £500 a year in addition to their pay, but they have rarely lasted long, and the average income of the officers is very much higher.'[13] The undesirable young men who had nothing to recommend them but the riches which their parents had passed on, might be safely left, one authority reported, 'to the tender mercies of their brother officers'; ragging, ostracism, and mock court-martials were indulged in, in some cases the offender being driven from the army.[14]

On his appointment to a regiment, education ended and soldiering began. The qualifications required of an officer were those which any gentleman might have: the habit of wearing decently cut clothes, an ability to speak without dropping his 'h's', an acquaintance with the outward manners of good society, and the skill to handle a knife and fork without exciting the disgust or reprobation of his mess-mates.[15] His expertise was small. A comprehensive knowledge of army buttons, facings, shoulder-straps and badges was one way to success, and for actual duties a familiarity with the drill book was likely to prove useful. An education in military subjects was so far beneath his dignity that it was looked down on with distaste.[16] What kind of officer emerged? In 1900 a contemporary drew up a picture of his colleagues:

> The officer gathers a certain amount of experience of men and things; he learns a lot about sport; he becomes an authority on wine and tobacco; he becomes, in fact, one of the pleasantest of boon companions, one of the staunchest of 'pals', but of *soldiering*, apart from the mere routine of barrack life, he learns little or nothing . . . active service is regarded rather as a new and most exciting kind of sport, a feeling which has been heightened by our numerous campaigns against savages . . . [17]

The reformers had broken the stranglehold of purchase, but lacked the power to install something more efficient in its place. Before 1871 wealth and family connection had regulated both entry to the army and advancement from one rank to the next; after that year, though wealth was ostensibly removed and examinations added to the criteria for entry, there was no question but that both influence and private means remained essential to an officer's career. Essential, perhaps, but no longer so crudely governing the system such that the means of moving from lieutenant to captain, or from major to lieutenant-colonel, were spelled out loud and clear. The system of professional advancement was no longer directly regulated by wealth, but nor was it ruled by ability and skill. Plodding advancement by seniority, or promotion without any guarantee of fitness, now governed promotions for junior and field officers; beyond the rank of colonel, high social connections continued to suffice.[18] The aristocracy retained its relative monopoly of the army's leading ranks.[19] The stalemate was clear. Cardwell and the Liberals had lacked the power, and indeed the wish, to tamper with the position of the army officer in society at large. With his continued hold on selection and promotion, his influence on government, and his support in the Commons and the Lords, the officer's position could not easily be disturbed.

One further aspect of the army has now to be described. It concerns the social origins of those who, more numerous if not always very vocal, comprised the army's 'other ranks'. Their backgrounds were as follows:[20]

Occupation (per 1,000)	1896	1897	1898	1899	1900
Labourers, servants, husbandmen, &c.	662	640	657	649	616
Manufacturing artisans (as clothworkers, weavers, lacemakers &c.)	120	148	139	141	142
Mechanics employed in occupations favourable to physical development (as smiths, carpenters, masons, &c.)	104	102	92	103	133
Shopmen and clerks	73	73	72	68	70
Professional occupations, students, &c.	11	10	9	9	10
Boys under 17 years of age	30	27	31	30	29
	1000	1000	1000	1000	1000

Whence came the 'labourers, servants, husbandmen, &c.' who formed so large a category — practically two-thirds — of those the army chose? In 1856 the average recruit came from a small town or farming community; a third or more were Irish.[21] He was in his twenties, physically mature, and likely to be of better health and stature than his contemporaries at home. In the years thereafter, the decline of agriculture and the numbers on the land served to close off this flow of volunteers.[22] By 1899 a majority of new soldiers were coming from the cities of Great Britain. They were young, physically immature, and often lacking trade or occupation.[23] The social origins of these urban youths are clear. Beneath the artisans and the labour aristocracy, and distinct from unskilled labourers in fairly regular employment, lay a stratum of the population confined to casual labouring or to frequent unemployment. Navvies, spademen, and unskilled workers on the docks might earn good wages in arduous and irregular employment; but for men who lacked the taste or physique for such work, casual labouring might provide their sole resort. Below them, the least fortunate of all the city-dwellers, came those without employment or remuneration of any real kind. It was among the casuals and the unemployed that volunteers were always to be found.

During the last half of the century the emphasis in recruiting shifted sharply to the young. Only a certain proportion of a regiment might legally be formed from 'boys' aged less than seventeen, but above that age there were no restrictions on recruitment, and the age groups finding most common representation were those of eighteen and nineteen: between them they furnished more than half of the recruits.[24] And the official figures may over-estimate the average age pertaining in the ranks for, in practice, evidence of age was not required and many a well-built youth of sixteen or seventeen successfully pretended to less tender years.[25] This recruiting of young men was neither efficient nor humane. A large proportion of the losses from death and invaliding occuring during the first years of a soldier's service was due to the 'extreme youth of the men who join, who cannot stand the labour and fatigue to which they are subjected'.[26] But the army was always short of sturdy volunteers and the young, in turn, looked on the army as a refuge from their trials.[27] One consequence of such flexible enlistment was that, at the turn of the century, of every five men offering themselves for service in the army, only two remained as effective soldiers at the end of two years' service.[28] The infantry regiments were particularly deficient. Needing the greatest numbers, they took the lowest physical categories and accepted the largest proportion of substandard men. Even then, they failed to fill their ranks.

Reasons both cultural and economic had divorced the army from the urban working class. To the skilled, and the unskilled in regular employment, the remuneration offered by the army could not match what they might earn otherwise themselves; but even in bad times, when work was scarce and hardship often to be found, the prospects of service in the ranks could scarcely overcome the antipathy felt towards the army by working people in the towns. Thus, in the hardest decade of the century, when the refuge offered by the army would surely have held some attraction for the decent working class, a volunteer thought it 'only natural' to find himself recruited together with 'the very offscourings' of the cities, amongst 'rogues and scoundrels', men 'with vice and ruffianism stamped indelibly on their faces'.[29] And more directly relevant to the period in question, the trade depression of 1892, the strikes in the Durham coalfields and the upheavals in the Lancashire cotton trade, brought in no immediate influx of urban volunteers.[30]

The antipathy between the urban worker and the army was mutual in its nature. The army considered the health of city-dwellers to be generally quite poor, and their natures unsuited to military service.[31] A committee investigating the perennial shortage of recruits ascribed part of the deficiency to prejudice alone: 'The prejudice against the Army prevailing in certain districts in the country, and in certain classes of society, where the conditions of service in the Army are not understood . . . '[32] But the Inspector-General of Recruiting in an earlier, more honest age had admitted not only that he could see no obvious improvement in the class of those enlisting, but that it would indeed be undesirable to enlist men who 'would not be content with the rewards and prospects of a soldier's position'.[33]

Passing from the composition of the army to the question of conditions for the ranks, we notice one outstanding feature. Life in the domestic barracks of the 1890s was geared, not to impending battles with the Germans, but to the preservation of military tradition. Drilling and guard duty, as an official pamphlet put it, were the two duties 'by far the most important that the private soldier has to do';[34] and their importance, unassailable in the days of Marlborough and Wellington, had not yet been challenged or cast down. In those earlier days, an army moved by advancing in long column, and fought in thin, extended line. The chief manoeuvre which the private soldier had to do was to get from a formation in which his firearm could be used, to one in which he might march from place to place. Thus the significance of drill: for drill alone prepared him for the move from line to column, and from column into line. By 1900, of course, the utility of a narrow line of red-coats, in wars against the Germans, was open to some doubt. But the drill remained and with it, the precept upon which good order in the British army continued to be based: 'The one duty of the soldier was to obey, and as long as he was acting in line or column he could hardly obey too mechanically, with too little thought.'[35]

The emphasis on guard duties can be no less simply explained. In the early nineteenth century army, recruited from among rural unfortunates and 'the very offscourings' of the towns, a strong guard around each barrack formed an obvious precaution. Ingress, egress, the custody of those in breach of regulations: guard duties were designed to supervise all these. By 1900, though, this earlier requirement had largely passed away. In its place a new necessity arose: for it was on the standard of the guards which each battalion now maintained, on their dress, their turn-out, their alertness to etiquette's fine points, that its reputation rested. The sentries at the gate represented the battalion to the world, and, in turn, it was on their show and their appearance that the battalion lavished energy and time.[36]

Between the officer and ranker there stood a gulf which had no bridge. Their contact in the barracks was naturally constrained: the captain gave the orders and the company obeyed. Outside the line of duty, relations were just as carefully defined.

> As everyone knows, with us both officers and men take part together in all kinds of sports and manly games, such as cricket, football, rowing, boat-sailing, etc., meeting in the most friendly manner in the world without any ill-effect on discipline . . . But though intimacy of this sort is rather encouraged than otherwise, and officers are expected to lead their men in their games, yet any further intimacy would be regarded as a very serious offence indeed. Officers and men will play together in a cricket match all day, but when the match is over, no officer would dream of walking up to barracks with one of his cricket playmates of a few minutes before. Indeed, did he do so, I fancy very serious notice would be taken of such a breach of discipline.[37]

The career of the private soldier before the First World War was marked not only by its obvious discomforts, its narrow prospects and rewards, but also by the confines, physical and mental, within which his activities took place. The days were passed in a variety of duties, 'of which not one tenth forms any useful training for war'.[38] These duties were not military but social, not presuming war but predicating peace. They reflected a military order in which the regimental honour, the proper discipline, and the correct relationship between officers and men, were preserved above all things; part and parcel of a social order, far from industry and trade, linking the sons of cottagers and the sons of baronets and squires.

2
A Unique Family

At the beginning of the twentieth century, the basic unit in the British army was that of the battalion. The battalion consisted of perhaps eight hundred men, arranged in companies and placed under a lieutenant-colonel. It was recruited, typically, from one small area within the British Isles. Each battalion, through its geographical location as well as through its history and campaigns, carried its own customs and traditions; and these traditions continued to hold strong even after the Old Army regiments — battalions in all but name — had been joined together, two battalions to a depot, in the reform of the regimental system in 1881. The battalion perfectly expressed the connection with the land and with certain social classes. Thus,

> The main strength of our military system has always lain in the fact that regimental roots were planted deep into the British countryside.... This ... built up a unique County and family *esprit de corps* which exists in no other Army in the world.[1]

Equally, the size and cheapness of the battalion system suited England's military requirements. In the late nineteenth century, these requirements centred on manning posts along frontiers in Africa and Asia, on garrisoning provinces of Empire threatened by occasional unrest.

In contrast, the organization of the French and German armies revolved on the division. This unit, introduced to warfare by France's revolution, was designed less to garrison large empires than to serve in wars between great powers. The division brought together artillery, engineers, transport and similar detachments, and joined them to a group of infantry battalions; at full strength it was ready to join numberless similar divisions in a drive across the Rhine. Each division was designed to be a fraction of an army, a fraction 'capable of independent movement on any kind of ground'.[2] Of course, neither France nor Germany kept armies ready at full strength. The division, much more than the battalion, consumed money and supplies. So the continental armies were constructed for the most part like skeletons whose muscles, flesh, and vital organs could, according to circumstance, be rapidly attached. And the system of conscription meant that the French and German populations contained millions of young men who, having done their time as soldiers, were still liable for further service should emergencies arise. The general staffs relied on these young men returning to their depots the moment they were called. The guns and uniforms were ready; the divisions had only to entrain.

The British army, on the other hand, was made up of volunteers. It was a body whole but miniature, designed for service in the Empire but not well suited to absorb thousands of new men. It had its own reserve: of soldiers recently discharged and of members of the part-time forces who had agreed to serve abroad. Once these were taken up, however, there were no further powers to compel male citizens to serve. Even if there had been, there were no half-empty units waiting to be filled. So when in 1899 Dutch settlers challenged British domination at the Cape, the expansion of the army was not easy to effect. A good number of battalions were already overseas while, of those in the home country, some were undergoing training and others were permanently stationed to guard against Irish and working-class unrest. The War Office lacked sufficient soldiers to send out to the Cape. More importantly, it lacked an army on the continental pattern, one that contained within itself the seeds of self-expansion. In such circumstances it could only raise more soldiers. The problem of expansion had to look after itself.

In the event, recruiting soldiers for South Africa caused problems which the War Office was ill placed to resolve. Patriots from the possessing classes, rather than youths and casual workmen, stepped forward to enlist; and these imposed their own conditions, rather than following some blueprint which the generals had laid down.[3] Units were formed in whatever ways the County families thought best. Ancient conditions of volunteering were resurrected. A committee of 'influential and patriotic gentlemen', acting like a private army, raised eight thousand mounted troops. Some volunteers equipped and organized themselves — the government providing transport to the front. Individuals raised units of their own. Lord Donoughmore, for instance, formed the Duke of Cambridge's Own, a troop of the gentle and the highly born who financed their own passages and gave their pay to charity.[4] By one means or another, sufficient soldiers were obtained. But these men were not only inadequately trained, they were simply shipped out to the Cape. There, added to already overloaded units, they formed conglomerations ineffective and ungainly: shadows, really, of those warlike and purposeful divisions which in an emergency the continental powers seemed able to deploy.

A Royal Commission of Inquiry examined the problems which the Boer War had raised. One recommendation in particular stood out: that the means of expanding the army should be worked on and improved. According to the commissioners, 'the true lesson of the war . . . is, that no military system will be satisfactory which does not contain powers of expansion outside the limit of the regular forces of the Crown, whatever that limit may be'.[5] In brief, the reserve and part-time forces had provided inadequate reinforcement to the British army at the Cape. The limitations on the supply of well-trained men, and the deficiencies in the organization of their units for the field, were the object of particular attention; for the government was turning increasingly to Europe, to the support of France and Russia in their clash with German power. If war broke out, the British government might wish to intervene.

> ' . . . this implied that we should have an Expeditionary Force sufficient in size and also in rapidity of mobilizing power to be able to go to the assistance of the French Army in the event of an attack on the Northern or North-Eastern parts of France.'[6]

The reform of the reserves, and the preparation of a force to vie with Germany's great army, were matters dealt with by R.B. Haldane, Secretary of State for War in the Liberal government which came to power in 1906. Haldane established the Special Reserve, designed to feed recruits into regular battalions, in place of the militia.[7] He replaced the Volunteers and Yeomanry,[8] bodies of amateurs who trained in evenings and weekends, with one auxiliary force alone, the Territorials; he based its structure on that of the division, and brought the new body under War Office control.[9] No less important, he arranged the regular battalions in groups throughout the kingdom. In the event of war, they could be brought together, twelve to a division; each division, at full strength, to contain some eighteen thousand officers and men.[10] Once these reforms had been completed, England and Germany would be able to cross swords. An expeditionary force, 'reckoned at six great divisions, fully equipped, and at least one cavalry division', would be at the British government's command.[11] It could mobilize and cross over into France as rapidly as its German counterpart might move.

By the close of 1909, the major part of Haldane's reforms had been put into effect. An expeditionary force had been created, and the various auxiliaries arrayed; and the formation of an Imperial General Staff to oversee policy was in the process of completion.[12] The way was open for effective intervention on the continent itself.

It was on 3 August 1914 that Haldane, acting for Mr Asquith, ordered the mobilization of the army to take place on the morrow. Immediately six divisions of regular troops were in full stride towards battle. Behind them the Special Reserve battalions were assembling the necessary drafts, and behind again stood fourteen divisions of the Territorial Force. Moreover, in those fourteen divisions every man had a rifle, every battery had its guns, and every division had its full complement of services.'[13]

3

The Real Business of War

In August 1914, when Great Britain went to war, her army mobilized much as Haldane had foreseen. An expeditionary force crossed over into France, leaving the British Isles to be defended by the Territorial reserve. Within days of the opening engagements, though, it became clear that new factors had entered into play. The task of helping France and clearing it of Germans was costing far more men, and demanding a far larger number of divisions than anything on which the British force could draw. In five days Sir John French, General Officer Commanding-in-Chief, lost fifteen thousand officers and men; the First Battle of Ypres, beginning in October, saw further losses amounting to more than twenty thousand.[1] Yet his strength in August, before battle had been joined, was only five divisions — less than one hundred thousand men. And even with a full seven divisions in action in the field, with the Special Reserve at home being drained to make up losses, the British Expeditionary Force (BEF) was still too weak to make real impact on the German military machine.

The government, pressed on by an enthusiastic public, looked for new forces to deploy. It looked, of course, to the wider reaches of the Empire and to the half-trained auxiliaries now guarding the UK. Garrisons throughout the Empire were hurriedly run down, and surplus units redirected to the front: these formed five divisions. After initial indecision, men in the Territorials were asked to extend the scope of their engagement to permit service overseas. Slowly, some of the Territorial divisions made ready for the fray. As they did so, the War Office decided to duplicate all the units in the Territorial reserve: to enlist, in the various localities, sufficient newcomers as would make up fourteen more divisions.[2] Beyond these steps, politics pushed forward where considerations of military efficiency shrank back. The wild excitement, the popular preoccupation with Germany were facts too powerful to ignore. The government decided to recruit as many men, almost, as were willing to enlist. By-passing the recruiting system which, for generations, had served the regular battalions, by-passing the County Associations around which the Territorials revolved, Lord Kitchener's appeal went out to the young men of the nation: he needed them for a New Army to do service overseas.[3] His appeal was successful. More than half a million volunteered during the first six weeks of war and still the flow continued:[4] men from the great cities of the kingdom and from its decent cottage homes, men breaking with tradition by leaving factory, pit and mill. By the last day of December 1914, taking the total of all forms of enlistment, well over a million men had been added to the military forces at home in the UK.[5]

As a result of this vast influx, the army soon extended from raw recruits parading in factory towns without rifles, uniforms, or even proper NCOs, to battalions of long-service soldiers manning trenches at the front. Their diversity was great: in terms both of their training and of the roots from which they sprang. The finest soldiers — that is, the most highly trained, the least diluted by reservists and young lads — were to be found in the overseas battalions as they returned to England from garrisons abroad. The average service in the ranks was at least four years, and these battalions, gathered twelve to a division, were sent into action as soon as they arrived.[6] In contrast, the civilian element was more apparent in the six divisions which had crossed to France in August. Each of these had needed, on mobilization, to be filled up by reservists: men who, having done some years with the colours, had passed back into society at large. A good proportion, perhaps 40 per cent, of the junior NCOs and men had been living as civilians when ordered to return.[7] One of Sir John French's lesser worries, before battle had been joined, concerned their readiness for duty: 'Many of the reservists at first bore traces of the civilian life which they had just left, and presented an anxious, tired appearance ... '[8] None of these soldiers, whether with the colours or back in the reserve, differed materially in background from the unfortunates taken in during earlier decades: young, physically immature, and often plucked from off the streets.[9] Still, the army altered men, and though its raw material was poor, it could take for granted the firm discipline, resistance to fatigue, and steadfast attitude to losses which, in time, its regime was able to instil. As for the reservists, returning to the army after months or years away, Sir John French trusted to 'the magnificent body of officers and non-commissioned officers' to make good their defects.[10]

The Territorial divisions contained a different class of men. In drill halls throughout the kingdom men had long gathered for military training during evenings and weekends.[11] The 1909 reforms had welded these auxiliaries into fourteen divisions and given them the responsibility, in the event of war, for defending the UK. Some joined the Territorials because they saw it as a duty; recent writings suggest that most of the adherents looked on their unit as a club.[12] In the cities, 'the mass of the rank and file was provided by the upper working class artisans and the clerks';[13] in no sense were these soldiers seeking refuge from the workhouse or the streets. And although Territorial units were attached to regular formations, their organization and recruitment lay in different hands. Their loyalties were moulded by the locality they came from and the parent regiments to which they were attached. Manchester, for instance, supported four Territorial infantry battalions, nominally the 5th, 6th, 7th and 8th battalions of the Manchester Regiment. Together, these units formed 'The Manchester Brigade'. Similarly, the 5th, 6th, 7th and 8th battalions of the King's Liverpool Regiment were Territorials and made up 'The Liverpool Brigade'.[14] In several of these 'city brigades', numbers of the officers and men were drawn from the same offices or works, officers sometimes being in charge of the departments in which their own Territorial soldiers were actually employed.[15] Territorials came from rural areas as well. In late 1914 regiments of yeomanry — Territorial cavalry — were beginning to reach France.

> I often rode amongst them, and was much impressed . . . . Although I now found that the old type of hunting farmer was not so fully represented in their ranks as formerly, yet a valuable leavening of this class still remained, and they were for the most part commanded and officered by county men of position and influence, accustomed to hunting, polo and field sports.[16]

But no simple picture of clerks drilling to their manager's commands, of landowners mustering their tenants in the shires, fits all fourteen Territorial divisions embodied at the outbreak of the war. Units of the Northumbrian Division, for example, differed greatly from the North Somerset Yeomanry or the Manchester Brigade. Recruited on Tyneside and the Tees, the division drew on miners from the Durham coalfields and shipbuilders from yards in the north-east. The miners 'produced an excellent type of recruit, hard, well-developed, and muscular';[17] although, as one officer describes them, 'not, perhaps, the easiest to lead'.[18]

The fourteen Territorial divisions were due for summer training when the war with Germany broke out. Immediately embodied, they prepared themselves for the defence of the UK. Doubts existed about their wholesale use abroad. The terms of their engagement precluded service overseas, but even when this had been surmounted — units volunteering 'almost to a man'[19] — regular officers questioned whether part-time soldiers could ever match the efficiency which British regulars displayed.[20] Sir John French's losses made such doubts seem academic. He pressed the government not to wait until the Territorial divisions were complete in all respects, but to send him reinforcements, a unit at a time, to fill out regular divisions. From September 1914 the Territorials reached France in battalions of infantry and regiments of horse; from November, they came out in whole divisions.

Still lower in the scale of military efficiency were the new-comers — the men who, in that intoxicated autumn, came flocking to enlist. For the most part they had had no training whatsoever for the war. In each area these men had a choice of destination. Some applied at regimental depots to join a regular battalion. Others enrolled in one or other of the fourteen duplicate or 'second-line' Territorial divisions. By far the greatest number, though, swelled the ranks of the new or 'Kitchener' divisions. By 12 September the first six divisions had been formed, the 9th to the 14th. These were quickly followed by twelve more, the 15th to the 26th — an aggregate of 350,000 officers and men. A fourth Army comprising six divisions followed, and finally a fifth.[21] The great majority of those enlisting joined as unknown individuals, all strangers to each other. They were formed into battalions, groups of a thousand men. Each battalion was broken down into four companies, each with its company commander — temporary officers immediately commissioned from the universities, public schools, etc. A month's trial for NCOs was in force in several units; in others, corporals and sergeants were elected by the men.[22] Without experience, without proper NCOs, without even uniforms or rifles, these men hoped to take on a German army equipped with machine-guns and artillery, trained and heavily dug in. Clearly, they could not be sent abroad without months of preparation. Most of them, indeed, remained in England in huts or under canvas for practically a year. Some reached France from mid-1915 onwards, although the last of the Kitchener divisions were not fully formed until later in that year. Many of the new divisions had their first real experience of fighting as late as 1 July 1916, the first day of the Somme.

From the moment war was entered, the efficiency of the British army entered a decline. Two factors were responsible for this. First, the rate of casualties, and second, a scale of volunteering which had brought into the army a whole new class of men. The fighting slowly stripped the army of its longest-serving soldiers. Sir John French's losses have already been remarked, and throughout 1915 they continued to mount up; the Kitchener divisions being still not fully ready, the regulars, aided by the territorials, carried the brunt of British efforts in France, the Near and Middle East. For a time the regulars replenished losses by drawing on reserves, but their supplies were soon exhausted. The territorials, in any case, had had no trained reserves at all. Amongst the regular battalions which had reached France in August 1914, barely one officer and thirty men remained by the turn of the New Year.[23] As wounded men recovered and new men were brought in from reserve, their numbers were restored; but the quality of the regulars had of course been 'watered down'.[24] By September 1915, even in regular battalions, ' . . . the presence of the comparatively few veterans was not enough to leaven the inexperience of the newcomers.'[25] Newcomers were now replenishing the losses amongst units of Territorials and regulars alike; these, and the conscripts who followed later, had had only 'perfunctory' battle training.[26] There were no more regulars to send. The staff at the base camp at Etaples, through whose hands passed all the reinforcements for the infantry in France, began allotting men to the various battalions whether regular, Territorial, or New Army, on a very simple basis. They made allotment, without any question of selection, whenever losses were incurred.[27] The outcome was quite plain: 'the old battalions were . . . hardly better trained than the new units'.[28]

What were the advantages and disadvantages, from a commander's point of view, of sending into battle great numbers of inexperienced young men? In the first place, their resilience could not match that which the pre-war regulars displayed. Sir John French inspected a Territorial battalion which, in its first brief action, had lost more than one-third of its officers and men.

> Whilst there was work to be done and an enemy to be held at bay, no other thought filled any of their minds than to die fighting, if necessary, to the last man. But when these Territorials returned for a term of well-earned rest to their cantonments, with the excitement and danger behind them, a severe reaction came upon them. The heavy losses amongst their friends and comrades bowed them down with grief; for they necessarily lacked as yet the professional training and stoicism of men whose real business is war.[29]

Their discipline, in short, had rested on courage and commitment rather than on inurement to losses and fatigue. And whilst this

battalion was among the first of the Territorial units to cross over
into France, and had been selected, therefore, as being in a higher
state of readiness than most, the hundreds of infantry units that
followed, whether Territorial or New Army, increasingly fell short
of the standards which the pre-war regulars had set. There were of
course exceptions. The 51st Division, a first-line Territorial unit
drawing soldiers from the Highlands, retained its qualities until the
last days of the war; so too did the 18th, a Kitchener division
drawing heavily on men enlisted from the prosperous Home
Counties.[30] At the other extreme, the 16th (Irish) and the 35th
(Bantam) divisions, both Kitchener formations, proved eventually
unfit for service in the line. They were withdrawn, their complexions
altered, and their ranks replenished with infusions of new men —
neither Irishmen nor Bantams. But there were real limits to what
such replenishment could do. In March 1918 an observer noted the
quality of soldier being sent up to the front.

> For two days companies of infantry have been passing us on the roads —
> companies of children, English children; pink faced, round cheeked
> children, flushed under the weight of their unaccustomed packs, with
> their steel helmets on the back of their heads and the strap hanging loosely
> on their rounded baby chins.[31]

By this stage of the war, GHQ could rely only on a handful of divisions
if, in any critical engagement, it was to be confident of achieving a
result.

> Among these were the Guards and a number of other British divisions,
> probably including — through their independent, stalwart outlook — all
> the Scottish ones; and every oversea division.[32]

A second disadvantage attached itself to soldiers who had so recently
joined up. They lacked real knowledge of the rudiments of war. For
months, many Kitchener battalions drilled without uniforms or
rifles, some of them receiving their equipment only weeks before
entering the line. They were short of experienced officers and NCOs.
For men recruited later, the position got much worse. In 1917,
'Many men came out quite untrained — sometimes only nine weeks
after enlistment.'[33] Accordingly, apart from submission to the
'system of suppression' upon which British discipline relied,[34] the
newcomers learned only simple skills. They knew how to dig and
man a trench, and how to clamber out of it to form the waves of an
attack. Outside of these parameters, the new soldiers were lost. In

1914 a series of complex battlefield manoeuvres, involving infantry, cavalry, and horsedrawn artillery, had safeguarded the BEF during the Great Retreat. But these were regulars, and therefore highly trained. In March 1918 the German thrust dislodged the BEF's Fifth Army from the trenches it maintained: now, whole units fell apart and straggled heedless to the rear.

Of course, their very inexperience offered some advantage to commanders such as led the BEF. In the first place, they could be sent to attack impossible positions, when the odds against survival might have daunted wiser men: ' . . . for a desperate effort, untried soldiers could be better than tried ones . . . the old soldier might use his skill not only to defeat the enemy, but to avoid taking the necessary risks in a stiff fight.'[35] Second, when offensives were frustrated and long lists of casualties incurred, it was possible for the BEF's commanders to pin blame upon the men. Writing of the new soldiers as they poured forward into France, Sir John Edmonds, the editor of the official histories, prepared the ground for an exoneration of the generals from any culpability for what happened on the Somme. The new divisions could not manoeuvre in a battle, they 'could not even keep straight on'.[36]

Apart from inexperience, a further factor undermined the efficiency of the British army as the war drew on. That factor related to the social backgrounds of the new officers and men. The shortage of 'good' officers became particularly pressing. Historically, the British army's military successes may partly be ascribed to the high proportion of officers in relation to its strength; something which the continental armies, being generally far larger, found it impractical to match.[37] The officers were there to give direction to their men. An officer during the war in South Africa had noted:

> The genius for being led is so ingrained in our men that independent, unsuperintended action can never be expected of them. No men will do better what they are directed to do, but no men are less likely to do the right thing in the absence of their accustomed director . . .
>
> [The British soldier] is neither cautious, nor cunning, nor apt to profit by practice or bitter experience. He prefers to trust to his phenomenal luck and phenomenal courage, but, better than all, to his officers.[38]

In 1914 the quality and numbers of regimental officers still held the key to military success. The quality of its officers, when the Territorials reached France, was the greatest problem connected with that force;[39] and the technique which Sir Douglas Haig perfected, of launching waves of foot-soldiers against machine-guns and barbed wire, placed special weight upon the captains and lieutenants. Without them, without the example which they gave, the scale and violence of the slaughter too easily snuffed out an attack: 'When British troops lost their officers, they were . . . apt to fall back, not because they were beaten but because they did not know what to do and expected to receive fresh orders.'[40]

By 1917 the supply of new officers was beginning to run short. Australian divisions within the BEF found a way to solve this problem: provided that a man had shown his ability in combat and carried the respect of those he was to lead, he could be simply lifted from the ranks. They could go on finding officers until the last day of the war.[41] The purely British units were less fortunately placed.[42] For them, ability was one thing and birth and education quite another; and a discipline based on a rigid separation between officers and men must have been undermined by a policy of promotions such as the Australians maintained.[43] Of course, the authorities were less conservative in distributing commissions than they had been before the war: they could no longer count on a substantial private income and an entry in Debrett's. The thousands of university and public school men provided an important reservoir from which new subalterns could be drawn.[44] Unhappily, the limits of this reservoir were not initially perceived. Many youngsters fresh from public school entered the ranks of certain Kitchener battalions: the casualties resulting when they were sent up to the front meant that, by 1917, their numbers had been recklessly drawn down. Again, the ranks of certain 'high-class' Territorial battalions had been full of potential officers; their casualties in battle further contributed to the shortage of lieutenants.[45] Eventually, men had to be commissioned who were not altogether fit. These were turned into 'temporary gentlemen, who wore riding boots and passed the port in mess'.[46] Siegfried Sassoon, with his County connections and six hundred pounds a year, was gladly taken in. Wilfred Owen was a teacher, his father was a clerk; he had been to grammar school and had not a penny to his name. But he too, despite his handicaps, received the King's commission.[47]

In like manner, the army now drew its other ranks from sections of society amongst which, before the war, the recruiters would never normally have strayed. No longer did its shilling attract only the unfortunate — the casual labourers and the lads from off the street. In August 1914 men came flocking to the army who had always kept themselves away; men from the very backgrounds which the military authorities had feared.

There was much that was brutalizing in the life of the manufacturing hands, and therefore much good cause for discontent among them. Moreover, in the towns they had plenty of companions against whom to sharpen their wits, and no lack of agitators to work upon their worst feelings.[48]

By Christmas 1914 the barriers were down. These men now furnished whole divisions: not just the manufacturing hands and their companions, but the denizens of workshop, pit, and mill. What did these newcomers make of the discipline they faced? Before answering this question, before treating of how, or if, their sharpened wits were blunted and their worst feelings reined in, it will be useful to make some further points about this flow of volunteers.

4

The Manufacturing Hands

It is no part of this analysis to give account of why men actually enlisted, or to link conditions in Great Britain with the fever sweeping France and Germany as well. We have, of course, volumes of eye-witness effusions, describing how men flooded to enrol, and a range of overall statistics setting out the volunteering for each month of the war. We lack, however, details of how the volunteering actually proceeded, by age or occupation, day by day throughout the first eighteen months of war. Such a chart, broken down for the separate regions of the kingdom, might shed more light upon the attitudes of the different classes to the war than can any number of the generalities commonly advanced — generalities touching the 'intense, almost mystical patriotism' which is supposed to have existed, or stressing 'the illusion of wonderful adventure' which drew so many civilians to the front.[1]

Neglecting then the broader problem of the factors which moved men to enlist, we concentrate upon the narrower one: of the consequences for the military authorities of taking in thousands of new men. Did the 'manufacturing hands' abandon pre-war outlooks on the day they joined the ranks? Were their pasts, as trade unionists, even socialists, so very rapidly effaced? Or did their 'brutalising' background and sharpened wits lead to those clashes with authority which army officers had feared? For whatever the gaps in the detailed picture of enlistment, there can be no doubts about the scale on which the working class took part. Nearly five million industrial workers had entered the armed forces by the time hostilities had ceased, and South Wales and the Clydeside, two centres of working-class unrest, had provided, relative to their populations, greater quantities of soldiers than the rest of the UK[2]. Nor were they unwillingly dragged in. More than 10 per cent of the industrial workforce joined up during the first two months of war and by January 1916, when volunteering ceased, nearly 30 per cent of the men employed in industry had stepped forward to enlist.[3] Before discussing the impact on the army of this influx of new men there are, as a preliminary, certain points worth making about the manner by which this entry actually took place.

In the first place, the numbers entering the army under the voluntary system, before the introduction of compulsion, were extremely large. In July 1914 the ration strength of the British army had amounted to 164,000 men — six skeleton divisions at home and numbers of battalions manning stations overseas.[4] Within a year, some seventy divisions were forming, training, or serving overseas; and still the flow continued: men to maintain the strength of these divisions and to create a vast engine of communication and supply. By late 1915 the rate of volunteering was beginning to fall off. Even so, by February 1916 a great army had been formed, by far the largest ever fielded by any country relying on purely voluntary means.[5] More than two and a half million men had willingly stepped forward, a greater number than compulsion was ever to bring in.[6]

In the second place, the shift from volunteering to compulsion was far smoother than the form of words suggests. Many of those called up under the Military Service Act, the vehicle of conscription, had already given token of their willingness to serve. They had done this at the invitation of Lord Derby. Derby, as Director-General of Recruiting, had sought to balance the wishes of the generals, anxious for ever greater numbers, against the fears of Labour leaders, anxious lest a general measure of conscription affect men's freedom to change their trade or place of work.[7] Attestation was the answer. Lord Derby asked men to say they would serve if called upon to do so; and, under his scheme, more than two million men thus registered their names.[8] Labour leaders joined other public figures in praising and encouraging this scheme.[9] Accordingly, when compulsion was actually brought in, many of those now entering the army had already signed away, in principle, their rights through attestation. The Derby scheme took the sting out of compulsion, preparing men for the duties they would face; not, perhaps, in its original conception but because of the consequences its priorities induced. Initially, both single and married men had been invited to attest. Soon, the government agreed that married men should not be taken before all the single men had gone.[10] Thereafter married men, even where willingly attesting, felt that they should not be called while single men were free; so, early in 1916, single men between the ages of eighteen and forty-one became liable for military service.[11] Even then, the claims of Labour were respected, and though men could be drafted for the trenches, they were not, in general, compelled to work for one employer or to do one allotted job. In May, married men found that they too were 'deemed to have been duly enlisted'; and the age-groups liable were also steadily enlarged.[12] Yet the new Act failed to flush out that quantity of shirkers which the generals were anxious to take in. Its enforcement lay not with the War Office, but with the government itself. Before 1916 miners and munition workers were free to join the army; after that date, the army could not take them, for it was placed, in order of priority, behind the navy, the air force, and many areas of industry itself.[13] So the stream of men enlisting never reached the levels which volunteering had brought in. In brief, compulsion produced fewer reinforcements for the army than had been provided under volunteering and, of the wartime conscripts, large numbers in any case had already freely given a commitment of their readiness to serve.

This massive volunteering, whether in the form of genuine enlistment or of merely being willing to attest, was sufficient, surely, to blunt the 'sharp wits' of the new soldiers coming from the cities, to instil obedience in those who had had experience of social and industrial unrest. And beyond the readiness of the 'manufacturing hands' and their 'companions' to leave their homes for military service, a further factor shielded the army from real discontent. That factor concerned the suddenness of the change in outlook once war had broken out. The army, it will be recalled, had long attracted the opprobrium of the decent working class. In 1914, this tradition still held force. It had been reinforced, if anything, during the years of agitation which preceded the outbreak of the war. The army had been used against the working class. In South Wales, troops had fired upon the strikers. In Liverpool, they had moved to break the dockers' strike. In the great railway centres, they had intimidated the railway companies' employees.[14] When working men now freely joined the army, they abjured some aspect of their past. The army had not changed. Its discipline still exacted a host of 'trivial formalities and unnecessary indignities' upon the rank and file.[15] Rather, the newcomers had changed: not, perhaps, as individuals, but in terms of what they seemed willing to accept. Before 1914, the working class had sometimes mocked the army. It viewed as 'outcast' those who took its pay.[16] Now, its members willingly stepped forward: to enjoy a level of subordination stricter than that which set the workman from his boss, and more far-reaching than that prevailing in their workplaces and streets. Their new trade demanded more of them than firing rifles or learning to salute. It asked them to relinquish all that they had built for self-defence. For while the labour movement — its unions, its parties and its press — had tempered the rulers' hold upon the ruled, the rank and file had built no such safeguards and were unlikely to construct them during the emergencies of war.

Their defencelessness was clear. Military discipline, in general, 'prevented agitation from the ranks in support of virtually any cause whether a political movement or a campaign to improve the terms and conditions of service.'[17] And, in particular, it was enforced without any of those safeguards through which, in England, the powers of the executive had been successfully contained. The contrast between the discipline imposed on British soldiers, and that in force elsewhere, will quickly make this clear. Section 98 of the Australian Defence Act, for example, spelled out which crimes, in the Australian forces, might earn the penalty of death. Soldiers who were insubordinate, who refused to enter battle, or who deserted to the rear, could not be thus condemned. And even where a death sentence could be legally imposed, it could not be carried into effect 'until confirmed by the Governor-General'.[18] Time and time again Sir Douglas Haig appealed to the Australian government to amend this Act.[19] It limited his sanctions and gave to simple soldiers the power to decide when, and under what conditions, they were willing to obey. Perhaps they rarely used it. But, as British senior commanders slowly had to learn, there were occasions on which Australians would refuse to carry out their orders — orders judged foolish, oppressive, or unfair:[20] ' . . . these troops had the habit of reasoning why and not merely of doing and dying.'[21] And if, on some occasions, privates in Australian battalions would brook the wrath of GHQ, they also resisted that degree of subordination which, on British soldiers, the military police had managed to impose.[22]

For men enlisting in Great Britain, there were few safeguards such as the Australians enjoyed. They could be condemned to death — as indeed they were — by a handful of captains and lieutenants, gathered perfunctorily in a tent,[23] for brief desertion or for an act of simple insubordination.[24] And there was no civilian agency, not even the High Court, through whom to enter an appeal. These powers Haig most carefully preserved. Without them, obedience might suffer and his armies fall apart.[25] Foreign observers could not conceal their surprise at the 'humiliating' discipline which the new soldiers from Great Britain seemed willing to accept.[26] Prince Rupprecht of Bavaria, examining captured British orders, commented on how 'very strict' a discipline the English had enforced. His own army suffered when men deserted or refused to do their duty, but for the most part he lacked that sanction — the firing squad — on which his British counterparts relied.[27] The Australian government's observers, too, found it hard to account for the docility which men brought up in a democracy now so willingly displayed. The editor of their official history accounted for this paradox by contrasting the democratic forms which English politics embraced with its 'largely feudal' practice and tradition.[28] Private soldiers born in the United Kingdom, he noted, accepted a vigorous subordination because, in the majority, they 'had been brought up to consider themselves inferior, socially and mentally, to their officers'. Australian soldiers, both officers and men, expressed a pride in their own political tradition — 'a fierce pride that their own people was strong enough to refuse this instrument [the firing squad] to its rulers'.[29]

Beyond the question of the scale of volunteering, and of the docility which an upbringing in the British Isles enjoined, there were other factors which helped to keep good discipline in place. One such factor concerned attitudes within the labour movement itself. The army, as Sir John Fortescue described it, had not only feared the sharp wits of the manufacturing hands, if that class were too widely present in its ranks; it also feared the 'agitators' to which that class was prey.[30] In 1914, however, the authorities could discount the malign influence of these. Rather the reverse: once the trades union and labour leaders had been reassured about the effect of wartime measures on the different industries and trades, they took for the most part a positive attitude to the army and the war.[31] Their outlook on a war with Germany lies outside the province of this book; some shrank back from the wild aggrandizement which allied war aims from time to time embraced but, on the other hand, 'Hang the Kaiser', a slogan typifying the worse feelings thrown up by the war, was an imperative framed by one Labour politician who reached the Cabinet.[32] A group of MPs around Philip Snowden opposed the war and pressed for a negotiated peace. Still, they did nothing to upset good discipline and little to defend the army's other ranks. The chronicler of capital courts-martial shows that these MPs barely taxed the government when they raised the question of the British firing squads in France; 'a little more care' in setting out their case could have made a policy of unchecked executions less easy to effect.[33]

There were further factors which cemented discipline when uniform was donned. Once enlisted and transported, say, to France, the new conditions encouraged men to strengthen rather than to question the army whose cause they had promised to uphold. At first, men had joined up with their workmates and their friends, preserving links and loyalties built up in civilian life. The slaughter in the trenches effaced this common ground. Freed from their pre-war attitudes and views, the survivors found a new vehicle for their loyalties. They came to cherish the standing of their regiment —

later, that of their particular division. A minority, perhaps, resented the disparities of power, the elaborate structures of authority and rank; but important factors strengthened the officers' regime. Volunteers for military service accepted that, however imperfect conditions in the army, the greatest goal was that of Germany's defeat. It behoved them, then, to support good discipline lest, in the attempt to temper it and better their conditions, the army suffer and the war be lost. Once the war had been agreed to, the discipline had to be endorsed; the relations of destruction had a logic of their own. No less, close contact with the army softened views which had once been more extreme. Ben Tillett, the leader of the dockers and in his day the associate of syndicalists and revolutionaries, confessed to Sir Douglas Haig that his notion of the British Officer had been shallow and ill-judged.

> 'At first, his impressions were derived from the picture papers and society journals. He thought them "fops and snobs". He is astonished now to find that "his friends" have unbounded confidence in their officers, and could not get on without them.'[34]

Whatever the confidence the officers enjoyed, the opportunity was not neglected at important moments in the war to tighten discipline by imposing those penalties for misbehaviour which the legal code contained. More than three hundred men were executed for military offences abroad during the years 1914–1919;[35] though full details have not yet been released, the evidence suggests that these executions were concentrated at times when their impact might produce its most powerful effect.[36] Thus, for most of the Kitchener divisions, the first real test of discipline must have come during the great bloodbath on the Somme. On 1 July 1916, the BEF lost more men on a single day than any other army in the war.[37] Little ground was gained and yet, in the weeks thereafter, the offensives — waves of foot-soldiers facing machine-guns and barbed wire — continued to be launched. Tens of thousands died without succumbing to their fears. Some, however, fled. In those autumn days, the BEF's commanders took the opportunity of underlining, in the minds of newcomers and veterans alike, the stern nature of the penalties for failing to obey. The following orders despatched from GHQ brought to the attention of every soldier in the army the sanctions which it was willing to employ.[38]

'*General Routine Order 1771*, September 4

(i) No. 12182 Private A. Murphy, 9th Battalion Scottish Rifles was tried by Field General Court-Martial on the following charge:-
"Deserting His Majesty's Service."
The accused absented himself and remained absent for six months.
The sentence of the Court was "To suffer death by being shot." The sentence was duly carried out at 5 a.m. on 17th August 1916.

(ii) No. 10018 Private P. Giles, 14th Northumberland Fusiliers (Pioneers) was tried by Field General Court-Martial on the following charge:-
"When on Active Service, Desertion."
The accused, after being warned for immediate duty in the trenches, absented himself and remained absent for a week.
The sentence of the Court was "To suffer death by being shot." The sentence was duly carried out at 5.30 a.m. on 24th August 1916.

(iii) No. 24/2008 Private F. Hughes, 2nd Battalion Canterbury Infantry Regiment, New Zealand Imperial Forces, was tried by Field General Court-Martial on the following charge:-
"When on Active Service, Deserting His Majesty's Service."
The accused left the front line trench and remained absent for ten days.
The sentence of the Court was "To suffer death by being shot." The sentence was duly carried out at 5.50 a.m. on 25th August, 1916.[39]

(iv) No. 2057 Private J. Higgins, 9th, attached 1/8th Battalion, Argyll and Sutherland Highlanders was tried by Field General Court-Martial on the following charge:-
"When on Active Service, Deserting His Majesty's Service."
The accused absented himself from the fighting zone till apprehended, a week later, disguised, in the vicinity of a base port.
The sentence of the Court was "To suffer death by being shot." The sentence was duly carried out at 5.33 a.m. on 26th August 1916.

(v) No. 4071 Pte J. Bennett, 1st Hampshire Regiment was tried by Field General Court-Martial on the following charge:-
"When on Active Service, misbehaving before the enemy in such a manner as to show cowardice."
The accused, from motives of cowardice, left the trenches during a gas attack.
The sentence of the Court was "To suffer death by being shot." The sentence was duly carried out at 5.40 a.m. on 28th August 1916.[40]

General Routine Order 1782, September 10

No. 18/313 Private H. Crimins and No. 18/356 Private A. Wild, both of 18th (Service) Battalion West Yorkshire Regiment, were tried by Field General Court-Martial on the following charge:-

"When on Active Service deserting His Majesty's Service."
After having been warned for a dangerous duty they absented themselves for four days.
The sentence of the Court was "To suffer death by being shot." The sentence was duly carried out on 5th September 1916.

General Routine Order 1796, September 18

(i) No. 20062 Private J. Anderson, 12th Battalion King's Liverpool Regiment, attached 8th Battalion, Loyal North Lancashire Regiment, was tried by Field General Court-Martial on the following charge:-
"Misbehaving before the enemy in such a manner as to show cowardice."
He left a working party, when under the enemy's fire, through fear for his personal safety.
The sentence of the Court was, "To suffer death by being shot." The sentence was duly carried out at 5.55 a.m. on 12th September 1916.[41]

(ii) No. 12923 Private A. Rickman, 1st Battalion Royal Dublin Fusiliers was tried by Field General Court-Martial on the following charge:-
"When on Active Service Deserting His Majesty's Service."
He absented himself from the firing line on July 2nd, and remained absent till apprehended on the lines of communication on July 20th.
The sentence of the Court was "To suffer death by being shot." The sentence was duly carried out at 6.10 a.m. on 15th September 1916.

General Routine Order 1814, September 25

(i) No. 5715 Private C. Depper, 1/4th Battalion Royal Berkshire Regiment (T.F.) was tried by Field General Court-Martial on the following charge:-
"When on Active Service, deserting His Majesty's Service."
He left the trenches with the intention of getting away to England, but was apprehended in Amiens.
The sentence of the Court was "To suffer death by being shot." The sentence was duly carried out at 6.10 a.m. on 13th September 1916.

(ii) No. 21373 Private J. Carey, 8th (S) Battalion Royal Irish Fusiliers, was tried by Field General Court-Martial on the following charge:-
"When on Active Service, deserting His Majesty's Service."
On two occasions he absented himself after being warned for the trenches till apprehended at some distance from the firing line.
The sentence of the Court was "To suffer death by being shot." The sentence was duly carried out at 6.5 a.m. on 15th September 1916.

(iii) No. 7595 Private A.J. Haddock, 12th Battalion York and Lancaster Regiment, was tried by Field General Court-Martial on the following charge:-

"When on Active Service, deserting His Majesty's Service."
The accused absented himself when on the way to the trenches, until found some miles away, five days later, attempting to hide himself.
The sentence of the Court was "To suffer death by being shot." The sentence was duly carried out at 6.14 a.m. on 16th September 1916.

(iv) No. 2120 Private P. Black, 1/4th Battalion, attached 1/7th Battalion, The Black Watch Regiment, was tried by Field General Court-Martial on the following charge:-
"When on Active Service, deserting His Majesty's Service."
The accused absented himself from his unit when going into action, and remained absent till apprehended in a town some miles behind the firing line more than a month later.
The sentence of the Court was "To suffer death by being shot." The sentence was duly carried out at 5.47 a.m. on 18th September 1916.

General Routine Order 1826, September 28

No. 19933 Rifleman E. Card, 20th Battalion King's Royal Rifle Corps, was tried by Field General Court-Martial on the following charge:-
"When on Active Service, deserting His Majesty's Service."
The accused absented himself from the neighbourhood of the trenches when under orders to move up into the front line, until surrendering himself on the next day in the neighbourhood of Amiens.
The sentence of the Court was "To suffer death by being shot." The sentence was duly carried out at 6.17 a.m. on 22nd September 1916.'

The sanction represented by these shootings went far beyond their effect upon the friends and fellow-soldiers of the unfortunates who died. The details here given were circulated in printed form and read out, by order, on parade throughout the BEF.[42] Such readings were intended to stiffen the faint-hearted, and deter potential miscreants and cowards. The ceremony appalled Australian officers and men who, ineligible for execution, nonetheless attended such parades; and the bloodletting surprised the Germans, into whose hands copies of the details inevitably fell.[43] No one could stand aside with the reflection that outright cowards alone were being shot. Men were executed for some momentary failing after facing lead and high-explosive for months and years on end or, again, for refusing some minor order when well distant from the front.[44]

It would be wrong, however, to suggest that a new-found enthusiasm for the army or a fear of punishment drove every trace of independent outlook from the minds of all recruits. Naturally, the more dramatic cases of indiscipline occurred later in the war, when goodwill had drained away, and when, in any case, men were being sent up to the front who had not the least wish to be there. Nonetheless, from the beginning, traces of pre-war attitudes were sometimes to be seen. Where sections of the working class joined up together, they sometimes jibbed at the indignities which the army's discipline supplied. One such section was recruited in the mining districts of South Wales. Its

'response to Lord Kitchener's appeal in 1914 was magnificent . . . the Cardiff "Dailies" reported that 141,000 enlisted from the South Wales coalfields in the first four months of the Great War, as the general belief was that the war would be over in three months, and the period of army service would provide a welcome "break" from the pits.'[45]

These volunteers appear to have been less malleable than most. Twice in four months, according to one of their number, the young miners comprising a battalion of the Welch Regiment refused all orders. In May 1915, while undergoing training at the hands of instructors drawn from the Metropolitan Police and the regiment of Guards,

'one of the young soldiers was struck on a very sore arm by one of these Sergeant-Majors with a heavy stick which they always carried.
'The boy sank to the ground in great pain, his comrades went to his assistance and loudly expressed their anger, actually threatening the offender.
'After parade, meetings were held and it was decided to refuse to "Fall In" the next morning. This was 100% successful, there was to be no further parades until the instructors were sent away. The 3rd Battalion Welsh regt. were sent to Porthcawl from Cardiff to "persuade" us to parade, they failed in their mission.
'We remained in our billets for four days, we were fed as usual by our civilian landlords.
'We were then informed that the instructors were transferred elsewhere and accordingly resumed our training . . .'[46]

That August, the battalion again refused orders to parade, until they had received an undertaking that Field Punishment No 1 — by which offenders were tied to the wheel of a wagon for a couple of hours each day — would be less frequently imposed.[47]

Another man volunteering at the outbreak of the war found himself with his friends, all miners, in a Rhondda Pals battalion (10th Battalion, Welch Regiment). The transition from the warm atmosphere of the coal pits to a bleak October under canvas proved too much for their lungs and, rather than endure ill-health, the battalion refused all duties. They were moved to warmer billets.[48] Lord Kitchener, for his part, had perhaps feared such outbursts from these men. From the outset he had tried to dampen any distinctly Welsh ardour which such volunteers might bring. He had given orders to prevent their language being spoken on parade grounds and in billets and, in contrast with privileges granted to both the Irish and the Scots, forestalled the formation of a distinctly Welsh division.[49]

There were other problems with good discipline during that first winter of the war. Conditions in the camps in England were not always very easy. It was a cold, wet autumn, and the War Office, taken by surprise, lacked the huts, tents, clothes and blankets to supply the units which continued to be formed.[50] The conditions sapped the spirits of the most ardent volunteers. Canadians, for instance, had travelled the Atlantic anticipating battles with the Germans: they faced nothing but an unending bitter winter in camps on Salisbury Plain.[51]

'The "training" became a fight against the weather for bare health and existence. The camps turned into archipelagoes of tents in a knee-deep sea of mud. The Canadian troops, coming to the mother-country with a glow of generous enthusiasm, had little expected these miseries, and reckless breaking of camp and disturbances in the old cathedral city of Salisbury were the result.'[52]

Some English units, too, were faced with problems of this kind.[53] Essentially, though, disturbances such as breaking out of camp were the products of frustration, of men's anxiety lest their time and energy not be put to good effect. These outbreaks had little in common with the deliberate disobedience of orders which, in 1915, certain units of Welsh miners appear to have displayed. Such disobedience was rarely seen in the first years of the war. All the more difficult, then, for the authorities to cope when, on 9 September 1917, trouble on as serious a scale broke out once again.

5

Not Irishmen But English Soldiers

At the outbreak of the First World War, the claims of nationalism upon the working classes who so soon, and in such numbers, were to fill the armies of the great powers, proved immensely stronger than the claims of common interest to which the socialists and internationalists appealed. Despite the size of left-wing parties in Germany and France, despite the growth of labour and its political ideals, no real opposition to the war took place. In Germany, a few members of the Reichstag endeavoured to stand back, but were overborne by the popularity of war with Tsarist Russia. In France, the handful who opposed were hampered by the manifest iniquity of a German army on their country's soil, and by the belief, held by socialists and radicals alike, that their republic was the incarnation of the Revolution. In Russia, the urban working class subscribed to the feeling which everywhere took hold. In Great Britain, there was no effective opposition to the war. Some intellectuals and certain fragments of the working class stood back, but those movements which not long before had disrupted national life appeared to wither when hostilities broke out. Despite the rise of labour, the growth of trade unions and the corresponding background of unrest, working men either freely joined the army, or quietly awaited those consequences — eventual military and industrial conscription — which a war with Germany entailed.

One small blemish marred this willingness to fight. Although a new spirit swept through London and Vienna, through Paris and Berlin, stilling oppositions, reconciling trade unions to governments, and bringing truce between masters and their men, before long it penetrated further. In different forms, it touched the cottagers of Kerry and the citizens of Prague. In London and in the cities of Great Britain, the war released great energies and led men to volunteer. By contrast, in the broader reaches of the Empire, hostilities with Germany had an unsettling effect. Far from binding subject peoples yet more closely to the Crown, it threatened dangerous repercussions. In South Africa, for instance, it strained relations between Dutch- and English-speakers. In both India and Egypt it lent to nationalists some hopes of furthering their cause. In Ireland, it furnished opportunity to the supporters of Home Rule.

The ministries were conscious of the risks which war must bring. All the great powers had their Irelands, their *irredenta*, or recruited soldiers from their subject lands. Germany had her Polish, Danish, Alsatian and Lorrainer soldiers; Russia her Muslims and her Poles; Austria the Czechs and other Slavs. The armies most seriously affected were those of Austria-Hungary. Drawn from ten linguistic nationalities, the Germans and the Magyars at times were thinly spread. The other nationalities, far from being 'patriotic, largely loyal to the Emperor, and not yet touched by anti-militaristic agitation,' as had been imagined from Berlin, were affected by pan-Slav ideals or wished for national independence.[1] Perhaps the Slovaks remained obedient and loyal, and great masses of the Croats unreservedly fought on, but the Czechs, the Rumanians, and others proved more or less disloyal.[2] Thousands of Transylvanians seceded or, being captured, formed Rumanian battalions in the service of the allies. The unreliability of the Czechs exceeded even this. They could not be used against the Russians without risking their departure from the lines; whole regiments deserted or were in open treason, and the laying down of arms became a common practice.[3] In the winter of 1914–15, a Prague regiment of infantry on the Eastern Front was reduced from two thousand to one hundred and fifty men within a single day; in the words of the Austrian Chief of Staff, 'without firing a shot it was taken prisoner, or rather called for in its trenches, by something like a Russian battalion.'[4] The allies recruited special legions from the Czechs, amounting to 130,000 men, whom they used against both Central Powers and Bolsheviks.[5]

Such dissidence was not confined to Austria-Hungary's armed forces. In the early periods of war, German units recruited in Alsace were sent to fronts which did not face the French, and individual soldiers from this province were ordered eastwards after deserters had disclosed the German plans.[6] And though, at the outset, Russia's border peoples affirmed their attachment to the Tsar, their loyalties were weak. Being a danger to the army, the Finns and others were not compelled to serve. As a precaution, those who were conscripted — Poles, Jews, Letts, Estonians, Armenians and Georgians — were employed on fronts some distance from their homes.[7]

The soldiers of Great Britain, like those of all great powers, were drawn not only from the heartland, committed to the war, but from amongst the peoples of the Empire as well. One part of that Empire comprised the self-governing Dominions; another, vast territories in Africa and Asia. The Dominions represented an access of strength reliable beyond anything on which the Habsburg emperor could draw. In July 1914, before war had broken out, both Canada and New Zealand made firm pledges of support. Australia was quick to follow.[8] With war declared, their aid was immediately spelled out: twenty thousand troops apiece from Australia and Canada, and eight thousand from New Zealand.[9] This help was promised before a single man enrolled. But the volunteers came in. Young men looking for adventure, immigrants from the Mother Country anxious to support her in the hour of her need: these were the types who clamoured to enlist: ' . . . all the romantic, quixotic, adventurous flotsam that eddied on the surface of the Australian people concentrated itself within those first weeks upon the recruiting offices of the A[ustralian] I[mperial] F[orce].'[10] Within weeks, the various contingents were sailing for the front. As the months passed by, the help rendered continued to increase. By 1918, Australia was providing five divisions for the BEF alone and, between them, the overseas Dominions furnished one-sixth of that force.[11] The enthusiasm of 1914 was clearly not sustained. Nonetheless, both Australia and Canada replaced losses and increased their contributions without resorting to conscription. Twice, in referenda, Australia's front-line soldiers were canvassed for their views: 'They themselves, when they enlisted, had not known the trials and horrors of war; and, now that they did know, they would not, by their votes, force any other man into those trials against his will.'[12] Underpinned by this voluntary spirit, and backed up by governments which refused to countenance 'Old Army' excesses, the quality of these Dominion corps stayed firm.[13] By 1917, they were being used as 'shock troops', to force the issue when Englishmen could not.[14] But Haig and his fellow generals bemoaned the price they had to pay. They inveighed against the unruliness of the men from the Dominions, their unwillingness to accept that level of subordination to which British troops had sunk.[15]

Still, these overseas divisions were no uniform creations, and their ranks reacted differently according to their different backgrounds and ideas. The Australian Imperial Force contained numerous immigrants from England. These were happy to carry out such duties as born Australians were not anxious to perform.[16] The Canadian forces contained thousands of English immigrants as well.[17] On the other hand, eight hundred Canadians, born and bred in Russia, were serving with the BEF when the Bolsheviks took power. After they had 'given indication of "Defeatist" tendencies', it was feared that their discontent might spread.[18] However desperate the military position — at a time when 'children, English children', were being sent up to the front — these veterans had to be removed. So, as GHQ instructed:

> 'the whole of these Russians, about eight hundred in all, will be trans-
> ferred forthwith for duty with Canadian Forestry Companies, such Com-
> panies being selected as are not situated in Frontier Departments. The
> disaffected men are to be distributed evenly amongst the Companies, and
> those of bad character separated.'[19]

Elsewhere, the help given by the Empire is less straightforward to assess. South Africa, for instance, was cool in its response. The six thousand British troops within its borders were quickly freed for service overseas, but the outbreak of rebellion, in part the consequence of war, diverted material and men. After the collapse of this rebellion, forty thousand South Africans entered German South-West Africa and, when the Germans had surrendered, a further force was sent into East Africa.[20] Beyond that, South Africa provided units for service in the Near and Middle East. Apart, however, from companies of 'natives' recruited for labouring purposes, she gave small assistance to the BEF in France.

It was Whitehall, though, which decided against making greater use of Africa's reserves. The Army Council had hoped to raise some fifty thousand troops in England's East African possessions. It was discouraged, in the first instance, by a report from General Smuts: he judged the natives to be 'unwarlike'.[21] But other factors undoubtedly weighed heavy. It was thought improper to unleash the coloured races on a European foe.[22] And in East Africa, the consequences for the post-war era were not to be ignored. The whites were heavily outnumbered and their situation might become even more precarious if the tribespeople were taught the use of arms.[23]

In Egypt, the position was complex. Turkish and religious propaganda, designed to stir up disaffection, was circulating widely; in the view of Sir John Maxwell, General Officer Commanding, every lie was immediately sucked in.[24] Certainly there were many factions in the wider population which would have welcomed the end of British rule. In these circumstances, the British government decided not to use the Egyptian Army in the maintenance of order and the defence of the Canal. 'Administrative problems' were cited as the reason, and despite the wishes of both officers and men in the army to fight beside the British, it was sent south to the Sudan.[25] In the civil sphere, though, Egypt was made to more than pay her way. Without her labour and draught animals, her fodder and supplies, the war against Turkey could hardly have gone on.[26] As the advance through Sinai and into Palestine continued, men of the Egyptian Labour Corps laid the water-pipeline, the railway, and many miles of road, at great speed and under difficult conditions; by August 1918 their numbers had risen to some 135,000 men.[27] Beyond the railheads, the mobility of the fighting units was maintained by supplies brought up by the Egyptian Transport Corps, some 170,000 of whose members served as camel drivers over a period of years.[28] In addition, tens of thousands of Egyptians were recruited as labourers for France.

It was on India's contribution, though, that the highest hopes were pinned. Within days of war breaking out in Europe, two divisions of infantry and two of cavalry were on their way to France; one division to the Persian Gulf; and the infantry units from a further two divisions to Egypt.[29] The earliest help that Sir John French received, after his losses at Mons and Le Cateau, came from two Indian divisions; and it was the Indian infantry, rather than the Egyptian or the British, which repulsed the first and most serious attack by Turkey upon the Suez Canal. Thereafter, this flow was steadily expanded until, by the time of the Armistice, half a million Indians were serving overseas. More men were killed from India than from any one of the Dominions.[30] Still, their help presented problems: problems relating to their loyalties, and to racist sentiment in the trenches and Whitehall. In the Near and Middle East, the authorities pondered the reliability of troops drawn from the Muslim areas of India in a war against their co-religionist, the Turk. In 1915 Sir John Maxwell reported the existence of a plot to undermine the loyalties of Indian troops, a plot having ramifications throughout Asia and elsewhere; that same year, units of Muslim troops were re-embarked from Lemnos lest they prove unreliable in the Dardanelles campaign. Simple racism governed British policy as well. The deeds of Sikhs and Gurkhas soon filled the chap-books of Imperial romance, but less well advertised were the slights offered to soldiers from the Indian sub-continent, both officers and men. The artillery was not entrusted to their hands and, amongst both cavalry and infantry, Indian officers were advanced less swiftly than their prowess might suggest. It was judged impolitic, and something of a risk, to appoint Indian officers to commands where white officers might find themselves in subordinate positions.[31]

Berlin's hopes, that the rise of nationalism in India and Egypt would impede the British effort, were not to be fulfilled. The German press had been tempted to consider upheavals in India as the natural consequence of war, and, from the outset, the German general staff regarded revolution in India and Egypt as being 'of the highest importance'.[32] In fact, no portion of the Empire gained its independence in these years. The main source of instability arose not in Africa and Asia, but within the British Isles themselves. It was Ireland which gave both government and army the gravest problems to resolve.

The rise of Irish nationalism has often been described; less simple, though, to trace its influence upon Irishmen enlisted in the army. Perhaps, at times, their loyalties were strained, but the British experienced few of the embarrassments which, after 1914, the Austro-Hungarians suffered from the Czechs. In the late nineteenth century the mood of Irish soldiers had given small cause for alarm. During the South African War, for instance, every Irish regiment saw service, and did so to such advantage that, in recognition, the regiment of Irish Guards was formed. Yet this was at a time when Irish nationalists were showing interest in the fate of the Transvaal and when a fringe of Fenians and exiles, taking matters further, had launched a military excursion to champion the Boers.[33] A cultural and political revival was slowly taking place and this, in turn, brought new successes to the Parliamentary party. Soldiers recruited in the South, while maintaining perfect discipline, shared some of the aspirations which the Irish Nationalists were hoping to fulfil. The candidate for Galway during the parliamentary elections of 1906 has described an incident which shows something of the mild confusion affecting Irish soldiers at this time.

'I had received another visit which had surprised me — from the Adjutant of the Connaught Rangers who came down to say that at the regimental depot were a certain number of married men having votes and that Shawe Taylor had been permitted to address them and I should have the same opportunity. I thanked him but made up my mind it would be silly to waste time . . . However, Harry Murphy insisted, we drove out and were received by the adjutant who took us into the mess for drinks while the men were being mustered . . . we went in to the gymnasium where were about thirty soldiers drawn up. I told them that I thought highly of Irish soldiers and had a brother serving; but that from my point of view the rule of Ireland by England was wrong and only existed by armed force: and that while this was so, I considered that no Irish nationalist should go into the British army and that I should do what I could to stop recruiting . . . About a dozen men had Gaelic and I made them a patriotic address in such sentiments as my vocabulary could express — and so finished. We moved out and as we went the men cheered — I thought out of courtesy. But the Colonel said to me, "They didn't do that for Shawe Taylor": and when we got into the barrack square the recruits took it up . . . On the polling day, the sergeant-major came up to me, saluted and said, "Twenty-eight voted, sir, and I'm sorry to say there's three of them gone wrong. Some of the rest were a little bothered by what you said about recruiting but I explained it to them." '[34]

After 1906 the tension between the Nationalists campaigning for Home Rule, and the Protestants in Ulster who vehemently opposed it, grew continually more bitter. The Ulster Volunteers were formed: 85,000 men enrolled, not in ragged bands, but in proper military formation. They were ready and able to resist the imposition of Home Rule.[35] The creation of a rival force, the Irish Volunteers, was a measure of the anger ignited in the South by Ulster's opposition and the British government's prevarication. Its numbers swiftly grew: past 100,000 at the end of May 1914 and reaching 180,000 on the eve of war.[36] Untrained, and scarcely armed beyond the few rifles which regular soldiers could be induced to sell, the Irish Volunteers formed a large and unpredictable new force: for, though they had been brought under his nominal control, they were by no means at the disposal of John Redmond, the leader of the Parliamentary party. The landing of weapons for the Irish Volunteers at Howth and the subsequent affray at Bachelor's Walk, when a detachment from the Scottish Borderers fired upon the crowd, filled the front pages of the press; 'within measurable distance of a real Armageddon', the British government was preoccupied with Ireland.[37]

After war broke out, Ireland's problems seemed quickly to recede. The wave of popular emotion sweeping Great Britain and the Empire touched both the north and south of Ireland. In the first flush of enthusiasm, both Protestants and Catholics stepped forward to enlist. The decision of John Redmond and of Sir Edward Carson to bury differences and stand by the British government was endorsed by much of their support. Redmond's declaration that Ireland would take responsibility for her own defence, his biographer suggests, 'interpreted faithfully the instincts of the vast majority of Irishmen':[38] certainly, it split the Irish Volunteers and encouraged thousands of army reservists (who, their loyalties divided by the struggle for Home Rule, were uncertain what to do) to obey the order to rejoin.[39] Berlin's hopes 'that Ireland would rise in rebellion the moment that war was declared' appeared to be frustrated and, as if in token, the King's Own Scottish Borderers, confined to barracks since they had fired on the crowd, were cheered through Dublin as men departed for the front.[40] The British government could relax its vigilance, reduce its garrison in Ireland, and concentrate on the raising of recruits.

The reliance which the nineteenth-century army had placed upon the Irish suggested that the numbers now forthcoming might indeed be large. The Napoleonic Wars had seen the enlistment of Catholic peasants in their thousands, the formation of whole regiments of troops; and while the relative decline in Ireland's population reduced the proportion of her soldiers in the British army — from but three thousand short of those of English birth in 1821, to only 12.9 per cent of the total strength in 1898 — on the outbreak of the First World War more than twenty thousand Irishmen were serving with the regulars and a further thirty thousand belonged to the Reserve.[41]

The Catholic peasantry were not alone involved. Many in the military establishment viewed with satisfaction the prospect of recruiting Ulstermen. Advantageous conditions of service were obtained for a division to be recruited in the North. The War Office agreed that the Ulster Volunteers should enlist as a separate unit, choose its own officers and regain such of its former officers as had been despatched elsewhere on mobilization. These conditions, apart from keeping alive the notion of an armed force representing Ulster, were sure to act as a stimulant to recruiting and morale.

The response of the population of the South, overwhelmingly more significant in point of numbers of recruits, was yet more critical if Ireland were to participate fully in this war. Much depended on the rapport established between its leaders, such as Redmond, and the British government and army. Many Irishmen based their attitude towards the war on estimates of the Asquith government's good faith, but concession could not be easily arranged by a Prime Minister constrained by opinion both in Ulster and on the British right. The uncertainty over the future of the Home Rule Bill held up the start of the recruiting drive, and the terms upon which the measure was suspended added to the deterioration in goodwill. The War Office was no more forthcoming in the concessions it supplied. Lord Kitchener refused to countenance the embodiment of the Irish Volunteers as a force for home defence, and derided the suggestion that such a step would encourage widescale nationalist enlistment. Far from supplying the arms and drill instructors now requested, he proposed to draft units of the Territorials into Ireland to ensure that its defence not rest upon the Irish, not one of whom, he once had said, could be trusted with a rifle in his hands. This attitude was common in the army. The organizer of recruiting in Ireland interviewed many officers who admitted that they were not eager to see great influxes of nationalist recruits: men whose discharge once war was over must strengthen the pressures for Home Rule. Captain de

Montmorency of the 10th Division was convinced that Irish troops would be subverted if they trained at home, and wrote to many senior officers proposing that they be trained in England and their barracks filled with Englishmen and Scots.[42] For many officers, the habit of mind which had led Lord Wolseley to refer to the Irish as 'cowardly skulking reptiles' was difficult to break, and they could not alter their opinions to accommodate a policy pressed upon them by Whitehall.

The rebuffs offered to its leaders were not immediately apparent to the population of the South. In the wave of emotion which followed the assault upon the Belgians, thousands of recruits poured in. By the end of September, three divisions of recruits for the established Irish regiments were forming and training. The 36th (Ulster) Division, exclusively Protestant and Unionist, was comprised overwhelmingly of officers and men from the Ulster Volunteers who, in keeping with the pledge which Sir Edward Carson had received, were to go to war 'as old comrades accustomed to do their military training together'. The official recruiting campaign was scarcely under way, and the military role which the government would permit the Irish Volunteers was already cloudy and uncertain, yet a further two divisions were soon recruiting in the South. At the Curragh, Sir Bryan Mahon was supervising the training of the 10th Division which, while drawing men from the Dublin Special Reserve and from the catchment areas of regiments based in central Ireland, did not maintain an exclusively Irish complexion; deficient battalions were filled up with Welsh miners, though Irish recruits were sometimes moved *en bloc* to regiments elsewhere.[43] In the training camps round Mallow, the headquarters of a 16th Division had been established, and the co-operative attitude of the officer appointed to command, Lt-Gen. Sir Lawrence Parsons, led John Redmond to believe that this unit would represent and be drawn entirely from the South. There was an impressive flow of suitable recruits. The barracks at Fermoy could only cope with half of the 'old men and young sportsmen, students, car drivers, farm labourers, Members of Parliament, poets, litterateurs' whom one enthusiast observed.[44]

The goodwill channelled into the 16th Division was far from nourished and enlarged. Despite representations to the effect that an English-style campaign, based on circulars, mass meetings and the like, would check rather than encourage the flow of volunteers, no thought was given by the authorities to the question of its adaptation to conditions in the South. An atmosphere of trust was missing. Employers were generally believed to be sacking workers to compel them to enlist, and government departments circularised their employees with thinly-veiled threats of dismissal.[45] The Redmondite press ran advertisements calculated to shame Irishmen into joining up.

'Lord Kitchener is very disappointed at the slowness with which the Irish Division in the New Army is filling up . . . should the vacancies in the Irish divisions of the New Armies not be filled up by Irishmen by 14 September, drafts for this purpose will be sent in from England and Scotland. This would be a discredit to Ireland.'[46]

The Prime Minister had promised that men who had already trained together in one district would 'to the utmost limit that military expediency will allow' be kept together if they joined up, but nothing further was done to implement the wholesale embodiment of the Irish Volunteers. One of their officers in Munster was twice rebuffed when offering a thousand men to the War Office for home or foreign service.[47] Sir Francis Vane, recruiting for the Munster Fusiliers, was offered nine thousand Volunteers from Cork, half of the city force, on condition that the defence of the railways, harbours, and so on, be allotted to the rest. This the War Office refused to countenance, though the members involved would have sufficed to bring the division up to strength.[48]

Similar obduracy was experienced by Irishmen resident in England who wished to form units of their own. The Irish Brigade raised on Tyneside received War Office sanction as a unit only after its first battalion had been disbanded and ordered to report to the Northumberland Fusiliers.[49] And where attempts to create a distinctively Irish force were not frustrated at the highest levels, they were thwarted by obscurantism lower down. General Parsons of the 16th Division complained that recruits were not coming forward in sufficient numbers to fill the gaps in the division, but refused the offer of Irish settlers elsewhere. These he dismissed as ' . . . Liverpool, and Glasgow, and Cardiff Irish, who are slum-birds that we don't want. I want to see the clean, fine, strong, temperate, hurley-playing country fellows such as we used to get in the Munsters, Royal Irish, Connaught Rangers.'[50]

General Parsons succeeded, moreover, in destroying at executive level the few distinctively Irish features which Kitchener had initially conceded. Neither badge, nor name, nor colours were permitted to emphasise that unity which Redmond hoped would form the basis for the army of a postwar and independent Ireland. Not one Colonel in the whole division was a Catholic, and commissions were granted overwhelmingly to Protestants.[51] Practically every candidate for commissioned rank whom Redmond recommended was turned down by Parsons, sometimes with farcical results. Serving in the ranks were to be found Stephen Gwynn and Professor Thomas Kettle, both Nationalist MPs of standing. Gavan Duffy, the bearer of a famous Irish name, came back from Australia in search of a commission, but Redmond's submission of his name produced only the reply that the army must take due precaution against the chance of commissioning drunks. Redmond's own son was refused, the general insisting that he could no longer sacrifice military interests to political expediency.[52]

The recruiting figures in the South of Ireland during the first period of the war reflected something of this unusual situation. On the one hand, the Irish nationalists had long been gaining ground, their efforts seeming likely to result in civil war; and, on the other, its leading representatives, abandoning their claims, were all agreed on supporting England in this, the hour of her need. Again, the British government, supported by the South's official leaders, now strove to harness for military service the new-found harmony and trust, while the War Office and regimental officers displayed only caution and reserve. The figures were as follows. After eighteen months of war, in only three Irish counties had more than 20 per cent of the men of military age come forward — which three were in Ulster — though in none of the counties of England, Scotland, Wales, did the percentage fall below this mark. Sixteen counties in the south and west of Ireland furnished less than 10 per cent. In August 1915, there were 416,000 men in Ireland qualified for military service, of whom 252,000 were actively engaged in occupations on the land; 100,000, it was estimated, could be absorbed into the army with small adverse effect on agricultural production.[53] Ireland, it seemed, was not providing all that she was able. 'The labourers and the cornerboys have gone,' explained the Queen's County constabulary report, 'and there remains none but shopboys and farmers sons who are averse to enlisting.'[54]

Why, though, were Irish shopboys and farmers' sons averse, when their counterparts in the rest of the United Kingdom were so evidently not? Opinion in England found its answer in the role played by extremists. The Royal Commission on the Causes of the Rebellion was later to summarize this view: it was 'owing to the activities of the leaders of the Sinn Fein movement that the forces of disloyalty gradually and steadily increased and undermined the initial senti-

ment of patriotism.'[55] Still, whatever the persuasiveness of this
analysis for the period after the uprising, it fails to account for what
happened in the period before, when recruiting figures had proved
disappointing, yet when few signs of anti-British feeling had actually
emerged.[56] Part of the answer must lie in simple economics: agriculture prospered as the demand for food increased, and that
element of destitution which throughout the nineteenth century had
compelled young Irishmen to join the British army, was partly
softened or removed.

Developments in 1915 served, in any case, to dampen loyal
feeling. The rebuffs encountered by Redmond's Volunteers, the pre-
ferences given openly to Ulster, and the losses — excessive, some
opined — suffered by Irish regiments abroad, underpinned a view
which certain nationalists were taking: that Ireland should have no
further part in what was England's war. Their murmurings were not
easy to subdue. The Irish leaders were assured, in confidence, that
losses suffered by the Irish regiments, though severe, were not excep-
tionally so; but in Ireland opinion had it that British generals were
principally to blame.[57]

Members of the Irish Republican Brotherhood, Sinn Fein and
organized labour worked upon these fears. A campaign against
recruiting had been put into effect. One case involving the distribu-
tion of leaflets was reported in July 1914, twenty-one in August,
forty-four in September, and fifty in October.[58] Leaflets were hung in
shops and bars, and distributed at the stations. They could be read in
copies of the *Evening Mail* on sale outside the Dublin theatres. While
Asquith spoke in favour of recruiting, James Connolly, commandant
of the Citizen Army, held a rival meeting to revive memories of
Bachelor's Walk.[59] The Irish dailies were countered by an under-
ground press which, continually closed by the authorities, re-
appeared the following week under different titles.[60]

Whatever their ultimate effect in Ireland as a whole, these efforts
had little impact on those who had already joined the army. A
captain of the Royal Dublin Fusiliers reported that numbers of
Special Reservists, men who had participated in the Dublin lock-out
of 1913, were often absent without leave, sneaking out of camp,
possibly to attend anti-British meetings.[61] Such incidents either were
extremely rare, or else went unrecorded. Indeed, James Connolly's
prognostication that, if the police or military were let loose on the
citizens of Dublin, 'the next time the Dublin Fusiliers were sent to
cover the retreat of the British, the Dublin Fusiliers would forget to
follow the British,' was based on wishful thinking.[62] Sir Roger

Casement's failure to gain recruits from amongst the Irish prisoners held in German camps was proof positive that their loyalties had not seriously been shaken. 'How could anything truly Irish really survive the free entry into the British Army?' Casement asked himself, and then supplied the answer: 'No. These are not Irishmen but English soldiers — that is all.'[63]

The reaction of the Irish soldiers to the Easter Rising showed that, for the time being, the British had no cause for alarm. Neither in Dublin nor in France was there any real manifestation, outside the rising proper, of anti-British feeling. The authorities, of course, had every reason to avoid embarrassing their Irish troops, and hesitated to subdue the insurrection with the three thousand or so which could initially be gathered: the real work of suppression did not begin until units of the 59th (North Midland) Division had arrived by sea. Nonetheless, there may be found no evidence supporting Padraic Pearse's statement of 26 April 1917 that Irish soldiers were defecting to the rebels.[64] In the days which following the uprising, the Redmondite press, now thoroughly pro-British, waxed eloquent about what the Irish regiments had done:

> '. . . not regiments of professional soldiery of the old stamp, but the reserves of the Irish Brigade who had rallied to the last call of the Irish leader, true Irish Volunteers. The 4th and 10th Dublins kept the glorious anniversary of their regiments' heroic landing at Sedd-el-Barr by defending their own city against the blind, self-devoted victims of the Hun. The 2nd and 3rd Battalions of the Royal Irish Rifles — these, to the cheers of the Dublin crowds, began the work of defence.'[65]

It is difficult to assess when, and in what form, news of the uprising can first have reached the front. Some units may well have had the intimation from the Germans. Rumours of the rising were current in the 36th (Ulster) Division while it was preparing for the June offensive; Major Crozier of the Royal Irish Rifles observed that his own men took little notice.[66] All leave to Ireland had been cancelled from Thursday, 27 April 1916; private letters to the troops were ordinarily censored; no newspapers appeared in Dublin until 4 May; and the *Continental Daily Mail*, ubiquitous throughout the trenches, was unlikely to contain material which would excite the feelings of the troops.[67] Such news as filtered through from Dublin to the Irish units serving with the BEF had no effect upon morale which can be traced through the daily diaries kept for each battalion. The 10th Division had suffered losses in the Dardanelles, and its Irish units had been reinforced with drafts from regiments based in southern

England; after a winter spent in terrible conditions, they had been further reduced by sickness and ill-health.[68] No mention is to be found in the diaries, at whatever level, divisional, brigade, battalion, of the political situation at home and of its effects upon the troops. The 16th Division was on active service on the Western Front after Christmas 1915; by Easter it was occupying flooded trenches in the Loos-Hulluck sector, was undertaking frequent, small-scale actions, and was subject to heavy gas attacks. The reaction of the troops to German propaganda showed that their loyalties held firm. The 8th Battalion, Royal Munster Fusiliers, was made the object of two placards constructed by the Germans, one of which read: 'Irishmen! Heavy uproar in Ireland. english guns are firing at your wifes and children. 1st May 1916.' The other referred to the surrender of British troops at Kut-el-Amara. The story that enraged Irishmen stormed the German trenches to seize the placards may be laid at the door of the recruiting officer; they were collected from an empty German dug-out by a lieutenant on patrol.[69] Nevertheless, the use to which the battalion chose to put them was more indicative of their loyalties than was the fiction. On 25 July 1916, the battalion diary noted, Lt-Col. Williamson presented the placards to the King, who asked that his thanks be conveyed to the battalion in return for this and other services. The conduct of the 9th Munster Fusiliers provided even more graphic illustration of the estrangement of Irish troops from nationalist opinion. They hung an effigy of Sir Roger Casement from a tree in No Man's Land: 'it appeared to annoy the enemy and was found to be riddled with bullets.'[70]

The authorities seem to have taken few very obvious precautions to protect morale. If indeed they did, small traces have remained, and it is upon a gathering of incidents that the story must rely. The 16th Division received an unusual number of visits from high-ranking officers in May 1916, visits most probably connected with the forthcoming offensive, but during which the opportunity of reinforcing the loyal martial spirit can have been hardly overlooked.[71] The colonel of the 1st Battalion, Irish Guards, was summoned to the War Office in June to discuss the Irish situation.[72] The 1st Battalion, Royal Munster Fusiliers, serving with the 29th Division at Messines Ridge, was withdrawn from the front line during Easter week, and a soldier of that unit remembers that 'we were of the opinion that we were not to be trusted'; the official reason given was that the battalion was being moved to the Lines of Communication as it was under strength.[73]

Though the authorities were faced with no immediate problem, they could count no longer on the unthinking loyalty of the Irish soldiers under their command. Like the Austrians in Brno and Bratislava, the army in Ireland was now one of occupation and, whatever the shortages of manpower on the Western Front, prudence required that a strong garrison remain. The War Office on occasion doubted the reliability of Irish soldiers in the execution of this task. A lance-sergeant of the 11th Battalion, Royal Dublin Fusiliers, remembers rifle stealing and the infiltration of Sinn Feiners into his unit at Wellington Barracks, Dublin, in September 1917. The unit was evacuated to England in November, as were all Irish reserve battalions, after a spate of rumours to the effect that a second rising was at hand.[74] Discipline was tightened up, and resulted in at least one instance of a strike. The garrison at Tipperary, composed of wounded soldiers from all fronts and from many different Irish regiments, was impelled by minor irritants during Christmas 1916 to refuse parade. English reinforcements were brought in to arrest the mutineers. A participant recalled: 'Orders were given by our NCOs to strip the bed irons and charge the magazine and capture the guns and ammo. and prepare for attack.' The army chose conciliation. 'During the day, the GOC arrived and we were invited to come out. He gave the usual speech and informed us all leave would be opened and any man who wanted could have his Xmas leave granted.' The same garrison had to draw rifles from locked stores when mounting guards, and to return them after duty.[75]

Steps were also taken to shield Irish troops from militant nationalist opinion. When Countess Markiewicz was due to speak at a meeting in Tralee after her release from prison in 1917, units of the local 7th Battalion, Leinster Regiment, were hastily transferred to England.[76] Nor did the authorities make the same mistake as the German government, whose policy of drafting socialists into front-line units merely carried to the trenches the ideas already rife among the civil population. General Maxwell, taking over the Irish command after the rebellion, suggested to the Adjutant-General, Sir Nevil Macready, that Irish prisoners might be allowed to expiate their guilt by joining up, 'and might usefully garrison such places as Sollum or elsewhere'. This scheme Macready rejected.[77]

However carefully the War Office might protect the Irish units from alien influence, it could do nothing to conceal the growing unpopularity of the army among the Irish population; and, as sympathy for the rebel cause grew after the execution of its leaders, estrangement between the civilians and the Irish troops increased. Stephen Gwynn, a captain in the Connaught Rangers, wrote that after the rebellion Irish soldiers found themselves 'in great measure cut off from the moral support which a country gives to its citizens in arms'.[78] Recruiting in Ireland practically dried up. Each of the Irish divisions was 4,500 men below establishment after the fighting on the Somme, July–September 1916.[79] In July the 1st Battalion, Dublin Fusiliers, was complaining that its latest draft contained men from many different Irish regiments; brigade headquarters replied that nothing could be done.[80] After the September fighting, there was every prospect of the Irish divisions disappearing through attrition: 45,000 men were needed to bring Irish units up to strength, 9,000 alone were fit for draft in Ireland, and of those, many were men returned from the front. Few shared the expectation of Macready, that a reinvigorated recruiting drive under the aegis of both Redmond and Carson would repair the situation, for only 13,000 men had volunteered from the whole of Ireland in the first eight months of 1916.[81]

In September 1916 Macready presented five alternatives to a meeting of the Army Council. It might introduce compulsory service in Ireland; amalgamate the 16th and 36th divisions; reinforce the Irish divisions with English troops; transfer all Irish units serving in non-Irish divisions; or simply allow the Irish divisions to die away.[82] Compulsory service, it appeared, would prove harder to enforce than had been the case in England, and would entail disastrous political consequences for the Irish Nationalist Party, the only ally in the South which England still retained. The Under Secretary informed the Lord Lieutenant of the problems which conscription would present. The scheme 'would probably require in addition to the police double the number of soldiers now in Ireland, would cause the wildest political excitement, and in all probability scenes of violence in various parts of the country.'[83] General Sir John Maxwell endorsed this view, and pointed to the effects which 100,000 disaffected Irishmen might have upon the army.

'If they were drafted into the existing Irish Reserve Battalions which are at the moment contented and loyal, they would probably poison the minds of these, and it would be a matter for grave consideration whether they could be trusted and armed while in Ireland. On the other hand, if they were all, including the Reserve Battalions, sent over to England to be trained and armed, this would at once give rise to the outcry that England does not trust Ireland and that this was an intrigue to get all able-bodied men out of the way in order to kill Home Rule.'[84]

In March 1918, when the need for reinforcements was to sweep aside considerations of this kind, the Chief of the Imperial General Staff, Sir Henry Wilson, was to assure the Secretary of State that 150,000 Irishmen could be absorbed into the army without any real danger; in 1916, however, this view did not prevail.[85] The Army Council's first choice among the five alternatives, therefore, was for the weaker of the 16th and 36th divisions to be added to the stronger; but the Irish politicians could no longer agree on a unity which the nationalists, in the first days of the war, had regarded as desirable.[86] The third expedient was proposed, considered, and accepted: that the Irish divisions be retained as separate units, but be filled up with Englishmen and others.

This decision was put into effect. On 26 October 1916 the Adjutant General, GHQ, France, received 'Approval from War Office for reinforcing Irish units with Englishmen, keeping the Regular Irish battalions supplied with Irishmen.'[87] By 24 November the 6th Battalion, Royal Irish Regiment, had received its first draft of fifty-eight other ranks, 'mostly Englishmen taken from surplus RFA recruits'.[88] The 16th Division, after nine months in the trenches, had ceased as a purely Irish unit to exist.[89]

The Easter rising and the sharpening of nationalism in Ireland did not impair the loyalties of those Irishmen already serving in the army. Unlike the Czechs conscripted by Vienna, these men did not rise against their rulers. They fought on without reserve. Their contribution, though, to England's efforts of necessity declined. Deprived of Irish reinforcements as recruitment rapidly fell off, and shorn of moral reinforcement as attitudes in Ireland changed, the 16th Division was slowly sapped of strength. British generals had long known the evil consequences of reinforcing one corps with drafts drawn from another; nonetheless, the 16th (Irish) was re-inforced, first with Englishmen, and then with Portuguese.[90] The policy bore unhappy fruit when, in the spring of 1918, units of the 16th Division were caught by the German Army as it swept towards the sea. The demise of the division, sketched out in chapter seven, belongs to a different period of war. By then, in fact, the BEF had changed. Among its thousands upon thousands it contained not disloyal Irishmen, for these had stayed at home, but a sprinkling of British soldiers who had grown more critical of the Old Army regime.

6
Unrest and Discontent

In the late summer of 1917 the British Expeditionary Force, France and Flanders, was deployed along a section of the Western Front extending from the coast of Belgium to the head-waters of the Somme. In the trenches, behind the lines, gathered in the base depots, and strung out along the lines of communication were gathered some two million officers and men. This great army, the largest which Great Britain has ever sent abroad, was manned, reinforced, armed, fed, and generally supplied, along routes which started principally in England: routes passing through the English ports, across the Channel, and thence through vast bases on the northern coast of France. By 1917 the web of routes and bases, spreading southwards from Dunkirk, had been so far perfected and enlarged that, for the scores of thousand different items pouring daily into France, each had as its initial destination a depot designed to check and sort and store; only then were supplies moved forward, as the need arose, to units at the front. The complex of base ports, base depots, advanced depots, and the network of British road, rail and canal communications established on French soil, bore the simple title: 'Lines of Communication, BEF'.

These Lines of Communication (LOC) were on the grandest scale. For sorting, storing and transporting, they employed one-third of a million men.[1] For labouring, they engaged nearly three hundred thousand more.[2] At one depot established near Le Havre, a single hangar measured more than half a mile in length, over six hundred feet in width, and contained some eighty thousand tons of military supplies.[3] From another depot near Rouen, the flow of food-stuffs to the trenches sufficed, on certain days, to feed one and a quarter million men — and Rouen was but one of half a dozen bases catering for the feeding requirements of the BEF.[4] And dozens of other depots were gradually set up: for uniforms, motor vehicles, sandbags and barbed wire, ammunition, tanks, horses and horse transport, for all the countless items which the BEF consumed.

The LOC handled not only guns and butter; they also handled men. Reinforcements for the artillery passed through the base camps at

Calais and Le Havre. Those for the cavalry landed elsewhere on the coast. The endless stream of infantry, however, came in chiefly through one place: through the base camp at Etaples, a small town in the Pas de Calais, some fifteen miles south of Boulogne. From small beginnings in 1915, the facilities around Etaples were steadily expanded until they comprised the largest reinforcement camp, and the largest base hospital complex, maintained for British troops abroad.[5] Etaples Base embraced railway yards, ordnance stores, training grounds, port facilities, a bakery, a prison, and all the encumbrances of an army far from home; but consisted principally of a series of Infantry Base Depots (IBDs) gathered on the rising ground to the east of the railway which runs north-south beside the town. Each IBD, consisting of 'whole streets of hutments and tents', surrounded by barbed wire, was designed to lodge and feed drafts for three regiments of infantry.[6] Reinforcements passed through the IBDs on their way forward from England to the front. Also in the depots were to be found men transferring to other theatres of the war or classed as 'Temporary Base' after hospital and convalescence.[7] Between June 1915 and September 1917 more than a million officers and men passed through the IBDs on their way up to the front.[8]

The importance of Etaples to the BEF in France lay not only in supplying reinforcements for infantry divisions. The Base, when it was running smoothly, also ensured that reinforcements reached their correct unit in proper physical condition. The problem was as follows. Men arrived in France as drafts from their respective regiments at home; but the BEF consisted of divisions, not regiments, strung out along the front. The men reaching Etaples, therefore, had to be lodged in depots, then grouped and re-assembled for service at the front. Lieutenant Wilfred Owen, arriving in Etaples in the last days of 1916, lodged in the IBD used by reinforcements sent from his regiment at home. Only on moving forward in the New Year to the 2nd Battalion, Manchester Regiment, stationed on the Somme, was he separated from fellow officers and men who, in turn, moved up to join other battalions of the same regiment on duty elsewhere in the line.[9] And GHQ presumed the drafts had little knowledge of trench warfare.[10] Thus the training programme, held on an area of dunes, designed to spread the lessons which the fighting had thrown up.

At Etaples, the troops met with conditions which most remember as oppressive. Not even the most experienced or battle-weary were given respite from the war. At the 'Bull Ring', as the training grounds were called, soldiers barely discharged from hospital and men who had seen much service in the trenches were put through the same

training as the latest drafts from England. A course in gas warfare
and ten days at the Bull Ring was the usual programme; ten days,
that is, of march and double-march across the dunes, supervised by
officers and NCOs of the 'blood on the bayonet' school.[11] An officer
remembers the training to have been 'demoralizing beyond
measure'.[12] Another man, newly arriving at Etaples, found the Bull
Ring to be 'like passing through hell for two weeks'.[13] A corporal
encountered several men returning to the front with wounds which
were far from healed: 'When I asked why they had returned in that
condition they invariably replied: "To get away from the Bull
Ring".'[14] If the accommodation was rudimentary, so also was the
food. Official rations on the LOC were more limited than those
provided at the front.[15] Even so, they purported to allow a daily diet
more generous than the single meal of bully beef and onions typical
of a whole host of reports.[16]

Not everyone described Etaples Base in terms of clear distaste. The
Adjutant General, BEF, responsible for the flow of reinforcements,
described the British convalescent camps in France as places 'where
men were exercised, well fed, encouraged to go in for games of all
kinds, and kept amused by entertainments when the day's work was
done'.[17] Amusements, games — these words occur in no other recollections of the base camp at Etaples. Certainly, a camp cinema
existed, and a couple of tea huts, but these brought little solace to the
soldiers passing through. 'I recall the YMCA hut as cheerless. . . . It
was not easy to get a pass out of the camp. . . . Every place was out of
bounds for us . . . '[18] Even Wilfred Owen, who compared conditions
at Etaples to life in a hotel, was writing an officer's account. He had a
tent to himself, a servant, and lunched on items more substantial
than onions and corned beef: 'We were in the camp of Sir Percy
Cunynghame, who had bagged for his Mess the Duke of
Connaught's chef.'[19] But Lt Owen escaped the Bull Ring, and during
this, his first visit to Etaples, spent only two days at the Base.[20]
Overhearing the rowdiness of Scots troops penned in their IBD,
Owen likened life there to a paddock — 'a kind of paddock where
the beasts are kept a few days before the shambles'.[21]

Two further features of the Base camp were recalled by all who
passed its gates. The first was the training staff itself. The instructors
at the Bull Ring, called 'canaries' from the yellow armlets which they
wore, had installed a harsh regime.

'The battles fought in the Bull Ring were the most exciting of the
War. . . . Nothing we encountered thereafter provoked such rage as we

felt when, shouted and cursed at, pursued and prodded, we charged with full pack and fixed bayonets, through barbed wire and into water, leaping trenches, climbing walls, downhill and uphill, running, stumbling, scrambling up again, while the Canaries chirped . . .

'No, the Bull Ring was not nice. I can truthfully say I had moments there as unpleasant as anywhere on the Western Front. I was never so angry elsewhere. The sectional rushes, the belly-flopping, the "on-the-'ands-downing", the marching, the manual drill, the saluting at every few steps when you were off duty, the air-raid alarms — what a bad war it was at Etaples!'[22]

The camp police, responsible for order, formed a second feature remembered by the soldiers passing forward through the Base. The police in any army are usually disliked, but a particular hatred surrounded the contingent at Etaples. They had not served at the front, it seems, but had been brought in from Aldershot; and it was the disciplinary standard of the glasshouse that they had been trying to impose.[23] 'Discipline was strict at Etaples. That does not mean discipline was good: it merely means that what the Army calls "crime" was extensively manufactured and severely punished. There was always somebody tied to a gunwheel.'[24]

For the rank and file, the harshness of the training, the spartan nature of the camp's accommodation, and the policy of the authorities in limiting visits to Etaples or even to the sea, compelled full use of the camp's facilities when each day's work was done. The recreation huts, and the area close to the bridge which crossed the railway into town, were particularly crowded on Sunday afternoons, no training being undertaken after church parade. The afternoon of Sunday, 9 September 1917 provided no exception. Nor was it exceptional that the military police should keep the bridge clear of troops; nor that the soldiers present should resent the actions of the police. At noon that day an NCO had warned the police that men from the New Zealand Base Depot intended raiding the police hut in retribution for the arrest of one of their number on an earlier occasion. 'As threats by Colonials were fairly common', no notice was taken of his words.[25] The threat to raid the police hut was not directly carried out, but an incident took place that afternoon which was to have graver consequences than any originally envisaged. At 3 o'clock the police at the bridge arrested a gunner of the New Zealand Artillery. He had committed no offence, he was later to allege, and was also gratuitously assaulted. He was soon released. The arrest, however, had been witnessed by others on the spot, and 'some feeling was shown against the police'.[26] By 4 o'clock a crowd had begun to gather, and in the next half hour or so was augmented by men leaving the camp cinema at the end of the afternoon performance. The crowd was now of threatening proportions. A New Zealander, on directly demanding the release of the arrested gunner, was taken into the guardroom and shown that, in fact, the prisoner had already been set free.[27] The revelation came too late. The crowd had grown until it pressed forward on to the bridge, and the military police were having difficulty in keeping order. An altercation between a police-man and an Australian took on more serious dimensions. A Scotsman undergoing training at the Base takes up the story.

> '[The] Red Cap tried to move him [the Australian] away without any result so he brought force into it and that started something that others joined in till the Red Cap must have lost his head and started using his gun. He wounded one or two but hit our post Corporal (an innocent minding his own business and passing by) in the head, he I believe died later; I knew him and a grand and good-living chap he was.'[28]

The crowd was naturally enraged.

> 'By this time hundreds had gathered and the Red Caps were having a tough time at their little huts on the Rly embankment being stoned by those who never missed an opportunity to get at them with a free hand to really enjoy it. The mob was angry and the Assistant Provo' Marshal soon turned on his horse when the stones started in his direction.'[29]

Nearly four thousand men were present, but not all of them wished to take the matter further.[30] One man remembers his group following its sergeant away from the demonstration, while thousands of soldiers had not yet left the different IBDs.[31]

> 'I was in the camp when someone said there was some shooting at the bridge which was close to our camp. . . . Our camp commander a staff officer of (I think) the KOYLI or DLI appealed very strongly to the men from his camp to report back and like true Scots we did. I think the absentees was no more than 7.'[32]

Numbers of the men in the depots, though, on learning of the shooting and the rush into Etaples, crossed over into town. And this despite the calling up of an officer and fifty men from the New Zealand Base Depot, of a further two hundred reinforcements, and of an assortment of officers from every IBD.[33] By 7.30 p.m. a thousand men had gathered in the town. According to the Base Commandant, Brigadier-General A. Graham Thomson, the crowd's hostility was directed against the police, and his officers went more or less unscathed.[34] The Camp Adjutant remembers a more dramatic sequence of events:

> 'Word of the incident went round to all the depots and that night . . . the men poured into the town and refused to obey orders.
> 'One of the Staff Captains at the office of the Officer i/c Reinforcements, a very brave man, stood on the parapet of the bridge, with a drop of about 40 ft. below him, and started to harangue the men but they disregarded him.
> 'Before this, he attempted to stop the men crossing the bridge by lining up a lot of officers from the camp about six deep but the men swept them aside. They swarmed into town, raided the office of the Base Commandant, pulled him out of his chair and carried him on their shoulders through the town.'[35]

Nor were the officers merely disregarded.

> ' . . . some of the officers attached to the office of the Officer i/c Reinforcements, myself among them, had to make our way down a path on the railway embankment in order to get to our billet in the town. We had a few stones thrown at us. Luckily we managed to get a lift on a passing engine.'[36]

The Base Commandant, in his contemporary diary, reports that the troops who had gathered in the town returned to camp that night.[37] Lady Angela Forbes, together with several female assistants, was responsible for two soldiers' buffets at the Base. Writing in 1922, she recalled the night of 9 September 1917 as being 'perfectly peaceful'; after a few words from a colonel, 'the mob were wending their way back to the camp'.[38] Another version of these incidents — based on recollection across a gap of sixty years and 'obviously . . . interspersed with a mass of rumour, hearsay and exaggeration'[39] — suggests that 'the rebels rampaged long into the night'.[40]

On the following day, Monday, 10 September 1917, the troops returned to training, and drafts continued to move to and from Etaples. Lt-Gen. Asser who, as General Office Commanding, Lines of Communication, was Brigadier Thomson's immediate superior, reached Etaples from Abbeville. He brought with him Major Dugdale, a police officer from GHQ. Certain measures were agreed on, to prevent disturbances breaking out again. A field officer was put in charge of Etaples town and all guards and picquets there, and a hundred men were sent from Le Touquet Lewis Gun School to Paris

Plage, a town adjacent to Etaples and just along the coast, in case the trouble spread. The forces of conciliation were similarly strengthened, by ordering all officers to be present in their depots between 5.30 and 10.00 p.m. A board of inquiry began to collect evidence as to what had happened on the Sunday.[41]

One further gathering was also taking place. A corporal had been arrested on the Sunday. He had joined a party of some seventy or so who, having split off from the main throng in Etaples, had then moved to the far side of the town. They had approached the road bridge across the River Canche; some of them were waving improvised red flags. On the bridge had stood a captain, four officers, and a mixed guard drawn from British and Canadian soldiers. In the charged atmosphere that evening, the captain had doubted whether his picquet would stand firm. He harangued them, urging them to carry out their duty. At this point the corporal intervened. He is reported to have said: 'Don't listen to the bloody officer. What you want to do with that bugger is to tie a rope round his neck with a stone attached to it and throw him into the river.'[42] A little later, the captain picked a sergeant and four privates, on all of whom he felt he could rely. They were ordered to arrest the corporal if he happened to return. He did return, and was promptly taken in. Next day, at 'one of the most hastily convened courts martial of the war', the corporal was sentenced to be shot.[43]

Neither the shadow of this summary court-martial, nor the stationing of further picquets round the camp, could moderate the temper of the troops. The crowds collecting during Monday after-noon and evening proved hardly less determined than they had been the day before. At 4 o'clock groups of men broke through the picquets on the bridge and held meetings in the town.[44] One witness recalls that a committee was elected, of perhaps six men chaired by a corporal of the Northumberland Fusiliers.[45] Some soldiers tried to stop traffic through the town, while others headed down the river for the detention camp. They were spotted at 6.30 p.m., addressed by the Base commandant and, according to his diary, were then led back to camp. A little later, a hundred men tried to enter the field punish-ment enclosure. Again, the commandant claims that they were persuaded to disperse. At 9 p.m. a crowd gathered at the railway station. A thousand men had assembled at the railway bridge, but 'were evidently from their temper not out to make any further trouble'.[46] Lady Forbes's tea-hut was located not far from the bridge: 'though we were crowded out there was not a pane of glass broken'.[47]

On Tuesday, 11 September the Base commandant resolved to seek reinforcements from outside. He urged the Chief Provost Marshal of the Armies who, together with Colonel Wroughton of the Adjutant-General's staff, had arrived that day, to put the matter direct to General Headquarters — 'troops from outside were urgently required'. The Provost Marshal promised to do this, but before GHQ could even be informed, Brigadier-General Thomson and his staff sought to hasten reinforcement. They tried to get in touch with 9th Cavalry Brigade direct: 'It was ... felt ... that Cavalry could usefully be employed.'[48] But the telephone call to 9th Cavalry Brigade was put through in error to Cavalry Corps HQ. Without breaking off the call or even speaking to the corps commander himself, the request was bluntly made: could two squadrons of the 15th Hussars, presently in Frencq, be held in readiness to move? To this request, no answer could be given. Within half an hour, however, a staff captain from Etaples had driven off to Frencq to inform the regiment what its duties would involve.[49]

At 2.30 p.m. Cavalry Corps HQ rang back. They would not move without permission from above. Etaples accordingly telephoned HQ, Lines of Communication, which in turn contacted GHQ itself. About 4 p.m. an answer was received. GHQ would not authorize the intervention of the cavalry. It would, however, send seven or eight hundred men of the Honourable Artillery Company (HAC), the first battalion of which was stationed at Montreuil.[50]

That afternoon there were further demonstrations. Just as GHQ was making its reply, men were defying orders and entering the town. A crowd of soldiers passed through the picquet on the bridge, marched through the town, broke the picquet on the bridge across the River Canche, and struck northwards towards Paris Plage. Eventually, according to the records, an officer met the demonstrators and persuaded most of them to return to camp with him. There they dispersed. That night, five arrests were made in Etaples town itself.[51]

Wednesday, 12 September saw an enlargement of these demonstrations. Tuesday's march to Paris Plage had not involved more than three hundred men. On Wednesday, in the attempt to stop the demonstrations, all troops were confined to camp except for training. At 3 p.m., however, a thousand men broke bounds, marched through the town and thence to Paris Plage. They then returned to camp. The picquets failed to stop them, and the Honourable Artillery Company had not yet reached Etaples. 'Some cars were interfered with' but no important incidents took place.[52]

That day, Lieutenant-General Asser made a further visit to Etaples. He gave final sanction to the bringing up of the HAC, but the continuing failure to contain the demonstrations perhaps raised doubts in his and other minds as to whether that unit could make a sufficient show of force. GHQ was also reconsidering this question. A wire reached Etaples, just as the thousand demonstrators were passing through the town, to the effect that the 15th Hussars, plus one section, Machine-Gun Squadron, were in readiness to move. Later in the day, word came through of further preparations. The 19th Hussars and four machine-guns could also move at one hour's notice. Etaples asked that these units should be kept at the ready.[53]

On Wednesday evening the HAC arrived: a detachment of four hundred officers and men. They at once took up their posts but, the day's demonstrations being over, had no duties to fulfil.[54]

Next morning all was thoroughly prepared. The Honourable Artillery Company was in position, the Hussars and the machine-guns were held in readiness to move. Etaples was confident that before the day was out it would have re-established full military control. It had informed the French authorities that order would be 'immediately' restored; now it was taking steps to carry out this pledge. All ammunition was collected from the soldiers in the IBDs, and, a rollcall being taken, it was found that only twenty-three men were missing. It was the turn, however, of GHQ to show unreasonable concern. Just after 11 o'clock on Thursday morning it wired that two infantry battalions, both from 7th Division, were on their way; at 12.45 p.m. it sent the further information that not just a regiment of cavalry, but an entire brigade, was now held at the ready. Etaples wired back: the brigade was not required.[55]

In the event, the HAC did the job unaided. Only two hundred men broke camp on Thursday evening, and they did so mainly by choosing more circuitous routes than that offered by the Three Arch Bridge. Indeed, in trying unsuccessfully to force the HAC's picquet on the bridge, 'two of the ringleaders were injured by entrenching tool handles'. The majority of the men were back in camp by 9 p.m.[56]

On Friday, 14 September the picquets provided by the HAC were dispensed with, and policing returned to a more peaceful basis. The original body of police, however, was not restored. Fresh personnel, to fill the ranks of the camp police, the foot police and the mounted police, had been drafted in, and was now in sufficient strength to handle all normal calls upon it. The HAC was removed from the forefront of affairs, one company being held in the town with the remainder in reserve.[57] Of the two infantry battalions sent by GHQ, the first, the 1st Battalion, Royal Welch Fusiliers, had arrived about midnight, and the second, the 22nd Battalion, Manchester Regiment, not until 4.30 on Friday morning. One company of the Fusiliers was sent that afternoon to guard the detention camp, while the remainder of the battalion stood at the ready. The 22nd Manchesters were kept in the camp nearby.[58] The awaiting cavalry units received the following advice:

'It is considered now that Cavalry will not be required at all unless situation materially alters. Adequate number of Infantry now available and ringleaders are being arrested. Trouble expected to subside rapidly.'[59]

This was shortly before midday. On Friday afternoon between fifty and sixty men again broke out of camp but were arrested in Etaples.[60] The authorities were now certain that the disturbances were over. On Saturday, 15 September the town of Etaples was thrown open to the soldiers in the IBDs. The 22nd Manchesters bathed in the sea, played football and watched a concert. They remained in the area until 17 September. That day the Royal Welch Fusiliers also left, as did next day the detachment from the HAC.[61]

What of the causes of the mutiny itself? The camp adjutant remembers as 'the chief cause of discontent' the fact that men who had already done much service at the front had to undergo 'the same strenuous training as the drafts of recruits arriving from home'.[62] Equally, once trouble did break out, both camp and regimental officers were ill-placed to restore discipline through those methods of persuasion available to officers who are well known to their men.

'It should be realized that each Infantry Base Depot was commanded by an elderly retired officer who had an adjutant to help him. The remaining officers, like the men, were either reinforcements from home, or had been sent down the line on account of ill-health, and therefore did not know them.'[63]

The transitory nature of the Base camp disrupted the usual regimental loyalties. Of the thousands of young officers, such as Lt Wilfred Owen, passing forward through the Base, many lacked experience and were still unfamiliar faces to their men. And by 1917 good officers and NCOs were needed above all at the front: permanent positions at the Base camps were filled by the old and the infirm.[64] When trouble did break out, therefore, only residual loyalties existed on which the authorities could draw. Much depended on the fear which the camp police had instilled. And thus the scale of the disruption when, on 9 September 1917, the camp police lost control. On this point all witnesses agree: the fracas at the bridge, culminating in the death of Corporal Wood, provided a powerful focus for resentment of the police. We have already noted Wood's standing in his regiment and the effect which his injury had upon the crowd.[65] The Base commandant's diary, in effect, attributes responsibility for the entire week of trouble to the military police, while the officers of the HAC, arriving in Etaples on the Wednesday, learned that 'riots had broken out . . . owing to the unpopular edicts and actions of a certain Provost Marshal' — the Provost Marshal, of course, being the officer responsible for the military police.[66]

If conditions at the Base camp, the loose hold of the officers, and the unpopularity of the military police are spoken of from many sides, less is known about the attempt to give some wider purpose to the demonstrations. The Base commandant explained the activities of the troops in terms of their desire to seek out, and deal retribution to, the military police; hence the march on the detention camp, the field punishment enclosure and the railway station, in all of which the police might have taken refuge.[67] Another witness remembers a different purpose directing the actions of the men. The plight of military prisoners was well-known to the soldiers at Etaples. Inadequately maintained and fed, and confined in cells situated in the lowest, dampest part of the dunes, men being punished for serious offences but who had been spared the penalty of death lived out their periods of sentence. Their release might only be a gesture but it would, it seems, have been viewed with general satisfaction.[68] Even so, the pursuit of the police, or the release of prisoners, could scarcely account for the continuing daily demonstrations; and their orderliness presents something of a puzzle. Riots, more or less destructive, were fairly common in the army, particularly in the closing period of war, and strikes — refusals of duty in support of specific objects — became quite popular. But the incidents at Etaples Base fall into neither category. It is the combination of the sudden riot on the Sunday afternoon, followed by demonstrations every afternoon and evening, which provides the most unusual aspect of the affair; and yet, apart from references to 'noisy meetings' and the like,[69] little is known of the kind of organization which was certainly thrown up, or of the deliberations of those who took part.[70]

The Commander-in-Chief, BEF, did comment indirectly on the troubles at Etaples. Writing two weeks after the disorder had died down, Sir Douglas Haig ascribed his difficulties to the presence in the ranks of men who voiced unrest and discontent.

'Men of this stamp are not satisfied with remaining quiet, they come from a class which like to air real or fancied grievances, and their teaching in this respect is a regrettable antidote to the spirit of devotion and duty of earlier troops.'[71]

These undesirables Haig likened to a leaven, a leaven which had spread throughout the ranks. How, though, had this leaven formed? Haig thought that the change from a purely voluntary army to one based upon compulsory military service provided something of a key. Being compelled to serve, some of the new men felt no loyalty towards the army and, when they came to be discharged, would leave it 'with relief'. He dismissed as 'negligible' their wish to serve their country.[72]

Thus the views of one man who, by virtue of his experience and office, was most fitted to assess the problems of morale. And yet, his arguments were flawed. The Australian people had resisted compulsory military service and, in consequence, every Australian in France was a simple volunteer. No one could doubt the spirit of self-sacrifice which had induced these men to serve. On Haig's own reasoning, therefore, the Australian divisions should have been most free of disaffection, among the least likely to rebel. Yet this was not the case. At Etaples, they formed the very faction which led the break-out at the camp, the leaven which caused the British troops to rise; on a wider canvas, there are innumerable sketches of the misconduct, in every theatre, of these Anzac volunteers. Their severest critic was Sir Douglas Haig himself.[73] And it was not necessarily the new men, the men who served against their will, who, on 9 September 1917, had followed the colonials across the Three Arch Bridge. One day after Haig had set out his complaints, excoriating 'the unrest and discontent' the newcomers had spread,[74] one man, a corporal, faced the sternest test of all. He was led out to be shot: a penalty he had earned for his deeds on 9 September. A regular soldier, with eight years in the army and two of them in France,[75] his kind was not the leaven but the very body of the bread.

So much, then, for Haig's contention that compulsory military service had introduced misbehaviour to his ranks. What of the 'real or fancied grievances' which the soldiers hoped to air? At that 'vast, dreadful encampment,' the Base Camp at Etaples,[76] these grievances ran deep. 'At Etaples, we were treated in a manner which made us ashamed to be soldiers. It made us bitter.'[77]

It would be wrong, however, to take issue with the logic which Haig's letter had displayed. Its contents were important, for they contained the simple truth. His letter noted that a change had taken place — a change in attitudes throughout the BEF. Haig held a minority to blame. That minority, he felt, had come in since conscription was enforced. But, no matter when they entered, their influence was clear: 'The influence of these men and their antecedents generally are not such as to foster any spirit but that of unrest and discontent . . . '[78] 'Antecedents generally' was a reference, of course, to the origins and outlook of a whole new group of men: 'the manufacturing hands' and their 'companions' whom the nineteenth-century army had been so unwilling to take in.[79] These men had shed 'the spirit of devotion' which had gripped Lord Kitchener's recruits.[80] Haig had grasped the problem which had surfaced at Etaples. The dissidents, he wrote, 'come from a class which like to air real or fancied grievances'.[81] In other words, a social and political element had unexpectedly crept in. Unlike the problems of desertion or insubordination, the new indiscipline might outrange the limits of what mere shootings could prevent. At 9.15 p.m. on Sunday, 9 September, close by the River Canche, a captain had found a sergeant and four privates on whom he could rely. The discipline had held. One arrest effected; one dissident condemned.[82] Next day, that discipline collapsed. One sergeant, four privates? They were nowhere to be seen. Out of the tens of thousands in the Base camp, not one would raise his hand. Of course, the officers had given orders, and put picquets round the Base but at 4 p.m., when the day's work was over, the troops quite easily 'broke through'.[83] Worse, these dissidents held 'meetings' in the town. What kind of discipline was this? And since no one was arrested, none could be condemned. If the captain gave his orders, he gave them in a void. This was the bitter medicine which Haig now had to take. One sergeant, four privates, could not have held the bridge. But a hundred loyal soldiers would have had a powerful effect. On that vital afternoon, Haig might have given ten divisions at 3rd Ypres for a battalion he could trust. By Tuesday afternoon, the battle had been lost. 'None of the picquets made any determined effort to prevent these men.'[84]

During the night of 9 September, the Old Army had died. It was still living on the Sunday; four privates and a sergeant had obeyed orders on that day. Riots in Base camps; arrest of malcontents: this is the story of all armies in great wars.[85] But at 4 p.m. on Monday, the position was quite changed. A new mood had arisen in all the IBDs. It was one, not of mere disorder, but of a determination to defy the regulations and cross over to Etaples. It continued through to Tuesday, and by Wednesday, the Base staff were treating their own impotence as a matter of routine. And GHQ reworked its calculations as the week drew on. It vetoed the use of cavalry; it brought up the 22nd Manchesters and the 1st Royal Welch Fusiliers, but kept them tucked quietly away. It employed, finally, part of the HAC — a contingent of young gentlemen straight out of public schools. Order was restored, but the price was very high. The sergeants and the privates could not be trusted to obey: so young officers were soon brawling with the soldiers who had taken to the streets. These fights could not go on, for no discipline withstands the strain of combats such as these. When the week was over, Haig quickly backed away. The town of Etaples was thrown open to the troops, certain officers removed, and reforms were soon effected throughout the back areas of France.

Thus, the rule book was re-written: not by generals but by the army's other ranks. Opinionated young officers could not see what Haig had done. Robert Graves had declared that, in such circumstances, the Fusiliers would be certain to obey, and, as late as 1965, Charles Carrington still believed that the Manchesters had restored order to Etaples. These two men were wrong. The generals had lost confidence in their hold upon the troops; after Monday 10 September they were no longer certain that their men would still obey. Another officer, R.H. Mottram, more clearly saw the change. He knew little of what had happened in Etaples, and cared little to find out. But one thing he knew well. A great change had taken place.

'I never knew the truth, and perhaps no one does. For some days a great docile mob walked about the streets, relatively harmless, and eventually returning to camp to be fed. Shortly after, the miserable failure of an offensive was brought to a close. But the effect was permanent. From this time there developed a new spirit of taking care of one's self among the men . . .'[86]

7
Shootings Out of Hand

A Sunday demonstration, sparked off by an incident involving one Anzac volunteer, scarcely threatened the British military authorities with a disaster comparable to those which their continental counterparts now faced. By September 1917, the fissures within many armies were running wide and deep. Those within the Austro-Hungarian armed forces, along lines of nationality, impaired their unity and strength; and were to lead, as 1918 drew on, to complete disintegration. The plight of Russia's army is equally well known. Her troops, now touched by revolution, were drifting back towards their homes. The French army was in a state of convalescence. It had survived widespread mutinies that spring, but was unfit for serious offensives. The German army was free of such a stain. In the German towns, however, the agitations of the socialists threatened to halt industrial production and bring disorder to the streets.

The troubles at Etaples were slight in comparison with these. Even so, a problem now existed which had not been seen before. The morale of the BEF was apparently impaired — 'deplorable' was the word used by a member of the War Cabinet to describe the condition of the army in late 1917.[1] An account of that impairment is difficult to give. 'Morale', a vast, elusive notion, is all too frequently defined through generalities like 'war weariness', too simply gauged by listing casualties and deaths. Rather than directly tackling this notion, it will be simpler and more illuminating, to examine GHQ's assessment of the problem: to scrutinise, that is, what Haig's staff said and did in dealing with the troubles which it faced. At Etaples, and in the months which followed, GHQ took certain steps to curtail the new phenomenon of rank and file unrest. These steps, and the thought which underlay them, shed light on the problems of the army and testify more readily than any judgements which the historian may make to the state of its morale. And such a scrutiny is unusually worth while. An examination of the cases of unrest, of measures to suppress them and place curbs upon their spread, illuminates the composition and traditions of the army, the recruitment, social basis, military standing, war experience and so on of the men and units which chanced to be involved.

First, then, GHQ's reaction to the problems at Etaples. From the confusion surrounding day-to-day decisions, it is evident that neither at GHQ nor at the Base itself had preparation been made to deal with outbreaks of this kind. At first, the Base staff had handled the affair themselves, trying on their own initiative to call up reinforcements; but GHQ had increasingly stepped in. Initially, it had shown its interest via telephone and telegraph, but as the week progressed officers had been sent down to gauge at first hand conditions at the Base. Their reports and all record of high-level deliberation have not survived; but something of the dilemma which confronted the authorities was reflected in a letter which the colonel of another unit addressed to his superiors when, a little later in the year, he too was pondering the lessons to be learned. Disturbances, he wrote, 'can, of course, be quelled by drastic measures, i.e. shooting those who are temporarily out of hand'. Still, 'if this procedure be solely relied on', more unrest might very well ensue.[2] Strong measures, in brief, might always be effective, but would have repercussions in other parts of France. The author of this letter wrote with the benefit of hindsight, after a policy of shootings had been put into effect; but doubtless such considerations, and the pressing need for caution, must have weighed with GHQ as it considered what to do. To fire on Anzac and British soldiers as they paraded through Etaples would have spread alarm through the back areas of France, and precipitated a crisis in Anglo-Australian relations; yet to take no steps towards the restoration of control threatened the basis of discipline itself. Just how difficult a path GHQ had to tread is shown by the variety of units which it brought up, or held in readiness, for intervention at the base. Its choice of units, culminating in the part allotted to the Honourable Artillery Company, sheds light on the dilemma.

For three days, it will be recalled, Brigadier-General Graham Thomson, the Etaples Base Commandant, had no troops available on whom he could rely. On the first day, his police were driven off, and every attempt to use infantrymen from one or other of the less affected depots, to use New Zealanders against a Scottish crowd, and so on, was thwarted by the unwillingness of the troops concerned to stop the demonstrations. He asked, therefore, that cavalry be sent. It was an obvious request. Cavalry units had always regarded themselves as an elite, and if brought up, together with their horses, might form a useful force in quashing demonstrations. Still, the use of cavalry represented something of a risk, and this risk GHQ seemed disinclined to take. Cavalry would be of little use in forming picquets on the bridge and railway embankment; it would be most effective in a dramatic clearing of the streets. Yet, if it undertook that duty, the troopers would of necessity need arms; when the shock and violence of the action, the provocation offered by the men on horses, and the certainty of casualties, might well excite the anger of hundreds who, far from being the ill-organized and unarmed demonstrators against whom, in civil questions, cavalry or mounted policemen traditionally are used, were the very men, their skills and rifles ready, who had chased the German cavalry from all engagements at the front. In the depots, the men had access to the arms. In the shelter of its streets, an infantry platoon might well have held Etaples against a cavalry brigade.

By Thursday, 13 September, the fifth day of the mutiny, these objections had in part been overcome. The greatest danger confronting the authorities now lay in permitting the demonstrations to continue, in allowing discipline to be wilfully defied. Accordingly GHQ sent into Etaples, or held in readiness for operations there, four separate units: a brigade of cavalry; the 1st Battalion, Royal Welch Fusiliers; the 22nd Battalion, Manchester Regiment; and a detachment from the 1st Battalion, Honourable Artillery Company. The 1st Battalion, Royal Welch Fusiliers was the regular battalion of an illustrious regiment, and one whose reputation was quite the equal of any unit whose drafts had joined the demonstrations at Etaples. On their loyalty, of all the regiments of foot, the army could surely place a maximum of trust. Robert Graves, who served with this battalion, maintained to Bertrand Russell that the Fusiliers would fire on striking munition workers if called upon to do so; and there seemed a chance, during their days of service at Etaples, that they might have to shoot down fellow soldiers.[3] The reputation of the 22nd Manchesters was less widespread. A service battalion, it had been created in the first months of the war. Nonetheless, overcoming its humble origins, and drawing soldiers from an area which Graves has classed as second only to the north Midlands in providing men of a reliable type, it was in 1917 serving together with the 1st RWF in 7th Division — 'one of the recognized top-notch divisions' in the BEF.[4] The division had been withdrawn in August into GHQ Reserve and had spent a month in billets.[5] In September, a more reliable infantry unit could scarcely have been found.

In the event, the authorities relied neither on the Fusiliers nor on the Manchesters. The Manchesters remained in camp throughout those days; and the generals at Etaples chose not to place in the

Fusiliers the kind of confidence which Captain Graves had so easily displayed in conversation — the battalion was not used directly to confront the demonstrating troops. A detachment from the HAC which, stationed at Montreuil, carried out guard duties for advanced GHQ and acted as a training unit for officer cadets was used instead.[6] Eight weeks later, when the Winter Palace at St Petersburg was stormed by Bolshevik workers and soldiers, the last vestige of a reliable force which the Provisional Government could find and place against them was a unit of officer cadets. At Etaples, the HAC was the one unit in which complete reliance could be placed. Drawn from the upper reaches of society, the cadets were certain to stand firm.[7] The attempt by soldiers drawn from the Scottish working class to reason their way through a picket of the HAC had not the slightest prospect of success.

So much, then, for the troops on whose loyalties GHQ felt sure it could rely. What, however, of those who made up the demonstrations? Little is known of their detailed composition, and the names of any 'ringleaders' have yet to be released. Still, some general observations may be made from what is known. The presence of both Scottish and Anzac soldiers lent the mutiny a cohesiveness which, by itself, a riot could not attain. In fact, the part played by Anzac soldiers on the opening Sunday at Etaples forms but one instance of the difficulties which arose between the British army, with its 'traditions of duty and long-suffering'[8] and its fixed gulf between officers and men, on the one hand, and a band of adventurers, all volunteers, who had crossed the world to fight in someone else's war, on the other. In addition to the Anzacs, many Scotsmen were present on that day. Discipline in the Scottish regiments was as fierce and narrow as it was easygoing among the Anzacs, and social differences were also very marked. Nonetheless, Scotsmen and Australians got on well together, and one historian has emphasised 'the quite remarkable friendship which ripened between the soldiers of the two nations' during the Great War.[9] At Etaples, this close relationship built a degree of trust and understanding which helped to convert a sudden riot of four thousand men into a series of daily demonstrations; it supplied, among the shifting and temporary population of a Base camp, the loyalties which, on the lower decks at Spithead and the Nore, had taken months and years to build.

The importance of the link between Anzac and Scottish troops becomes evident when we consider the conduct of men drawn from a community which had reason to mistrust and fear the Scots — the Catholic Irish. While Scottish troops were thronging through

Etaples, men of the 16th (Irish) Division refused active part in what was taking place. 'All they did was to raid the canteen and sit outside and get drunk and encourage the others.'[10] The attitude of the Irish soldiers at Etaples Base was probably connected with the deteriorating condition of the 16th Division and its eventual disintegration, the consequence of the rise of nationalism in Ireland; but it also forms part of a continuing hostility between the Irish and the Scots.

News of the Etaples incidents never reached the press, and Sir Douglas Haig, writing to refute his critics, went to some pains to deny that 'any discontent exists in our ranks'.[11] Still, whatever the success in suppressing information, it was scarcely possible for his staff to assume that the troubles had blown over, to take no steps to head off further discontent. At Etaples, a number of reforms were effected in the administration of the Base. Brigadier-General Graham Thomson was soon replaced, as were the commanding officer and adjutant at the Royal Scots Base Depot.[12] Two weeks after the opening demonstration, there came the most significant concession: training at the Bull Rings was to a large extent closed down, reinforcements reaching Etaples now going straight up to the front.[13] And concession spread wider than the confines of Etaples. In the words of one man present that September, but who declined a part in the opening affray, it was 'the belief of thousands . . . that it changed the whole phase of routine and "Bull" from Base to Front Line'.[14]

Concern over the condition of the army led the military authorities, in late 1917, to undertake a close investigation of the BEF's morale. The use of sampling techniques permitted the Military Censor, examining the letters sent homewards by the troops, to make the following assessment:

'The Morale of the Army is sound. In spite of increasing references to peace which occupy so much space in the newspapers, in spite of the Russian debacle and the Italian set back there is ample ground for the belief that the British Army is firmly convinced, not only of its ability to defeat the enemy and its superiority man to man, but also of the dangers of a premature peace.'

The examination of the Armies one by one, however, brought the Censor to the following conclusion.

'There is a very striking difference between the results of the examination of the Second Army which at the time was bearing the brunt of the fighting and that of the other Armies . . .'

In the Second Army, the letters which the Censor judged a favourable sign of the soldiers' morale were almost evenly balanced by those he took to be unfavourable; in the other Armies, the favourable greatly exceeded the unfavourable. Most of the letters examined (and in this the Censor based himself not only on the 17,000 letters specially selected, but also on a general impression arising over the previous three months) contained no passages bearing on morale, but were 'merely cheery ordinary letters'. In sum, 'War weariness there is, and an almost universal longing for peace but there is a strong current of feeling that only one kind of peace is possible and that the time is not yet come.'[15]

The morale of the Second Army, then, had by no means broken down, and a majority amongst the British troops in France remained convinced that the war must be fought through to its end. In 1917, though, the Russian forces had collapsed, and that same spring the French armies had been wracked with discontent. The riots at Etaples and the increasing numbers of offenders indicated that, in the British army, the spirit of 1914 did not survive intact. The Censor's survey work was recognition that a problem now existed which had not been seen before.

For the high command, the problem was intensified by the public airing of doubts and reservations following the costly battles of 1917. General Smuts, reporting to the War Cabinet on his investigation at the front, had found that many officers were concerned about the effects which criticisms of the army's leadership in the *Continental Daily Mail* — a journal more widely read and credited in the trenches than any other — might have upon the men.[16] Sir Hubert Gough, commanding the Fifth Army, was distressed by reports that a civilian touring the front had mounted a wagon in the streets of Peronne and shouted that everyone at home was fed up with the war; that 'if only the soldiers refused to fight there would be peace'.[17]

The authorities agreed that what was needed was a period of rest. A quiet winter would both improve morale within the army and reduce anxieties at home. Haig had set out the considerations in a paper for the Prime Minister in October 1917.

'The armies have undergone almost superhuman exertion and hardships during the last few months, and unless the demands made on them during the winter are reduced to a minimum they cannot be expected to respond fully to the further heavy calls entailed by a renewal of the offensive next year.'[18]

And though General Smuts had concluded that, for the time being, morale remained firm, he stressed that the men must be rested and not be overworked; to fail in this would be to overstrain the army.[19]

It proved, however, virtually impossible to retire units which had been engaged in heavy fighting to areas behind the front, and to provide their personnel with leave. The French were pressing that the British take over a longer portion of the line and, more importantly, the collapse of Russia was allowing Germany to enlarge her forces in the West. At GHQ, the Director of Military Operations had come to the conclusion that the Germans would launch a great offensive in the spring.[20] Throughout the winter, therefore, infantry units which had taken part in operations throughout 1917 were applied to the construction of large and elaborate defences.

The work of digging and entrenching fell heavily on front line troops and labour companies alike.[21] The burden was exacerbated, though, by the government's policy of withholding reinforcements from the commander in the field, and by the success of certain units in avoiding non-military duties. In January 1918, for instance, the army was 100,000 men below establishment.[22] At the same time, the soldiers from the white Dominions, their governments mindful that they had been sent to fight and not to dig, gained exemption from the task: they alone received a full share of rest and recuperation. In the circumstances, the morale of two important sections of the army became unsettled by the strain. The first comprised those units from the Catholic south of Ireland; the second, men of the Labour Corps itself.

Deprived of a decent flow of native reinforcements, and enjoying only qualified support from family and friends, Irish soldiers were bound to feel uneasy as their casualties increased. An old suspicion grew: that English generals were indifferent to the fate of Irish units. In autumn 1917, during the Battle of 3rd Ypres, the 16th (Irish) Division suffered heavy losses as it stood for hours awaiting the signal to attack — an attack then carried out without artillery support. Nationalist MPs threatened to air the matter publicly, unless they gained an investigation into the manner in which the division had been handled.[23] Such publicity Haig was able to avert. Abnormal weather, he suggested, had held up the assault; and Irish losses, though severe, were not greater than those of the other units participating in the operation. More frequent reliefs might have cut down losses, his critics were assured, but such reliefs 'would have left the army without any fresh reserves necessary to ensure the success of further efforts'.[24] The anxiety of MPs was thus successfully allayed;

less simple, though, to resolve the underlying problem. The 16th Division's last hours came in March 1918, during the German spring offensive. In circumstances veiled in confusion and in doubt, the line held by the division's three brigades was smashed and driven back.[25] By 3 April, over seven thousand officers and men had been killed or wounded, and eleven days later, only enough men remained to form a composite brigade. Other divisions could be restored by reinforcement; for the 16th, this help was not to hand. First bulked out with Portuguese, it then did a spell of duty in the back areas of France. Such treatment was a source of shame for both officers and men. Soon, the 16th ceased as an Irish unit to exist. When the division returned, reconstituted, from England in August, only the Royal Irish Fusiliers remained amongst troops from London, Leicester, Somerset, Northumberland, Scotland, and Wales.[26]

The Labour Corps formed a second segment of the BEF to start showing signs of strain. From small beginnings in 1916, when units from South Africa and the West Indies had arrived in France, the recruitment of foreign labour rapidly progressed.[27] By 1918, a 'huge organisation' had been formed.[28] A quarter of a million men from China, Egypt, India, South Africa, Fiji, the West Indies, and elsewhere, had been added, and the administration and allotment of all labour, including British and German prisoner personnel, had been brought under centralised control.[29] Under military discipline, and forming an integral part of the BEF, the Labour Corps undertook such work on road and railway building, and the construction of defences, as would free British troops for service at the front.

'The bulk of the labour units was employed on work connected with roads, light and normal gauge railways, quarries, forests, depots, dumps, railheads, hutting, horse-standings, camps, salvage, casualty clearing stations, water-supply, drainage, agriculture.'[30]

There were limits to what the Labour Corps might do. Units formed from British conscientious objectors or German prisoners, for instance, could not be exposed to German fire. Units recruited in China and in Egypt 'had not engaged to do work in the shelled areas'.[31] Men of the Cape Coloured Labour Battalion, on the other hand, were enlisted soldiers and could be used right up to the front.[32] Again, units made up of men from the Indian sub-continent were the 'least perturbed' by shelling, and some men from the West Indies worked within range of German artillery as well.[33] For the most part, though, the work of the Labour Corps was concentrated on the Lines of Communication and in the rear zone of the defence. During the week ending 16 March 1918, when a great German offensive was daily expected to unfold, four thousand Chinese and three thousand Indian labour personnel were helping the Fifth Army to strengthen its defences in the most vital sector of the front.[34]

It was not, however, considerations of legality alone which prevented a greater concentration of 'coloured labour' on the work of digging at the front. In a sentence full of underlying meaning, the official histories touch upon the further problems which the authorities had faced.

'The immobility of the coloured labour, consequent on the fact that in most cases it had to be segregated in special camps, would have prevented its employment on any considerable scale in the forward zone, whatever its morale.'[35]

It 'had to be segregated', of course, partly because these men were not wanted in French villages and towns, least of all in the brothels and the bars, and partly because GHQ had fears for their efficiency unless they were kept in sealed camps. Doubts exist as to whether all these men had freely given indication of their willingness to serve.[36] In any case, once indented and on his way to France, the average coloured labourer might be no more free, and in receipt of no wider measure of protection, than the inmate of a Nazi labour camp.

A sapper, who rose eventually to colonel, recalls conditions for labour units at an Ordnance depot just south of Dieppe.

'Early after my arrival came black men of the S[outh] A[frican] N[ative] L[abour] C[ontingent]. They were housed in a wired compound (like a POW camp) away from other troops. They worked as labourers on Railways, loaders for Ordnance and general labouring — sometimes they worked for me. The men only came out of their compound for work otherwise they were completely segregated like prisoners. Later the labour supply was augmented by Chinese labourers and tradesmen (carpenters etc.). These men on a rota basis were given days off to go to town (Dieppe).'[37]

These conditions, imposed in the Chinese case alone on up to one hundred thousand men, may well have contributed to the problem of 'morale'. On 5 September 1917, a few days before the outbreak at Etaples, two Egyptian labour companies, stationed at Boulogne, struck work: they alleged that their terms of contract required their repatriation, but they had been frightened by an air raid and suffered also from the cold.[38] The following day, they again refused to go to work and attempted to break out of camp. Themselves quite unarmed, they were shot down by their guards: twenty-three were killed, and twenty-four wounded. That afternoon, they 'went to work without further trouble'.[39] Four days later, the Commandant, Calais Base, learned that No 74 Egyptian Labour Company had refused to work. He conferred with his superior, called up the guard, and when next day, 11 September, the company again refused, this officer was ready. Four Egyptians were killed, fifteen wounded, and twenty-five given prison sentences within the day.[40] One month later, a 'disturbance' took place in a Chinese labour company stationed in the First Army area: five Chinese were killed and fourteen wounded.[41] Similarly, strikes organized by men of the South African Native Labour Corps were 'overcome': the casualties were not recorded.[42] In December 1917 the guard opened fire on the men of No 21 Chinese Labour Company, stationed at Fontinettes, near Calais: four were killed, nine wounded, when the rest went back to work.[43] In later months, the authorities appear to have been more successful in suppressing strikes and demonstrations among the Chinese and other Labour Corps without spilling an excess of blood. In February and March 1918, in the Calais area alone, further disturbances took place; and were put down without fatality.[44]

This resort to carnage — 'shooting those who are temporarily out of hand'[45] as the policy was officially described — was backed up by public denials that such a policy was being put into effect. 'No armed force has ever been used in France to compel the Chinese labourers to do their work or to remain in any locality' explained a memorandum drawn up by the Director of Labour, GHQ, for Haig to sign and release to the British press after criticisms had been voiced about the ill-treatment of these men.[46] This course of action proved successful. Public anxiety was allayed while, for the military authorities, opening fire on unarmed men remained an effective way of suppressing strikes and demonstrations.

The demise of the 16th Division and the rumblings within the Labour Corps had no exact equivalent amongst units recruited within the confines of Great Britain. During the German spring offensive, all energies were bent on the defence, and only the onset of defeatism — the demand, as the Censor had described it, for 'a premature peace' — could have disrupted discipline at so critical a time. After the repulse of that offensive, though, the position was quite changed. The Germans halted, then fell back, and their retreat became a rout. This defeat was matched by setbacks for Austria-

Hungary and Turkey. The lifting of the danger, the realization that the war was ending, affected all the allied peoples, not least the men serving Britain's manufactories and with her regiments abroad. Writing in July 1918, the Chief of the Imperial General Staff, Sir Henry Wilson, anticipated the changed mood in Britain as a whole. 'The moment the anxieties of the present situation are allayed we shall be faced in this country with grave industrial unrest, and a strong recrudescence of pacifist feeling.' 'It must be realised,' he continued, 'that all enthusiasm for the war is dead.'[47] These words, of course, applied to the civil population, but as events turned out, they apply to British troops as well. 'Unrest' and 'pacifist feeling' mean different things in armies than they do among civilians, but the parallels are clear. The first outbreak of unrest amongst British troops in France was taking place even as Sir Henry was writing his report.

Sunday, 21 July was celebrated by the Belgians as a national holiday and, their country being occupied for the most part by the Germans, festivities were held in France. At Beaumarais, near Calais, these events provided something of a holiday for the allied troops who went along. During the afternoon, however, British soldiers 'became troublesome' and in the evening about two hundred of them entered Calais contrary to orders and held a demonstration against the military police. By 11 p.m. the trouble had died down.[48] Next day the Calais Base commandant visited Beaumarais and addressed the Scottish troops in 'M' Infantry Base Depot. He reproached them for their misbehaviour, and asked them to represent their grievances in less unruly form. Their attitude he described as 'quite orderly'.[49] His intervention proved ineffective. That evening, parties of men again entered Calais and sacked the police billet.[50] The following day, Tuesday, 23 July, picquets were posted at all entrances to the town.[51] These picquets remained in position for some days, but men detailed for this duty could not be relied upon to prevent disaffected soldiers from entering the town. The Base commandant had occasion to admonish men from 'L' Depot who, when on picquet duty, had failed to carry out his orders. Prisoners undergoing field punishment were moved out of the area, and on 24 July two companies from the 1st Battalion, East Lancashire Regiment, were sent in to deal with the unrest.[52]

To the military authorities, though we are not admitted to their thoughts, it may have seemed that disturbances on the scale of the demonstrations at Etaples were in the offing; and the precautions which they took may most helpfully be seen in the light of the lessons which had been learnt a year before. The prisoners were at once despatched elsewhere, troops were brought in from other units to reinforce the picquets, and the GOC, Lines of Communication, and the Base commandant, himself a brigadier, made speeches to the men.[53] These steps proved sufficient, and, in any case, the troops appear to have been less inflamed than they had been the previous year. Not all the soldiers at the Base, indeed, shared the feelings of the Scots troops taking part. One of the men warned for picquet duty recalls the situation:

'The 51st Division came out of the line for a rest. . . . For some reason they were not paid out. They went out of Camp and into the Town of Calais and had a rough time with the Military Police. We heard that the Jocks had thrown some Red Caps into the sea at Calais.

'This affair lasted some days when one evening about three hundred reserve men at the Base were ordered to fall in with arms and ammunition at the entrance to the Camp and told by a Major on the Camp Staff that they might have to open fire on these men if they did not return [to] Camp peacefully. The men on parade were Southern Irishmen and some of them said why not remember Bachelor's Walk. . . .

'In any case some of the Officers of the 51st Division spoke to their men, after that they marched into camp without further trouble. We were all very glad that we had not to fire.'[54]

A repetition of the Etaples outbreak was avoided at Calais. Nonetheless, trouble continued to occur. Early in September 1918 a disturbance broke out among the reinforcements at Beaumarais, principally in 'M' Base Depot. The Assistant Adjutant and Quartermaster General, Brigadier Wroughton, visited the Base. Later in the month, responding to reports of unrest, he made another visit, but found that officers had exaggerated the indiscipline which had actually occurred.[55] At Etaples, too, the authorities were having difficulties once again. In late August 'Some trouble occurred among the patients of 51 General Hospital (Venereal cases) and a guard of 100 Canadian Infantry was posted in one of the huts of the Depot under orders of GOC Etaples.'[56] These skirmishes proved but a prelude to the serious outbreaks of indiscipline which were shortly to take place.

8
This Irregular Method

The first signs of disaffection in the army after the Armistice were to be found in France, in the camps and depots of the Army Service and Army Ordnance Corps. The work of both these Corps lay in supplying the material requirements of the BEF. In essence, the Ordnance processed and stored the items which the Service Corps moved to and from the front. The Ordnance Corps, under the control of its Director, operated a variety of depots and stores, and numerous shops for manufacturing and repairing. Its installations, concentrated around Calais and Le Havre, were responsible for 'almost all that the soldier in the field needs except rations';[1] its stores held some twenty thousand different types of item, while its workshops, employing about ten thousand men, undertook a variety of services 'unrivalled in the business world'.[2] The Army Service Corps, on the other hand, under the Director of Transport, was responsible for the BEF's transport arrangements in Flanders and in France. Its Director controlled movement through the ports and docks, and was responsible for railways, canals and roads.[3] This Corps was organized partly in transport companies — that is, horse and mechanical road transport — and partly in workshops maintaining vehicles and equipment. Though the two Directors were on the staff at GHQ, both the Army Ordnance and Army Service Corps formed part of the Lines of Communication, BEF, and it was the General Officer Commanding, LOC, who was responsible for discipline itself.[4]

By 1918 the Army Ordnance and Army Service Corps were drawn for the most part from two large groups of men. The first group comprised the skilled and semi-skilled, men more useful in the workshops than they could have been with rifles at the front.[5] The second group, on the other hand, had already done long tours of duty in the trenches, but through wounds or sickness, were now consigned to working in the rear.[6] In general, men of the Ordnance and Army Service Corps worked longer hours than was the case in industry in Britain, and received lower rates of pay. By the November of that year, one officer reported, the men were getting restless, being 'more than ever inclined to contrast their lot with that of the men employed in England on munitions'.[7] There was clear dissatisfaction; and Major-General Sir Charles Mathew, the Director of Ordnance Services (DOS), was giving thought to a proposal to reduce workshop hours to nine per day, six days a week. Even so, it seemed, such a working week would still compare unfavourably with the five and a half day, forty-eight hour week worked generally in England.[8]

The Director's subordinates were coming under pressure. On 1 December 1918 the Chief Ordnance Officer, Calais, reporting on the long hours being worked by the men in his command, suggested that they be limited to forty-eight per week. The Deputy Director of Ordnance Services (North) favoured the reform but, recognizing that concession would affect all the ordnance establishments in France, submitted the question to the DOS in turn.[9] A few days later, Major-General Mathew spoke to the Quartermaster General at GHQ, who raised a similar objection. The QMG pointed out that the question of shortening hours and raising wages in the Ordnance services, and the desirability of bringing practice in France into line with that in industry at home, affected other services as well. Could the matter be raised with him officially?[10] There, for the moment, the matter rested. Official channels dealt slowly with the problem while, in the camps and workshops, the troops considered their position.

On Saturday, 21 December the Director of Ordnance Services again discussed the question with the Quartermaster General. The QMG had referred the proposed forty-eight hour week to the other Directors based at GHQ, but had not come up with a solution.[11] That very day, however, the DOS received fresh news about the disposition of his troops. In the afternoon, men in the ordnance workshops of the Tank Corps refused to take on extra work.[12] A report also came through from the Deputy Director of Ordnance Services, Southern Area [DDOS (South)], about the spread of the unrest. On Wednesday, 18 December men in the ordnance workshops at Le Havre had struck. They set out their demands. They asked for 'shorter working hours, an extension of time at which they have now to report in camp, a holiday at Christmas and New Year, and an increase in bread ration'. They made no demand for demobilization.[13]

These strikes met with no uniform response. At the Tank Corps workshops, 'practically the whole of the workshops establishment' was put under arrest,[14] but the DOS took a more conciliatory line at Havre and at the other bases. He ordered officers to keep in close touch with their men, so that reasonable grievances might at once be heeded; and asked the chief Ordnance officer at each base to make it clear that, while irregular methods of ventilating problems 'can only bring discredit on the Corps,' full consideration would be given to complaints.[15] It was not difficult for Major-General Mathew to urge conciliation — he was not responsible for discipline as such — but he took active steps to make the policy effective. He pressed the question of the bread ration at Le Havre on the relevant authority and, in a report to the Quartermaster General, made clear his opinion that half measures would not now be enough. More generous leave would not resolve the problem. Men compelled to stay in France after others had been discharged 'should not be at any disadvantage as regards pay, etc., as compared with their fellow workers who are fortunate enough to be sent home early'.[16] The Quartermaster General, too, had veered towards this view. He informed the various directorates at GHQ at the start of the New Year that a letter had been written to the Army Council suggesting that men retained in France against their will should be paid civilian rates.[17]

Men from the Army Service Corps were now quite separately drawn in. On 3 January 1919 the Deputy Director of Transport, Northern Area, Lines of Communication [DDT (North)], the immediate subordinate, with his colleague in the Southern Area, L of C, of the Director of Transport at GHQ, learned of some difficulties at the Base Motor Transport Depot, Calais — in the nature of a strike, though its course is not recorded.[18] It was sufficiently serious to warrant his visiting Calais, a visit followed on 4 January by a trip to GHQ. At GHQ it was agreed that some concession should be made over working hours and leave; and the same day, visiting other units, the DDT (North) found working hours, while by no means uniform, to add up to something in the order of a six and a half day week. Men in the workshops of the 3rd Auxiliary Petrol Company, for instance, were working nearly nine hours a day and received only a half holiday on Sunday. The soldiers of the 6th Auxiliary Petrol Company were putting in eight and a half hours per day, but their half day holiday on Sunday could not be guaranteed, and, living well outside Calais, three hundred men were spending much of their free time on travel to and from the workshops. At the prevailing rate of leave, men were allowed home every twelve or thirteen months.[19]

A conference at GHQ on 8 January took up the question of working hours for Army Service Corps artificers and drivers. A forty-eight hour week, with one day free of work, would next be introduced. The Quartermaster General was willing to go further, to reduce workshop hours to forty-four; but it was pointed out that, in those units containing both artificers and drivers, the hours for one group could not be reduced to forty-four while those for drivers remained at forty-eight. At the heavy repair shops, however, whose complement contained artificers alone, working hours could certainly be reduced.[20]

Next day, these changes were announced — but only for the Army Service Corps units at Calais and Boulogne, where there had been trouble, and not for those at Etaples and Dunkirk, where there had been none. At the Base Motor Transport Depot, Calais, the centre of events, the authorities decided to go further.

'Certain suggestions were made as regards changes in the permanent staff of the camp and the necessary action is being taken . . . the working hours of the BMTD [Base Motor Transport Depot] have been reduced to 7 hours a day, with a complete holiday on Sunday.'[21]

The Deputy Director of Transport (South) had also attended the conference at GHQ, and he agreed that, in his area, the new hours should now be introduced. His assistant, a lieutenant-colonel, made visits to transport units and repair shops around Rouen and Le Havre, where he gave instructions for the working week to be suitably reduced. At these two bases, though, as this officer discovered, it was not days and hours, but the demobilization question, which was coming to the fore.[22] Under the existing regulations, soldiers in supply, transport, and the like would be the very last to leave: for on them now fell 'the brunt of the military work — that of clearing up the aftermath of war'.[23] The lack of any quota was resented by these men, and, on 12 January, the Director of Transport, GHQ, was informed that an allotment for demobilization, however small, was a concession he should certainly consider.[24]

By now, worries about demobilization were affecting the army Ordnance men. On 3 January, nine men from the depot at Le Havre had called on their commander.

' . . . the Deputation were perfectly respectful and their statements quite reasonable. They represented the very strong feeling which exists regarding the restrictions placed on the RAOC in connection with the Demobilization Scheme and urged the possibility of its ultimately seriously handicapping their future prospects in civil life.'[25]

These representations were passed on to GHQ, and, on 12 January, the regulations changed. The embargo on the demobilization of Ordnance men would now be lifted. A quota of tradesmen was to be demobilized each week. Storemen and clerks, however, could still not be released: their work remained essential.[26] On 25 January the Chief Ordnance Officer, Calais, informed the Director of Ordnance Services that, unless a proportion of these men were also soon discharged, he was certain they would strike.[27]

In late January, the restriction on the demobilization of Royal Army Service Corps men was similarly lifted. The demobilization quota would be small — only fifty other ranks might be sent home each week from the units supervised by the DDT (North) — but the authorities were satisfied that evidence of good intention had been given to the men.

'It is hoped that the raising of the embargo of the RASC as regards demobilization and the fixing of a number to be demobilized weekly, small as it is, will go a considerable way towards allaying the discontent which has existed amongst a portion of the transport personnel who did not consider themselves being fairly treated as regards demobilization.'[28]

Dissatisfaction with the rate of demobilization, and concern about the lengthy hours of work, was now spreading to all the great base areas in France. On 13 January 1919 a hundred Labour Corps men, working in an Ordnance depot at Dannes, struck work and returned to camp. They objected to the substitution of time work for task work. The strike was quickly over.[29] On 15 January, soldiers serving with the Royal Engineers, Calais, learning of the concessions granted to the Ordnance and motor transport men, asked that their working hours 'be made the same'. Next day, their hours were reduced to forty-four.[30] On Friday, 24 January the marines and crane drivers — all British soldiers — at Dunkirk docks struck work, demanding that a definite date be fixed for their demobilization. Replacements were brought in, but were by no means as efficient. Accordingly on Monday, the fourth day of the strike, a settlement was made whereby a hundred men would be demobilized each week.[31]

Men of the Ordnance Corps at Calais Base had been among the first to complain about the lengthy hours of work, and they now set out to raise further matters with the authorities concerned. On Tuesday, 21 January a deputation from Valdelievre Camp, Calais, called on the Chief Ordnance Officer at the base.[32] Four questions were discussed. The first concerned the rate of demobilization; the second, the hours of work; the third, the catering arrangements; and the fourth, the hour by which, on evenings off, the men had to be back in camp. The Chief Ordnance Officer promised to give these points 'the utmost possible consideration,' and ordered improvements to the catering at once. He noted the mood of the deputation. It was 'quite friendly and they seemed satisfied with the consideration promised'.[33]

However friendly the tenor of this meeting, a further difference was souring the atmosphere at Calais. One member of this deputation was a certain John Pantling, a private soldier. A few days earlier, Pantling had been charged with an offence. His trial and punishment aroused the anger of the men. The Chief Ordnance Officer considered the offence and punishment to be unconnected with Pantling's position as a spokesman, but the men did not agree.[34] Years later, one witness recalled what had happened on the night of the arrest.

' . . . it was pay night but an angry crowd of men demonstrated outside the commanding officer's office demanding his release; all thoughts of pay were forgotten . . .

'The officers temporized, but we . . . smashed open the clink ourselves and released our comrade.

'An attempt to re-arrest him was made about 10.30 p.m. but failed, as by pre-arranged signal we swarmed out like bees.'[35]

This account differs in some detail from anything which John Pantling's officers wrote down. According to their diaries, Pantling was tried and given a minor punishment, not imprisonment, some time before 20 January; on that day he joined a deputation to meet the CIOM (North), and on the 21 January he attended the meeting with the Chief Ordnance Officer himself. Next day, as a gesture of goodwill, 'the COO remitted the remainder of this man's punishment'.[36]

Whatever the details, it is clear that discipline at Calais Base, and in particular in the camp at Valdelievre, had been deteriorating for some time. On 8 November 1918, for instance, the camp Commandant was relieved of his post following 'an incident' that day.[37] Men who served there have left ample testimony about the rise of discontent. One of them recalled a confrontation 'some twelve months or more before the end of the war'.

'We were demanding that the working day should finish at 5 p.m. instead of 6 p.m. and as we failed to secure this by negotiation, a committee of the works decided that all men should leave at 5 p.m., ignoring the official hours. This failed as the response was only partial, and a staff sergeant, who had been most active in promoting this was moved and, we have reason to believe, victimized.

'However, the hours were shortened by a half hour.'[38]

There was a difference, then, between the troubles at Calais and those which had touched the army at Etaples. Its root lay in the different populations of these bases. Etaples existed for infantry contingents, reinforcements for the various divisions as they passed up to the front. Calais, on the other hand, existed mainly for supply. Its facilities were staffed by Army Ordnance and Army Service men, Royal Engineers, and others. These corps were drawn, as has been seen, from two large groups of men: from 'temporarily enlisted artisans', skilled in repair and manufacture, and from troops debarred by injury from duties at the front. The first group, the historian of the Ordnance Corps maintains, were 'embued with a trade union spirit and devoid of the tradition of the "Old Contemptibles" '.[39] The second group, whether Old Contemptibles or no, 'keenly resented' a demobilization plan which promised to keep them in the army until all others had gone home.

> 'To contend that they were less deserving of release than their comrades who had borne the heat and burden of the day in front line trenches would fail to recognise the position as it then stood. For some two years past all non-combatant Corps had been shorn of their fit men and their ranks filled with the disabled, who had often far longer service than those at that time at the front.'[40]

The Calais men, by virtue of their skills and their position astride the main lines of supply, were vital to the army and, by the same token, were well placed to voice underlying discontent.

> 'I think it found more expression in the different supply corps at the base because we were more static, we had a real hard-core of trade unionists and Socialists and because we had built up a mass circulation of the *Weekly Herald* . . . We had, over the preceding months while the war was still in progress, raised the circulation from a few copies per week to a total of 500 in the Valdelievre Camp alone . . . '[41]

Against this background, the arrest of Private Pantling in January 1919 had consequences altogether different to those which followed the arrest of a solitary New Zealander at Etaples Base in September 1917. That New Zealander known, in all likelihood, only to his immediate contingent, was one of many thousands passing weekly through the Base. His arrest aroused the Anzacs and the Scots; but their protest, hurriedly set loose, could only slowly and indirectly touch the armies at the front. Pantling, on the other hand, had spent months, even years, in the workshops at Calais and was known to hundreds of the men. They had put him on the deputation to see the COO. Without their labour, and that of the thousands of other troops doing duty at the Base, supplies and rations would immediately run short.

On Wednesday, 22 January the Chief Ordnance Officer, Calais, decided to remit the rest of Private Pantling's punishment. But Pantling was unmoved. On Sunday, four days later, he addressed a further meeting. He was arrested and charged with seditious conduct 'on account of what he said'.[42] The Ordnance men felt that Pantling had been victimized again; 'it was not so', the Deputy Director or Ordnance Services (North) lamented in his diary, 'as it was an independent action by Private Pantling.'[43]

On Monday, 27 January the men at the Base Workshops, Calais, stayed away from work and picquetted their camp. The Chief Ordnance Officer met a deputation.

'The delegates informed him that they were instructed not to negotiate on any matter unless Private Pantling was released at once and that the men had stayed away from work on account of his arrest. The COO informed them that it was impossible to release Private Pantling without a trial and that he had not been victimized as being a delegate and generally explained the position. The delegates would not listen to any reason and the matter ended.

'The COO then issued and posted circulars to the men explaining the position, giving all the facts, asking them to judge the facts squarely and return to work, and pointing out the results of their not working. These circulars were torn down.'[44]

The stoppage, at this point, affected only the Ordnance workshops in Calais. That same morning, however, another group of Ordnance men from the depot at Vendroux was due to meet the COO.[45] Work there was proceeding normally, but the troops had plenty of complaints. Conditions in the camp were deplorable, a former soldier has maintained, and Saturday and Sundays were worked like other days.[46] The deputation told the COO that there could be no discussion until Private Pantling was released. This the COO refused to countenance. That afternoon, therefore, the men at Vendroux Depot left their work, and together with the Valdelievre men and some women from the Queen Mary's Army Auxiliary Corps, marched into Calais.[47]

'Our bands were in attendance and the frightened French shopkeepers put up their shutters as 4,000 very determined men marched through the streets. The headquarters were surrounded and a deputation entered.

'After a futile attempt to induce the besieging army to withdraw, the general agreed to release our comrade (who had been transferred elsewhere) and that he should be in camp by Tuesday midday.'[48]

The course of this unusual interview is not officially recorded, but its outcome is agreed upon by all: Pantling would be released 'without prejudice' and would return to camp next day.[49] 'Without prejudice', of course, did not preclude his later re-arrest and trial, though this was not apparent to the crowd that afternoon. It was Brigadier Wroughton, of the Adjutant General's staff, GHQ, who had authorized the release of Private Pantling: a concession impelled not only by the temper of the crowd but also by conditions in the other camps and depots. He found, on arriving in Calais, that 'all work was stopped and the town picquetted by strikers'.[50] The strike was being systematically extended. The Director of Transport, GHQ, learned that

'the Ordnance personnel . . . were endeavouring to prevent our MT Depot and Auxiliary MT Company from working, with a view to forming a strong combination . . . I found that the men in the Depot had been ordered not to work by the Ordnance, and that the vehicles of the Auxiliary Company were not being allowed to work except on local Supply and Medical Services. The men had left the Depot and so I could not speak to them.'[51]

On the railways, too, the flow of British traffic came swiftly to a halt:[52] the railway units of the Royal Engineers stopped work, and then, apparently, the French civilian railwaymen refused to touch these trains.[53] The strike was spreading to Dunkirk, where 'practically all [the service troops] downed tools'.[54]

Next day, Tuesday, 28 January 1919, all work was halted at Calais.

'On Tuesday morning parties of picked men were sent out to visit the different camps in the area, help them to put their strike organization in order and supply picquets if necessary (but it wasn't).

'I was with one of these parties and visited several small camps and found them all solid. We then split into small groups and scoured the nooks and crannies of the dock area. I will quote two instances just to show the atmosphere.

'Myself, a solitary party of one, I found a group of five or six NCOs doing some clerical work.

'Myself: "What are you doing here? Don't you know there's a strike on?" NCOs swinging round on their office chairs — "sickly grin".

'Myself: Question repeated with expletive and still no answer. "I've no time to waste arguing with you, come on now, out of it." Result: All troop out, myself bringing up the rear.

'Another comrade in our party, also on his own, found a camp that was not then out and the guard made an attempt to arrest him; the rest of our party now reassembled when our comrade appeared in a somewhat dishevelled state:

' "Come on boys," he said, "the b——s have tried to arrest me!"

'Not more than half an hour later the men were out and the guard had been removed.

'On returning to camp we found the same sort of reports coming in from all quarters and nearly every camp embracing all the departmental corps were out comprising some 20,000 men.'[55]

This great strike, by its place and timing, put the army under strain. In food alone, the depots at Calais and Boulogne had supplied half the BEF, the 'highest daily feeding strength' relying on Calais amounting to two-thirds of a million men.[56] In petrol, 'the whole of the filling for the British armies in France and Italy' had depended on work done at two bases, Rouen and Calais.[57] In artillery, the BEF's entire stores were located at Calais.[58] In road transport, the BEF's mobility rested on supplies from Calais Base. The Mechanical Transport Depot located there received and dealt with 'all demands for spare parts, tyres and accessories for all mechanically propelled vehicles with the armies at the front'.[59] In fact, Calais' importance had risen after the Armistice, the other bases being rapidly closed down. 'By the end of 1918 all our armies were based on Calais.'[60] On Monday, 27 January 1919 these flows — of supply, leave, and demobilization trains, of lorries and horse transport, of clothing, petrol, foodstuffs, guns, of supplies of every conceivable description — reduced suddenly to nil.[61] And the authorities were faced with more than plain refusals. During these days the 'Calais Area Soldiers and Sailors Association' was launched, based on the system of committees which had spread throughout each camp. The Association 'took over control of all army units in the area, taking over, in most cases, the Officers also. It issued daily orders signed by the committee officials — and it all seemed so natural.'[62]

No sooner had the strike reached its zenith than its decline set in. Instrumental in this was the fact of Private Pantling's release. He had been returned to Valdelievre Camp, as promised, at noon on Tuesday, 28 January.[63] He was received with acclamation; but, from that moment on, the question which had exercised great numbers of the troops — the arrest of Private Pantling — appeared to be resolved. That afternoon, the railwaymen were persuaded to return to work, and were followed, in due course, by the Army Service men. Next day, only the Ordnance remained solidly on strike.[64]

Two tactics were now open to the army. The first, obviously, was to continue to persuade, to get the Ordnance men to resume working once again. On Tuesday, 28 January the Director of Ordnance Services came down from GHQ. He tried addressing some fifteen hundred men. The strike committee stopped him, but agreed to talk with him at 10.a.m. next day. But, before Wednesday's talks got going, the committee had a new condition to propose. They would not talk, they said, until the guard thrown up around another camp, containing disaffected infantry, had also been withdrawn. Major-General Mathew returned, frustrated, to Calais Base Headquarters where, a little later in the day, he told General Sir Julian Byng, General Officer Commanding, Fifth Army, that the strike, 'which was pre-arranged and only precipitated by the arrest of the RAOC representative, had its origin in Bolshevism'.[65]

A second tactic, less gentle than the first, was also being prepared. Shortly before 11 a.m. on Tuesday, 28 January the staff at GHQ sent orders to Fifth Army. Fifth Army was to release an infantry brigade 'for special duty' in Calais.[66] The brigade was to move with as many officers as possible, and up to two hundred boxes of small arms ammunition. Each company in each of its battalions was to carry three machine-guns.[67] In addition, the 1st, 2nd, and 3rd Guards Machine-Gun Battalions were to concentrate in an area nearby.[68]

The staff of Fifth Army, BEF, at once detailed 105th Brigade, from 35th Division, 'to assist in quelling riots' in Calais.[69]

9

It's Us That's Going to Talk to You

When plans for demobilization had been initially discussed, during the period of war itself, two notions of how best to do it came quickly to the fore. The first suggested that those who had served longest with the colours should be released before those who had but recently joined up. To many soldiers this notion seemed altogether just, but Whitehall turned it down. The government, anxious to return to conditions of full employment once the war was won, had other priorities in mind. According to its view, men should be demobilized according to industrial requirements. Thus, those possessing important skills and capabilities could be released at once. Those less happily endowed should be discharged thereafter, and only when the state of the economy assured them of a job. And it was along these lines, of giving prominence to the needs of industry and commerce, that a scheme for the demobilization of the army was actually laid down.

Two factors served to undermine the workings of the scheme. The first was its complexity. The 'industrial group,' the trade or calling, and the marital status of every soldier had to be recorded and delivered to Whitehall. There, the War Office laid down different categories of officers and men. The highest priority was accorded to 'demobilizers,' men required to staff the demobilization centres in England and elsewhere. Next came a group called 'pivotals,' men vital to the task of peacetime reconstruction. The total of these two categories was not to exceed 150,000 men. The third category consisted of men arranged in forty-two groups who had received definite promise of employment; the fourth, those needed to accelerate industrial production. Remaining categories of men, neither asked for by employers nor adjudged industrially essential, would be eventually released by trades in order of importance. Questions of age, length of service, and marital condition were only of importance in deciding order of release within the category to which a man had already been assigned.[1]

A second undermining factor concerned the haste with which the government's scheme was put into effect. The paper work could be started only after the Armistice on 11 November 1918, but the War Office believed that the substantial period then elapsing before the signing of a peace would allow time to implement the plan. For time, above all, was needed to classify the six million men in uniform into twelve categories of officer and thirteen of 'other ranks'.[2] But, in the flush of victory, few politicians cared to emphasize the wisdom of delay. The Prime Minister, in particular, found it inexpedient to campaign for re-election in the absence of definite progress towards demobilization; and the optimistic note sounded by him and his supporters created the impression that demobilization could be carried out at once, that a return to a peacetime footing might be swiftly undertaken. This impression, as the Chief of the Imperial General Staff, Sir Henry Wilson, reflected, 'had as a natural consequence come to be entertained amongst the troops on service in the various theatres of the recent war . . .'[3]

Although most soldiers looked forward to demobilization once victory had come, the terms of the Armistice placed duties on the army which had not been properly foreseen. The allied armies were called on to reclaim the whole of France and Belgium, and to occupy parts of Germany itself. The enemy surrendered not only territory, but also quantities of ordnance, transport, and military supplies. After 11 November 1918, therefore, the British army was engaged in consolidating these gains and in supervising the concessions which Germany had made. At the same time, individual soldiers, conscious that victory had been won, were looking forward to their return to civil life. 'Much difficulty therefore is now experienced,' wrote the diarist of a battalion on occupation duty on the Rhine, 'in making Men understand that a State of War continues to exist and that an Army has to be maintained in the field.'[4]

If the pace of demobilization was much affected by the terms of the Armistice, the smooth departure of those actually entitled to discharge was compromised by late and hasty changes in the priorities laid down. Ahead of the 'demobilizers' and 'pivotals', the Government now unearthed a new and prior claim: the shortages of coal demanded that the miners be released. The demobilization of the coalminers — specifically of face workers in good health — regardless of age or length of service began within two days of the Armistice, when the Adjutant General, GHQ, addressed a letter to all commanding officers asking them to hasten their return. Drafts of miners were soon arriving in Boulogne and by 5 December 1918, from that port alone, nine thousand men had been sent home.[5]

By the year's end, the government's demobilization scheme was showing signs of strain. The new duties imposed by the terms of the Armistice sat uneasily with the note of optimism encouraged by Lloyd George; and the complexities of priority laid down within the scheme hardly suited the improvising spirit with which the government faced the exigencies of peace. By 31 December, 300,000 men in all had been released, the great bulk of them neither 'demobilizers' nor 'pivotals'.[6] This was not a substantial total, and it convinced some soldiers that they were being held to contracts indeterminate in length. But, before examining the reactions of those still doing duty, it will be of interest to study the behaviour of some artillerymen, ex-coalminers, as they travelled homewards to the pits.

The miners reaching the base port at Le Havre in the first week of December had every reason to co-operate with the base administration. These men, from the Royal Garrison, the Royal Field, and the Royal Horse Artillery, were bound for England, Scotland, Wales. Their stay at Le Havre would of necessity be brief: a few days to complete formalities and make up drafts for home. Still, the depots were not prepared for the flood of new arrivals. The accommodation was congested and much of it was canvas; the food was poor, and the canteen tents not large enough to cater for the men. The comparison with the officers' quarters was particularly striking. There, aspects of the Old Army had maintained themselves intact. One man recalled the condition of these messes — fine food and drink, china, silver, the servants constantly at hand. It was 'like the Savoy Hotel'.[7]

On Monday, 9 December a minor incident occurred. An artilleryman, it appears, complained about his meal to a cook, who referred him to an NCO.[8] An argument developed, the NCO was punched, and the matter ended with the soldier being arrested and put into the cells. Not quite the end, however. Hundreds gathered demanding his release, and when NCOs attempted to disperse them, the crowd became enraged. The rest of that day and half the night were given over to eating, drinking, and destruction. Four huge wholesale canteens supplying the forces' needs were looted and set alight, an officers' mess was raided and the disturbance spread to other camps nearby. The officers fled, and attempts by NCOs to restore order met with no success. French fire engines, arriving to deal with the blaze, had their ladders broken and added to the flames. At one point, the men, many of them armed and now the worse for drink, seemed about to turn upon each other, for the tents of the Royal Garrison Artillery downwind were much threatened by the fires which other troops were spreading. Eventually, when the riot was exhausted, order was restored. But several camps had been destroyed, and thousands of front line troops had cast off the discipline — the social relations, in fact — of an army which they had now come to detest.[9]

These men were not detained. More than a thousand soldiers embarked at Le Havre on 15 December 1918 for the United Kingdom, about a thousand a day following in the period thereafter.[10] And they appeared unmoved by the damage they had done. On their way down to the docks, it seems, the men threw off their equipment and their arms, as though to divest themselves of all connection with the army; and a newspaper reporter, watching the reception laid on in Folkestone for the first batch of arrivals, testified to the 'playfulness and boisterous merriment' which marked the conduct of the troops.[11]

At Etaples, too, the miners in process of demobilization were also giving trouble. A mere sixty-five were gathered at the Royal Army Medical Corps depot there, but they found occasion to threaten the commanding officer with the prospect of a riot if drill were to be continued and their departure slowed. The officer did not take the warning seriously. On 14 December, though, the Deputy Assistant Adjutant General, responsible for discipline among all the reinforcements passing through Etaples, sent word that a muster parade should be held at once, that neither NCOs nor men should be forewarned: and that their kits should then be searched for arms and ammunition. At the RAMC depot a number of revolvers were found and promptly seized. The haul at the other base depots is not recorded.[12]

The destruction visited upon the base camp at Le Havre was not to be repeated, but discipline seems to have been deteriorating throughout the BEF. The damage done to trains and billets, for example, had simply not existed while the war was on. In February 1919 the Quartermaster General reported on the damage done to trains. It had 'lately reached such proportions that it is impossible to effect repairs'. He cited an account, one of many similar received, on the condition of a leave train once the soldiers had got off.

'Dirty — many stoves missing — many stove pipes missing where stoves have been left. Benches have been burnt in several trucks. First-class French coach DPY 140 has been entirely gutted; not only have cushions been taken out but the general structure of the inside of the coach has been destroyed, apparently with an axe. All windows broken — sashes, straps, cords, and curtains cut out or in other ways destroyed.'[13]

An officer confirms this rise in vandalism from another point of view.

'I noticed that the troops in transit were showing signs of revolt. They were beginning to resent discipline and retention — they were anxious about their civil employment too and the fact that those who had stayed at home or had obtained early release were getting the best jobs. One sign which I myself observed was deliberate damage done to houses at Folkestone, used as a transit camp. Plaster was knocked off the walls in great chunks by rifles being roughly pushed into it — many of these houses looked as if they had been bombed! This damage must have caused a tremendous amount of compensation to be paid to the owners. To protest against this senseless damage would have invited assault and battery.'[14]

The town of Folkestone provided the backdrop for more than mute dissatisfaction with the army and its ways. The first great demonstration on English soil against the slow pace of demobilization took place on the coast. In the last days of 1918 thousands of British soldiers returning to France after a period of leave were gathered in the rest camps just outside Folkestone. They had begun discussing the position, many seeing no reason why they were being demobilized so slowly. On the morning of Friday, 3 January 1919 they marched down to the Harbour and thence in good order through the streets to the Town Hall. A few men entered that building, climbed out on to the portico, and then delivered speeches. 'On all sides the men expressed dissatisfaction with what they considered the slow rate of demobilization.'[15] The Mayor addressed the troops, who greeted him with cheers. He had been in touch with a senior officer, he said, and if they returned to camp they would receive good news. 'To this the large crowd replied by singing *Tell me the old, old story*.'[16] In due course the main body of the men marched back to camp, where they held further meetings and discussions. That afternoon, a second march was held, and a number of soldiers who, acting under orders, were about to board the boats for France, were prevailed upon to stay. A further meeting was convened around the Town Hall but, after speeches, soon ended when the men dispersed.[17]

Throughout the day, nothing had marred the peaceful nature of the demonstrations. The evening passed without any incident at all, the soldiers going to the various places of amusement or staying in the camps.[18] It was at this point, however, that the military authorities, in their attempt to head off further trouble, unwittingly added fuel to the flames. Numbers of men due to return to France forthwith, were granted an extension of their leave in order to get their applications for demobilization prepared: to get, that is, a contract of employment both properly drawn up and sanctioned by their Local Employment Board. Next morning,

'When it became known among the men about to embark that some of their number had obtained an extension of leave, discontent immediately arose among the rest. Some men alleged that they were in the same position as the men to whom extension of leave had been granted, while a great many others complained that they were in complete ignorance of the 'contract' system, and had they known of it, would certainly have been able to make arrangements with their pre-war employers. The dissatisfaction was heightened by the allegation that some of the 'contracts' on the strength of which men were being kept back, were bogus contracts, which would not bear examination, and were simply exhibited as an excuse for getting an extension of leave.

'The result was that, on the one hand, those to whom extension had been granted were not allowed by their comrades to go back to London, while others who were quite ready to return to France were prevented from going on board.'[19]

Thus the War Office's account. In fact, events that Saturday morning were more dramatic than this communiqué suggested. An armed guard had been placed on the harbour early in the day, but, the demonstrators 'intimating' that they were prepared to go back to the camp and get rifles for themselves, it was immediately withdrawn. Strike picquets took up their places at the approaches to the quay and British soldiers were prevented from embarking.[20] At the railway station, too, a newspaper reporter noted the demeanour of the men.

'The mutineers . . . tore down a large label: "For officers only", which was posted above a comfortable waiting room. I mention this as it typifies one of the many causes of the trouble — the bitter resentment felt at the easy conditions of the officers as compared with those of the men.'[21]

The demonstration proper was much larger than it had been the day before. Ten thousand marched ten abreast through the streets of Folkestone, and the procession, reaching the Town Hall, spread out until the open space and the streets near-by were 'absolutely packed' with men in khaki.[22] Speaker followed speaker, the meeting culminating in the formation of a Soldiers' Union and the appointment of nine delegates to confer with the authorities.[23] What was wanted, they agreed, was 'justice'.

'Many of them had enlisted as soon as the war broke out, and now they were being kept in the Army while other and younger men who had only seen a few months' service were being demobilized first.'[24]

General Dallas, General Officer Commanding, Canterbury, arrived and after some discussion agreed to see the delegates. The meeting then broke up, the soldiers accompanying the delegates as they set off to confer.[25]

The conference lasted several hours. Two general officers, in constant communication with the War Office, put the army's point of view; the nine delegates set out the wishes of the men. Eventually, a compromise was reached. Its terms were these:

'— That the men should be dealt with individually.
— That those whose "contracts" were completely in order should be demobilized.
— That those who had genuine "contracts" which were not yet fully in order should be allowed to avail themselves of their week's extension of leave.
— That a similar extension should be accorded to men who could show reasonable grounds for claiming that they were in a position to obtain "contracts", and on the understanding that, if they failed to do so, they would return to their units at the end of the period.
— That men having no "contracts" or prospects of "contracts" should return to duty at once.'[26]

The men agreed to hold no further demonstrations, and the authorities promised not to victimize the leaders. And it was along similar lines that a dispute of this kind at Dover, involving rather fewer men, was also soon resolved.[27]

In the following week, the demonstrations spread. On Monday, 6 January 1919 soldiers from the Shortlands Depot, Royal Army Service Corps, marched into Bromley, and two hundred men of the same Corps, stationed at Osterley Park, Isleworth, drove up to Whitehall in army lorries. They hoped to lay their case before the Prime Minister himself.

'We are all time-expired infantrymen drafted into the ASC,' a sergeant explained to a reporter, 'and we have been informed that that branch of the Service would be the last to be demobilized. Most of us have had over two years in France, and have been wounded.'

The Prime Minister being unavailable, they spoke to a brigadier from the Ministry of Labour. He promised an immediate investigation, and said that men who could prove that they had a job to go to would be demobilized within ten days.[28]

Next day, there were even larger gatherings in Whitehall. In the morning, a number of soldiers arrived whose anxieties were clear. They were nearing the end of a period of leave, they said, and were due to return to theatres overseas — principally to Salonica, from which remote spot they were unlikely quickly to return. The Assistant Secretary of Demobilization then addressed these men.

'I would ask you to remember that there are other men in Salonica whose leave would be prejudiced by undue ration given to you . . . even apart from the question of demobilization.'[29]

They thereupon dispersed. In the afternoon, more than a thousand soldiers turned up in Whitehall in army lorries adorned with slogans, which they had driven from their camp at Kempton park. They assembled in the War Office quadrangle, and would not move until they had seen a senior officer. Eventually, a major-general addressed them, berating them for their unsoldierly behaviour. If they had grievances, he said, they must submit them at their own headquarters and to their own commanding officer. He knew that a few agitators were fomenting trouble, and that most of the men would be ashamed of the action they were taking. Sobered by these words, the men walked quietly away and drove off in their lorries.[30] In Bristol, men of the Bedfordshire Regiment marched from their depot carrying a banner, and interviewed the mayor.[31]

On Wednesday, 8 January there were further, larger demonstrations in Whitehall. Four thousand RASC men marched there from Park Royal, and asked that the Prime Minister should see a deputation. The request was refused. General Sir William Robertson then addressed them. They informed him of their grievance: most of them had been transferred to the RASC after serving in the infantry abroad; they wished to be demobilized at once. Robertson promised to investigate the individual cases, to demobilize a fair percentage as soon as possible, and to send an officer that afternoon to inquire into conditions in their camp. Thus reassured, these soldiers returned to camp.[32] Similarly, numbers of men from all branches of the army, on leave from theatres overseas, assembled in the War Office quadrangle; and, after an examination of their papers, many were granted a discharge or a further period of leave. In Maidstone, several hundred soldiers of the Queen's, the Gloucester, and the Wiltshire Regiment took to the streets: 'I well remember the regiment going on strike and marching through the streets of Maidstone protesting about the very poor rations we were receiving." They held a protest meeting in the High Street, and then marched on the Town Hall. The mayor promised to forward their complaints, and before long it was announced that their commanding officer had granted a number of concessions, including the abolition of full equipment drills.[33]

The best organized, if not the largest, show of disobedience took place at Shoreham, Sussex. The thousands of soldiers gathered in that camp, all of whom had seen service overseas, organized themselves, elected a committee, and decided on a strike.

> 'The reason for their grievances was that they considered the methods of demobilization were most unfair. Men who had been in the Army only a few weeks or months were being demobilized because their bosses could pull a few strings in the right quarter whilst others who had been right through the war from the beginning were still patiently waiting . . .
> 'When the mutiny broke out the officers tried to crush the uprising by the usual Army methods of putting the mutineers in the guard room on a charge. A mass raid on the guard room would then take place and all the prisoners released. This occurred on many occasions . . . '[34]

Just as long as the arrests continued, so long did the men refuse to parade or to carry out their orders; but when the commanding officer gave up the attempt, some men did co-operate in cleaning and in other duties. 'There was no interference from the others when they did so. No punch ups or anything of that description.'[35] Problems of administration were decided by a committee elected by the men, but the commanding officer remained in nominal control: 'On the whole it was an orderly affair.'[36]

If real power was vested in the troops and their committee, they were concerned more with the prospects for discharge than with experiments in rank-and-file administration. On Sunday, 5 January the committee passed the day in making preparations for a march on Brighton to interview the mayor. At 7 a.m. next day the men assembled ready for the march, but, before leaving, agreed to listen to their brigadier. He pointed out that thousands of soldiers could not be demobilized without some measure of delay, and promised to forward to Whitehall any genuine grievance submitted by the men. He offered to talk with them again at 11 a.m. This offer was declined, and the march set off for Brighton. Soon,

> ' . . . the whole route from the camp was alive with masses of khaki-clad men. At Southwick they were joined by the men of the RME, and on their way to Brighton every soldier in the streets was invited to join in the procession.'[37]

The troops marched into Brighton, gathered round the Town Hall, and waited for the mayor. There were songs and speeches. A reporter spoke to one member of the march.

' "We demand demobilization as soon as possible," said this man, who was wearing two wound stripes. "There is far too much messing about," he proceeded, "doing physical jerks, washing up pans and dishes, and generally doing women's work while we might be at home doing our own jobs. Why cannot we be discharged . . . " '

The RME men were angered, in addition, by the fact that they were being paid 1s. 6d. a day, while men doing the same work in civil life, in the engineering industry, were earning £3 a week and more. One speaker put it to the crowd that they had assembled not only for themselves, but also on behalf of their less fortunate comrades in France.[38]

When the mayor spoke to the deputation, speedy demobilization remained the burden of the case. The mayor then addressed the crowd. He promised to forward their complaints to London, and to get in touch with a cabinet minister known personally to him; he had heard, moreover, from their commanding officer, who was prepared to forget the demonstration if the men returned in proper order to their camp. The men decided to return to camp, to hold a meeting there.[39]

That evening, Monday, 6 January 1919, a vast assembly gathered at the Shoreham Depot. The commanding officer, a brigadier, was present. 'Demobilization was pressed home by the men's leaders with great earnestness, this being the outstanding grievance', but the officer could hold out no hope of immediate relief. The men resolved not to parade next morning, but to march instead into the town of Worthing.[40]

Bad weather prevented Tuesday's march from taking place, so the troops held a meeting at the camp. The enclosure was packed, and numbers of men were unable to get in. The meeting discussed the text of a telegram to the Prime Minister — it demanded the 'instant' demobilization of all the men at Shoreham — and then gave a hearing to a general officer who had asked to speak. He offered discharges at the rate of twenty-five per week, but this was ill-received.

'He began by saying in his Oxford accent, "I have been sent here from the War Office to talk to you men," that was as far as he got when some old warrior in the audience got up and shouted in his cockney accent, "Don't you believe it cock it's us that are going to talk to you," which they then proceeded to do.'[41]

The troops decided to stand by their original demand, and the meeting then broke up.

Around midday on Tuesday an incident took place which well
illustrated the temper of the men. According to the local press, the
men released from custody a prisoner who, they felt, was being
victimized. The full story, a participant recalls, was rather more
dramatic.

'Unfortunately some young hot-head got the idea to throw a brick
through the window of the officers' mess. He was arrested and put in the
Guard room. A mass raid was carried out and he was released. Now the
CO was most annoyed and angry about this and accused the mutineers of
breaking their pledge and the prisoner must be handed over at once.'[42]

The demand was not accepted, but the men met to debate it.

'On receiving the CO's ultimatum a meeting was called at the usual
place. . . . There was the chairman on the stage surrounded by his committee members and in their midst was the prisoner whom they had
released. There was a lot of argument going on. Some were for defying the
CO whilst others took the view that the prisoner should be handed over,
about 50-50 I should say, and there seemed to be complete deadlock on
the question.
    'Then followed what I should describe as a good example of the
wisdom of Solomon. Someone proposed that they should ask the prisoner
himself what should be done. This was carried and he agreed to surrender
himself to the authorities.
    'So he was solemnly escorted back to the guardroom and handed
over.'[43]

Later that day, the authorities met the strike half way. Of the troops
at Shoreham, 250 men from the London Command Depot were to be
demobilized each day, but those from the Royal Garrison Artillery
would have to wait a while. The Depot men agreed to go back to
their duties while awaiting their discharge, but promised to strike
again if, within two days, the RGA men had received no satisfaction.[44]
On Wednesday, 8 January the majority returned to work; others
were discharged and some remained on strike. Perhaps the army
demobilized at once those whom it identified as leaders. In any event,
when the RGA men met next day to reconsider the position, their
resolution wavered. Lloyd George's message to the troops — that
demobilization would not be quickened and would, on the contrary,
be delayed if the men took the law into their own hands — was read
out, their commanding officer spoke, and finally, 'in a spirit of
patriotism', the men decided to go back to their duties. By Friday, the
strike was over.[45]

Why did the army give way at Shoreham and discharge so many men so quickly? There are no official reasons given, but a number of considerations must have carried weight. In the first place, up to seven thousand troops were out on strike and showing exceptional determination: 'short of putting them up against the wall and shooting the lot', it was hard to see how discipline could have been restored.[46] Second, neither time nor place were suited to a show of force. This was no wartime camp in France, but Brighton two months after the Armistice. Third, it was doubtful whether the army had sufficient loyal troops in England to put the demonstrations down. The Guards Division and the cavalry were still serving overseas, and the loyalty of such Guards units as found themselves in England could no longer be assumed. At Shoreham, a Guards battalion, while unwilling actually to strike, would make no move against those who had entered on that path.[47] And at a demobilization camp in Purfleet, Essex, such troops became unruly.

'The guardsmen mutinied and prisoners were released from cells. The CO, with supporting officers, addressed the men who replied with snowballs and my most vivid recollection was seeing the CO's hat removed by a well-directed shot.

'The men demanded more passes to London and other facilities, which I fail to recollect — and wanted an assurance of non-victimization. This assurance was given and the disturbance ended.'[48]

These were difficult times for the army. In England, infantrymen, as much as the troops of service and supply, were beginning to be drawn in. The Chief of the Imperial General Staff feared that the army was being turned into a rabble.[49] Nonetheless, though he might rail against the politicians and their promises, his colleagues had not yet lost control. The disturbances at Folkestone had caught them unprepared, but they had learnt the lesson: on Saturday, 4 January 1919, the second day of trouble, the War Office ordered Haig to send the cavalry back home.[50] In the days that followed, Lloyd George was induced to make appeals to the men, the newspapers warned against imperilling a victory gained at such a price, and stern words were said about the uselessness of protest. More important, the War Office put pressure on the Cabinet to take a fresh look at demobilization schemes which antagonized the veterans and at rates of pay which made all soldiers clamour for discharge.

These measures had effect, but they took a little time; and, in the interim, the army had to improvise. The troops at Folkestone were placated, the strikers at Shoreham rapidly discharged. In Whitehall, appeals and promises were thrown into the fray. Trouble was stored up for the future — troops in Palestine and Egypt were incensed when they learned, weeks later, that fellow-soldiers had been discharged during their period of leave — but, in that vital week, the line was held. When, four weeks later, the next round of demonstrations started in Whitehall, the outbreak was rapidly controlled: concessions over demobilization and rates of pay had eased the general temper, and there was, moreover, the cavalry to hand.[51]

What of contemporary developments in France? In January 1919 the infantry were giving little trouble. It was only on the Lines of Communication, and chiefly in the base ports, that the Ordnance and Army Service troops had given voice to discontent. Friction over working hours and conditions in the camps had linked up with frustrations over the slow pace of demobilization; and agitation and indiscipline had led, quite quickly, to organized unrest. The great strike in Calais in the last days of the month not only promised to unite such troops throughout the back areas of France, it threatened to isolate the BEF from its reinforcements and supplies. But senior officers were acting to contain the discontent. On Tuesday 28 January Brigadier-General Wroughton, on behalf of GHQ, ordered the release of Private Pantling — a move calculated to drive a wedge between the strikers. At the same time, GHQ detailed 105th Infantry Brigade 'to assist in quelling riots' in Calais.[52]

At this point, it seemed that official policy was working. Pantling's reappearance at his camp led many soldiers to go back to their work; meanwhile, three infantry battalions were secretly converging on Calais. But all was not yet over. New factors had entered into play which no one had foreseen.

10
The Power to Enforce Their Will

During the month of January 1919 thousands of British soldiers had been passing through Calais. These men, from every unit in the army, were *en route* to and from the front after periods of leave in Britain. They knew nothing of Vendroux and Valdelievre, of the declining discipline amongst the units at the Base. Nonetheless, the outbreak of strike action affected them at once. From the beginning of the stoppage on Monday, 27 January, the Ordnance men picquetted every military installation, and the leave men were thus brought face to face with the Ordnance demands. More directly, the running of leave and demobilization trains was halted by the strike. Thousands of soldiers were thus stranded in Calais.[1] While the military authorities examined the position, five thousand leave men took action for themselves.

On Tuesday, 28 January the troops in No 6 Leave Camp East, situated just outside the ramparts to the north-east of the town, refused to proceed inland and demanded ten days further home leave in which to find employment. Some walked down to the docks, hoping to board the leave boats and then return to England; the rest remained in camp and appear to have elected a committee.[2]

The military authorities were at once distracted from their efforts to break the strike of Ordnance and Army Service men. The Calais Base commandant and Brigadier-General Wroughton convened a meeting of the striking leave men. At four o'clock that afternoon the two officers listened to the soldiers' demands for further periods of leave and, after some deliberation, delivered a reply. No further leave could possibly be granted, but an officer from GHQ would investigate complaints about demobilization.

'The men refused to accept decision and three delegates returned to Base HQ with the Generals. Most of the men followed. At 11 p.m. the Base Commandant addressed the men, told them nothing could be done and advised them to return to Camp. This they did and no damage was done.'[3]

While the Base commandant was thus furnishing advice, he was at the same time trying to contain this new and harmful outbreak of unrest. A brigade of infantry had been ordered up to cow the ordnance men; it was now needed against a strike of front-line troops themselves. 105th Brigade arrived by lorry at 8 p.m. that evening. The 4th Battalion, North Staffordshire Regiment, was sent at once to No 6 Rest Camp West and established picquets along the moat, thereby frustrating moves towards the quay; the rest was stationed in reserve. The night passed quietly in all parts of the town.[4]

Wroughton and the Base commandant had been placed in a difficult position. The latter was a man with experience of administration rather than of suppressing insurrection, and though Wroughton, a staff officer from GHQ, had visited Etaples in September 1917, the addition of five thousand disaffected front-line troops to the strike of Ordnance men removed the problem from those realms entrusted to a general of brigade. A new dimension had been added to the situation. No longer were skilled tradesmen the only class involved: men were now entangled who had had great experience of war — men drawn, moreover, from units superior in reputation to the battalions making up 105th Brigade. Nonetheless, the staff at GHQ resolved to meet the strike head on. Late that Tuesday evening two entire divisions, the 31st and 35th, less artillery, were ordered to entrain. General Sir Julian Byng, General Officer Commanding, Third Army, was deputed to command.[5]

The role now thrust upon 31st and 35th Divisions, in the duty of repression, marked a departure from what had earlier been planned. When the question of overseeing the demobilization process had originally come up, GHQ had instructed the staff of Third and Fifth Armies to choose one division each, for duty in this sphere. The 30th and 33rd Divisions had been the ones selected.[6] A division would also be required, in the army's view, at the Demobilization Staging Camps — camps whose place in the process of demobilization was thus officially described:

' . . . plans had been worked out for the movement of men from Concentration Camps to Staging Camps, where they would be sorted into five groups, for dispatch to selected ports at Home, which were affiliated to the ultimate dispersal stations in each area.'[7]

The 59th Division was to staff the staging camps. In December 1918 one of its brigades was allocated to the Dispersal Camp for miners at Dunkirk, and before the year was out the rest of the division was split up and moved to other staging camps.[8] The French authorities, however, now disrupted all that the staff at GHQ had done.

'They began to protest against the whole principle of sorting our men on this side of the Channel; which from their point of view was a tax on the railway facilities . . . If we wished to sort our men we ought, they argued, to do it after they had reached England. So the scheme of Staging Camps was eventually abandoned, in favour of one which required only direct transportation to the base ports.'[9]

When the staging camps were closed, the 30th, 33rd, and 59th Divisions were transferred for duty at the base ports to staff the transit camps established on the coast;[10] in the context of this move, they were probably too dispersed and dislocated to be used in the new and unexpected task of suppressing disaffection in Calais. To these three divisions, therefore, the 31st and 35th were hastily now added. All five divisions drew on undistinguished regiments from the English North and Midlands — regiments, it was said, providing the most dependable troops in the BEF.[11] The 59th (North Midland) Division had made its name in Ireland. It had been transferred right across Great Britain in April 1916 for use against the Irish nationalists in Dublin.[12] The 31st and 35th Divisions, though, had achieved some fame in France. The 35th, originally the Bantam Division, had shown its quality on first entering the fighting; by 1917, though, it had more or less collapsed. It had been withdrawn from the front, completely remoulded, and the name 'Bantam' officially forbidden. In 1918, of all the divisions in the BEF, the German Foreign Office had laid particular emphasis on the 'barbarity' practised by the 31st and 35th divisions on captured German prisoners.[13] At the time of the Calais mutiny, a participant recalls, the troops of these two divisions looked like ' "bits of boys" who were sent out just as the war ended.'[14]

On the morning of Wednesday, 29 January 1919 the men of the No 6 Leave Camp East woke to find their way to Calais quay barred by soldiers of 105th Brigade, 35th Division. A few hundred decided that the demonstration had gone far enough, and marched to the railway station for dispersal to their units. The great majority of both NCOs and men, however, stayed solidly on strike.[15] A strike committee took over the office at the camp, displacing the commander and requisitioning a car. The strikers then brought their case to the attention of the Calais Ordnance and Army Service troops, concurrently on strike, and tried to win over the men of 105th Brigade.[16] They won some sympathy from the Ordnance men, but little from the infantry brigade. The Ordnance men, entering the third day of their strike, were due to meet the Director of Ordnance Services at 10 o'clock that morning but refused to enter these negotiations while the leave men were hemmed in by 105th Brigade.[17] The troops of that brigade, however, showed no sympathy at all. A staff officer reported:

'During the day several attempts were made to cross the Bridges of the moat by parleying, but without success, except in the case of the Soldiers Delegates who were sent under escort to attend an interview with General BYNG.'[18]

General Sir Julian Byng had arrived in Calais on Wednesday at about midday. Having spoken with the senior officers concerned, he arranged a meeting with the soldiers' representatives — representatives, that is, from both the striking service units and the troops defying orders in the leave camp. He met the two sets of representatives that very afternoon. The service troops received a promise of further talks next day, to be attended by the Director of Ordnance, the Director of Transport, and so on, brought down from GHQ;[19] but the leave men, it appears, were given no undertakings as to what General Byng might do.

That evening, General Byng's staff worked out a plan of action. They decided to crush the Leave Camp strike and to send the troops back to their units. Half an hour after midnight the General Officer commanding 35th Division received his orders, thus:

'The GOC Troops CALAIS has decided that the OC [the Leave Camp] is to be reinstated tomorrow [i.e. Thursday 30 January]. You will therefore arrange for this to be done with such force as you consider necessary.

'The above camps will be occupied by you. It is understood that there are about 3,500 men in the camps of which a certain proportion are quite ready to rejoin their units. All such men will be given the opportunity of doing so. Leave trains will start leaving at 2 p.m. 30th.

'You will explain to all ranks under your command that the camps are being taken over to allow those men who wish to return to their units to do so. At present they are being intimidated by men who have just completed their fortnight's leave in England and who are now demanding to be sent back to England for an additional ten days in order to be demobilized out of their proper turn. Those who do not wish to return to their units will be confined to their camp until the GOC Troops CALAIS has decided as to their disposal.'[20]

Towards eleven o'clock on the morning of Thursday, 30 January, 35th Division began its operations. Basically, 104th Brigade was used against the camp itself, while 105th Brigade blocked the approaches to the north and west. 106th Brigade stood by in reserve and also watched the east.[21] Divisional HQ drew up a record of events.

'1112　105th Infantry Brigade report by telephone that 104th Infantry Brigade have surrounded southern part of mutineers' camp. The mutineers crowded round apparently quite peaceably.

1135　105th Infantry Brigade report by telephone that 104th Infantry Brigade are in the mutineers' camp, No 6 Camp East, and that the mutineers are being divided into two parties.

1150　104th Infantry Brigade report that 'sheep' are coming in quickly, about 1000 already. Sergeant of Scottish Rifles taken and under escort. He and other delegates attempted to prevent 'sheep' coming in, so he and the other three were placed under arrest. . . .

1330　[Order No.] G.A.2 sent by D.R. to Base Commandant stating all mutineers have given themselves up except four ringleaders who have been arrested. . . .

1330　All 'sheep' from No 6 Leave Camp East moved with equipment to No 5 Camp, where they were fed.'[22]

Events inside the camp were more dramatic than this summary suggests. The men of 105th Brigade entered the camp and surrounded the tents and huts; their commanding officer then addressed the mutineers. He relayed the guarantee of General Byng: that those who wished to break off the strike could do so. The general promised that no reprisals would take place. The four-man committee next addressed the men, urging them to continue with the strike. Ignoring their committee, the men moved towards the gate. The four delegates were arrested as they tried to discourage the defectors.[23]

Just as 104th Brigade was laying siege to the strikers in the Leave Camp, a meeting was beginning at Base Headquarters, Calais. It brought together, on the one hand, delegates from the Royal Army Ordnance Corps, the Royal Army Service Corps, Queen Mary's Army Auxiliary Corps, and so on; and, on the other, the appropriate officers brought down from GHQ, plus the Base commandant and Brigadier-General Wroughton.[24] None of the participants was in compromising mood. The Director of Ordnance Services, GHQ, felt particularly bitter. The Ordnance men, unlike the other service troops, were still on strike, and only one man was allowed to work — a demobilization clerk.[25] Major General Sir Charles Mathew, the Director, had informed General Byng on his arrival in Calais that the Ordnance men's strike had its origin in Bolshevism, that the strike was a pre-arranged not a spontaneous affair, and that a handful of militants were compelling the majority to stay away from work.[26] He had come to the conclusion, he continued, that the organization of the strike was inspired by 'cleverer brains' outside France. The soldiers' grievances were without foundation, their demands unreasonable and 'made with the object of showing the power of the organizers to enforce their will on their superior officers'. 'Incendiary' newspapers had in no small measure contributed to the spirit of unrest.[27]

As the conference opened, the Ordnance men pressed upon the officers a solitary demand. A discovery of some importance had been made in the hours since Private Pantling's release, by one of the strikers who had versed himself in military law. A soldier released under the kind of pressure which had been brought to bear on the first day of the strike might be re-arrested and tried on the original charge at any time. This anomaly the delegates at once set out to right. They would take no part in the business of the day until Pantling had been tried. The officers demurred, but the soldiers' delegates were adamant. Were there not enough officers present to constitute a court, they asked? Pantling stepped forward, a court convened, and a verdict was brought in. Pantling was acquitted.[28]

Delegates from the different units now submitted their demands. The Ordnance men asked for a thirty-six hour week, a speed-up in the rate of demobilization, an extension of café opening hours, and improvements in the rates of pay. They asked, also, for official recognition of the soldiers' council, and for permission to attend a meeting at the Albert Hall in London in February.[29] The RASC delegates were rather less ambitious.

> 'They pointed out that they would like a half holiday in the week, though they did not press for a reduction of work below 45 hours per week: they also raised some objection to teaching learner-artificers and further stated that transport was being mis-used.'[30]

These requests presented no insuperable difficulties, save that the Director of Transport, taking them up after the meeting, found that if an extra half day's holiday were granted every week it would involve such lengthening of hours worked on other days as might not 'admit of the personnel getting away in time to see the picture palaces and to enable them to get seats before the whole of the house was filled.'[31] Scarcely problems to undermine the army; and no more far-reaching were the points raised by the delegates from the Queen Mary's Army Auxiliary Corps.[32]

The conference between the officers and the soldiers' delegates lasted about five hours, without producing a definite result. The Ordnance men's demand for recognition of a soldiers' council was rejected: 'there was no necessity for such a Council — all complaints could be put in the ordinary way and taken to a General Officer if necessary.'[33] At the end of the meeting the delegates were told that the men must unconditionally return to work next morning; and were given until 6.30 p.m. to accept this ultimatum. Accept it they did, however, and all the troops, including those from the Ordnance Corps, decided to return to work.[34]

The accounts of the conference to be found in the official diaries suggest no reason why men who had been so intractable should now so readily give way. One explanation has appeared in print.

'The vote on the proposals was so rushed that it was only taken in one camp, Valdelievre, where only a few men, largely the weak-kneed variety were left.

'The reason for this was that a large French cinema had thrown open its doors to our men for a special show of British pictures. This was an unusual attraction and it appealed to the men, who felt that they were in such a strong position that a night's enjoyment could well be afforded. Whether the brass hats had a hand in this I cannot say, but the results were doubtless received with sighs of relief.

'The consternation of the men of Valdelievre Camp on returning about 11.30 p.m. and finding that a vote had been taken of the few men left in camp, resulting in a narrow majority for resumption of work, can well be imagined.

'The language used was unprintable, but the damage was done, and naturally the other camps fell into line with Valdelievre, which had been recognized as the headquarters of the strike.

'Another factor which was also largely responsible for the disinclination on the part of the committee to continue to extend the struggle was the collapse of the expected general strike which had begun on the Clyde on the same day as our own, and to which our eyes were anxiously turned.'[35]

It is an open question whether these troops, who had shown such determination, could have been so simply deceived. Of greater weight, surely, in its effect upon the vote was the text of two army orders published in London that very afternoon. The first, Army Order 55, abolished the existing system of demobilization and substituted one which gave priority to factors such as age and length of service. Such a system had long been seen as just. And yet, under the terms of this new order, the maximum rate at which the troops could be demobilized remained exactly as before. There would be no acceleration in the process of discharge. Why then was Army Order 55 so important for the strikers in Calais? 'The Order was accompanied by a Royal Warrant (Army Order 54 of 1919) increasing the rates of pay of men in the Army. The increases were on a generous scale . . . '[36]

There ended the great strike of British soldiers in Calais. Considerable in size and ending in a measure of concession, this strike remains without parallel in the history of the army. In January 1919 two mutinies existed side by side. With one, the authorities sought negotiations; the other was surrounded and put down.[37] The picture is quite plain. GHQ could rely on loyal units to crush the strike of infantry, but it felt quite helpless against the troops of service and supply. Had it turned to force, had it arrested every Ordnance soldier in Calais, the troops at Dunkirk and at the other British bases might simply have downed tools. With neither stores nor transport, and cut off from the sea, the British army not only could not fight, it could scarcely eat or move.

Conciliation of the service troops did not end that January day. On Monday, 3 February 1919 a further conference was held at Base Headquarters, Calais. The points which the soldiers' delegates had raised were once again discussed.[38] And elsewhere on the Lines of Communication the good news contained in Army Orders 54 and 55 was diligently spread. On 29 January the RASC men in Dunkirk had given notice that, unless their allotment for demobilization was substantially increased, a strike would start in six days time, and would take in the Ordnance, the Engineers, and other Base units in the town. So, when the negotiations ended in Calais, the Director of Transport, GHQ, hurried over to Dunkirk in order to confront the men. He asked them

'not to do anything until after they had carefully discussed the new regulations for demobilization, which had been published as an Army Order dated 29th January and of which a report was given in *The Times* of which I left them a copy.

'I urged them not to take any drastic action without first fully considering what it meant and begged them to carefully weigh the reasons which I had put before them . . . '[39]

The strike did not take place, and new, shorter hours of working were put into effect. Elsewhere senior officers addressed the troops. The Chief Ordnance Officer, Boulogne, for instance, invited Lt Col. Stewart Wallace to give a lecture on 'Citizen-Soldiers and Demobilization' to the RAOC detachment at Henriville Camp.

> 'He fully explained the problem of demobilization in its relation to the larger problems of democracy, and also the methods adopted by the highest authority to demobilize the troops, consulting at the same time the national and military needs as well as the circumstances of each individual of the millions concerned. The men received all his remarks with applause.'

The Chief Ordnance Officer felt that much good had been done 'and the present unrest materially reduced'.[40]

Precaution moved hand in hand with such conciliation. While the Calais strikes were still in progress, GHQ began to move forces into other base ports and towards important centres in the back areas of France. On 29 January four battalions of the 61st Division were placed at the disposal of GOC, Lines of Communication, for the purpose of maintaining order, and were at once despatched to Havre, Etaples, Abbeville and Boulogne. GHQ still preferred, however, the divisions it had earlier selected — the 30th, 33rd, and in particular, the 59th. The units of these divisions, too widely separated to be of service when the Calais strikes broke out, were concentrated once more, and allocated to areas where further trouble might occur. When the 31st and 35th Divisions left Calais, their mission now completed, the 59th moved in to take their place; the 30th Division was then concentrated in the region Boulogne-Etaples, and the 33rd in the areas Dieppe-Rouen and Havre. The first ten days of February saw a continuation of such moves.[41]

These precautions proved sufficient. Once the demobilization system had been altered and rates of pay improved, no further and important strikes took place. In the short term, these measures proved successful. In the long term, the solution was more drastic: the great mass of the soldiery was steadily discharged, the dimensions of the BEF cut back, and, insofar as an army still had to be maintained, a new and youthful age-group was conscripted for service in the ranks. In the Near and Middle East, though, the authorities tried a different combination. They sought to keep the wartime soldiers loyal by concessions over pay, without supplying those measures of demobilization which, in France and Flanders, had reduced the army to a fraction of its strength. But their efforts met with a rebuff.

11

A Dangerous and Growing Unrest

In 1914, when war with Germany broke out, a modest force of Indian infantry and English Territorials defended British rule in Egypt. They held its towns, its countryside, and the banks of its Canal. Further units were gradually brought in, and a long, slow offensive against Turkey planned for and prepared. As the British army steadily moved north, the Turkish enemy gave way until, by the time of the Armistice, the Egyptian Expeditionary Force (EEF) had conquered Palestine and entered Syria itself.

Whatever the scale of operations, whether in the desert or in the hilly country of Judaea, the EEF's supplies and reinforcements depended on lines of communication stretching south to the Canal. There were strokes of generalship, of course, but for the most part military success depended on a clear superiority in communication and supply. Pipes were laid across the desert, new roads and railways laid down, and thousands of camels and their drivers employed to provision and support the front.

The great base at Kantara formed the epicentre of all this. At its wharves on the Canal ocean-going ships loaded and unloaded, and from its camps and depots roads and railway lines ran to all parts of the front. Its population, entirely given over to the war, fluctuated between twenty and forty thousand, and beyond that its supplies and reinforcements sustained an army of up to 160,000 animals and half a million men.[1] 'Reared on a dreary wilderness of sand, it resembled a penal settlement of tents and timber,' recalled one soldier who spent time at the base.[2]

It was in Kantara, on the night of the Armistice, that the first serious trouble among British troops broke out, and in the months that followed, disaffection in the theatre was to centre on that base. The authorities had expected that the celebrations attending the Turks' capitulation might lead to some disorder, but the success of their precautions left them unprepared, perhaps, for the size of the disturbance when the Germans sued for peace. In some camps there was noise and jubilation, and in others good humour turned to fray. General Headquarters, EEF, sent home reports of 'incidents' among the troops in Beirut and Alexandretta, and of 'disturbances' in Cairo and elsewhere.[3] What GHQ described as a disturbance, though, was referred to as 'rioting' by the officers responsible for order at Kantara; they turned out a battalion of the Rifle Brigade under arms on the night of 11–12 November 1919,[4] in their efforts to contain

' . . . a wild outburst of pent-up anger against ruthless conditions — in fact an insurrection of the rank and file that set the officers quaking with fright. The canteens were raided wholesale and the piano of a sergeants' mess was pitched into the Suez Canal.'[5]

These troubles soon subsided. But now that hostilities were over, certain questions loomed large for British troops. Their disquiet centred on 'food and leave and an attempt to apply more discipline; and developed more after the terms of demobilization were known'.[6] The prospects for demobilization excited much concern.

'After the 11th Nov. . . . our hopes and expectancies became most pronounced and the burning question of when a move was to begin became an obsession with us all. Many men, like myself, had been engaged on Gallipoli and had been out for well over three years without having had any home leave. To defer the hopes of such was to impose a peculiarly cruel strain on their patience and the crescendo of complaint grew louder with the passing of weeks and months.'[7]

Two distinct grievances were beginning to arise. The first concerned the rate of demobilization which, by all accounts, was going to be slow; and the second the fact that, when demobilization did occur, 'Men who had been on Active Service for 2 or 3 years without leave, were seeing men being sent to the Demobilization Camp who had only been out weeks or months.'[8]

By the end of 1918 little progress had been made. No one had left the theatre, although gathered at the demobilization camp, Kantara, were some 3,460 miners and 605 'demobilizers and pivotal men' awaiting embarkation.[9] The mood was deteriorating.

'I arrived in Kantara Jan. 1919 . . . to learn of grave discontent amongst the troops of Egyptian Expeditionary Force in that area. We new arrivals were soon informed of the reasons for the situation. It appears that the politicians at home and the military authorities in the Middle East were very cagey in authorising Demobilization. We heard of ugly incidents further afield than Kantara; amongst other things, the firing of an ammunition dump and open acts of insubordination and indiscipline. This state of affairs apparently had been brewing for some time, and the authorities must have realised the widespread indignation of ALL troops, and their determination to secure justice and some positive and honest action.'[10]

Officialdom had good reason to be cagey. The Turks were beaten, but two considerations served to stifle all promise of release. The first concerned the scale of territories now seized. Some had been promised to the Arabs, some to the French, while some were to remain within the British Empire itself: all required strong garrisons until the Peace Conference could meet. The second consideration turned on the role of British troops. Egyptian units had been judged unreliable from the first days of the war, and had been sent south to the Sudan; the Egyptian Expeditionary Force was Indian and British. Indeed, by the time of the Armistice diversions to France and other theatres had reduced the British element to unsettling degree. Brigades in ordinary infantry divisions, for instance, now consisted of one British and three Indian battalions.[11] Less than one-third of the Army Service Corps was made up of British personnel.[12] Given the conditions in the aftermath of war, it was important that the proportion of British troops among the infantry should not further fall, while, among the troops of service and supply, Indian soldiers could not in any case replace the skilled and semi-skilled.

The slow pace of demobilization was undoubtedly the source of much dissatisfaction but, as was the case in France, grievances over discipline and pay were also openly expressed. The Adjutant General's report for December 1918 noted several serious incidents. Soldiers of the Anzac Mounted Division surrounded a village near Ramleh and assaulted every male they found.[13] Four times that month New Zealanders, a few British troops among them, looted shops and damaged property in Ismailia. At Port Said, Australians did battle with Italians and problems were caused by colonials breaking ship while on their way from France to Australasia. 'In all the above disturbances,' the report concluded, 'regrettably few arrests were made.'[14]

In 1919 these troubles broadened to take in the troops of service and supply. On 28 January GHQ informed the War Office of the mood of railway units. 'If these men consider no improvement is evident in conditions or rates of pay and work, matters may come to a head in a month.'[15] Despatches of 2, 14 and 18 February spoke of growing friction and unrest. On 20 February the War Office was informed that the railway troops were comparing rates of pay and bonus for doing different jobs: the less fortunately placed were beginning to complain.[16] That same month, men of the Royal Army Ordnance Corps, stationed at Kantara, organized a strike. The official record provides a full account.

'Serious trouble arose at KANTARA about the middle of the month with personnel of the Ordnance Depot there. . . . This unrest culminated on 13 February in a general refusal on the part of the majority of those employed in the Ordnance Depot to parade for work in the morning. No work was done in the Depot on that day except in a few Departments. On the following day work was resumed as usual, the GOC, Kantara Area, having given the RAOC personnel an assurance that their grievances in connection with demobilization and leave would be represented to GHQ. . . .

'Later in the month some signs of unrest began to be noticeable amongst MT personnel at Kantara. . . . the situation was eased by direct reference to GHQ and no trouble has resulted.'[17]

The Ordnance strike, and the unrest in Motor Transport, came some two weeks after the troubles at Calais. In France, it will be recalled, the disruption had been halted by the supply of some concession — the provision that men should be demobilized according to their age and length of service, and that there should be some increase in their pay. So why, in Palestine and Egypt, did War Office concessions fail to have effect? Partly, it seems, because so few men received promise of release, under whatever scheme, and partly because the troubles in the theatre meant that men eligible for demobilization just could not be released. The demands of occupation pressed more severely on the army here than was the case in France, and, in March 1919, those demands were actually increased. The authorities arrested anti-British leaders, nationalists who hoped to press their claim for Egypt's independence upon the Peace Conference itself. Disturbances broke out. There were riots in the cities, and, in the countryside, the peasants cut railways and roads. Cairo and Alexandria were isolated, and communications with the south cut off.[18]

This emergency, and the British need for reinforcements, pressed harshly on certain groups of men. At Kantara, for instance, nearly eight thousand troops were awaiting embarkation, but were not allowed to leave. Those already on the troopships, about to sail for England, were told to disembark.[19] These troops were then detailed for further active service.

' . . . the whole camp were paraded and addressed by the Camp Commandant to the effect Demobilization was Suspended it was received without comment, the reason for suspension a Political uprising in the Sudan. Some time later a squad of about 40 of various units all unknown to each other were paraded equipped with rifles bayonets fifty rounds .303, and field dressing and sent to a fair sized Village named Bel Beis in the Sudan. We were told that Rioters done some looting and attempted to release Turko-German P.O.War.'[20]

For the moment, the men due for demobilization accepted redeployment. The uprising was endangering their friends. The feeling nonetheless persisted that the Turks and Germans being defeated, there was no good reason why men enlisting for the duration of the war should have to carry on.[21] Before long, men whose passage home had been deferred began to organize themselves. The diarist of the 19th Battalion Rifle Brigade, a unit reinforced that March by a detachment of these men, reported on the progress of events. His difficulties began on Easter Monday, 21 April 1919.

'About noon an anonymous letter from the reinforcements . . . was given to the Adjutant, intimating that if a guarantee regarding their speedy transport home was not given at once all duties would cease. A parade was ordered at 1.30 p.m. for the GOC, but the men refused to fall in under the orders of the Bn authority, but of their own accord fell in under their 'leader' who gave them detailed orders for the parade, which they strictly carried out. The GOC, P.L of C (General LLOYD) who was accompanied by GOC Kantara Area (General PEARLESS) addressed the men, and they listened to him respectfully. Later, when warned for the afternoon guard mounting the men flatly refused to parade, & the usual afternoon parade did not take place. Early in the afternoon the four delegates interviewed the CO & Adjutant, whom they informed that they were about to proceed to Demobilization Camp for orders which they would communicate on their return.'[22]

The four delegates returned that evening. They informed the adjutant of the advice they had been given: to carry out a minimum of guard and other duties, only those, in fact, which they considered necessary themselves. Next morning, it was the delegation, acting on behalf of all the soldiers, who organized the mounting of a guard, and every day thereafter they met the adjutant and told him which duties they would agree to carry out.[23]

   Clearly, something remarkable was taking place in this part of the theatre. Men from different units had linked together to carry though a strike. Over Easter, troops in the Demobilization Camp, for instance, got together and decided what they would and would not do.

' . . . it was unanimously resolved to:-
1. Refuse all duties except essential ones.
2. Send messengers to call in ALL guards, as they would not be relieved. They came in.
3. Appoint a deputation to lead an organised march to Headquarters & *DEMAND* to be heard.
4. *DEMAND* the immediate resumption of demobilization.
5. An assurance of no victimisation.

The march took place & to our surprise troops from units outside the camp joined us, & marched behind in support; amongst them, Australians & New Zealanders.

'The only troops not associated with this demonstration of solidarity were the Indian Sepoys.

'The GOC wisely consented to hear our deputation, the leaders of which, were a sergeant & a Schoolmaster.

'The deputation came out & said — "We were to assemble on parade ground & GOC would address us!" It was put to the vote, & we agreed to hear him.

'We were told, "That in all his years of Service he hadn't experienced anything like this, & he was sure we would have second thoughts & act as good & loyal British Soldiers!" Murmurs of "BULLSHIT!" which rose to a crescendo of uncomplimentary shouts. The assembly broke off & converged upon the assembly point, & it was decided to continue the policy of "Strike" except for a few essential duties.

'Headquarters, seeing that the GOC's appeal had only stiffened our determination & the support from units outside the camp, sent for our deputation & said, "They would see what could be done!" but, "Would we resume our duties in the meantime?" The answer — "No! Not until the order for Demob came through!" '[24]

Elsewhere in the theatre, men taken from the Demobilization Camp to help suppress the rising began to chafe at the delay. One detachment had been sent south to the Sudan.

'April had arrived no mention of our return to Kantara a lot of cribing went on some Spokesmen took over issued an order no more Guard duties, Strike to be returned to Kantara, this was followed by a visit from the Camp Commandant who made threats regarding our behaviour, he got a hot reception and left in a hurry, later, we were sent back to Kantara to our dismay, a Strike was also on there.'[25]

Eventually, the army seems to have decided that it could no longer hold such men. On 27 April 1919, for instance, the 19th Battalion Rifle Brigade received orders to return all 'reinforcements' to the demobilization camp in preparation for their transport home. The strikers agreed to restore discipline, and all left the battalion camp under the orders of their officers.[26]

The Easter strike had been launched by those who, having seen demobilization within their grasp, had been sent back to active duty. They formed, however, only a fraction of the British forces in the Near and Middle East, and their strike action brought no relief to other British troops. News of this action, though, spreading through the theatre, had influence elsewhere. At Kantara Base a committee was set up.

'I received a typed slip of paper from the Sergeant in charge of records at our Military Hospital in which it was asking our unit to pick 2 Members to form a Committee to go into the question of demobilization. I presume the reason the Sergeant handed the note to me was that I was known in the Mess to take on anyone who was prepared to talk Politics. I held a meeting in the Mess of members of our unit, giving them some details regarding the sending of troops to South Russia and the flare up in India. . . .

'I later got an Invitation to a meeting which was arranged in secrecy on the outskirts of the Base, with instructions that each delegate should proceed on his own, and each in different directions, so as to avoid any detection on behalf of the military Police. This we did and got down to ways & means of organising the whole of the Middle East Forces. We met under these conditions for a few weeks then it was reported to us we were in contact with every unit from Cairo to Damascus. We could now approach Head Quarters to lay down our demands.'[27]

The members of this committee were drawn from transport, ordnance, and engineering units: the very branches of the Service which, a few months earlier in France, had formed so vigorous a combination. These troops had reason to complain. GHQ had informed the War Office that, given the demands of occupation, no motor transport men could be returned to the UK.[28] And even when certain skilled men in the Ordnance Corps were not required and might be demobilized at once, the army was unwilling to release them: lest their departure anger others who, having greater claim to be demobilized in terms of age and length of service, remained yet vital to the army.[29]

The committee did two things. It pressed the army for more rapid progress with demobilization, and it took a hand in the running of the base. The Kantara Base Commandant, it appears, had to liaise with a committee member in arranging guards for Base headquarters, the cashier's office, and the military canteens.[30]

'We met General Oswald Williamson and his staff at Head Quarters.

'We demanded that they should look into the rationing at one of the ROC units and that the men who had been put under restraint because of their protests should be released. We demanded the use of an Aerodrome in which we could hold a meeting to explain our proposals for demobilization, and that later we would report to the GHQ what our proposals for demobilization were to be.

'Our greatest tussle was over the use of an Aerodrome for a meeting.

'The General said such a proposal was against all 'Kings Rules & Regulations', and that it was not in his power to grant it. He asked the question suppose we do not grant it, what will you do? Our reply was that we looked upon our endeavours as a safety valve in a very explosive situation and if it was not granted we should resign as a committee and let things take their natural course. We were later granted the use of the Aerodrome . . . we were given permission to hold a mass meeting in one of the Aeroplane Hangars. This was a very exciting event, some of our Committee Members proved to be very able speakers.

'As the Chairman rose to address the crowd, one soldier in the audience rose to ask what form of procedure the meeting was going to take; and suggested we should start by singing the National Anthem, to which suggestion the Chairman gave his consent. The Crowd at once began to sing that well known Soldiers Song *Take me back to dear old blighty*. This at once put the meeting off to a very good start.

'After which the Chairman asked for their loyal co-operation in persevering the job we had in hand of working out some practical proposals to get a speedy demobilization under way.

'Then followed the Chairman's suggestion of reading out the Committee's proposals to lay before Head Quarters at their next meeting. What emerged were the following resolutions:
1. That those serving longest abroad without Home Leave be the first to be demobilized—
2. That sufficient transport should be allotted for this purpose to demobilize all those with over 12 months service to be Home within three months—
3. That a priority cable be sent to the War Office asking for these terms to be accepted, and replied to within 8 hours—
4. That a Destroyer Boat be sent to receive a High Ranking Officer with a full account of our demands, and conditions prevailing in the Middle East.

'The Resolutions were submitted to General Williamson and his Staff.

'They agreed to forward the proposals to the War Office at once.'[31]

The committee circulated other units, even those far distant from Kantara, with news of these events. On 12 May 1919, one day after the great meeting at the Base, the men of the 347th Motor Transport Company, Palestine LOC, stationed at Ramleh, received a report on the negotiations between the committee and the GOC, Kantara; it had been sent by the committee. Two days previously, a detachment of the same company stationed at Haifa had received a round robin. This material was handed to the company's officers at once, the men having promised to bring to their superiors 'any written matter' arriving from outside. 'Throughout these days,' the diarist of the company recorded, 'the behaviour of the men was beyond reproach.'[32] Again, on 12 May the Commandant, Port Said, noted that meetings of the rank and file were being called because of the slow pace of demobilization; he did not give them serious attention.[33] On the other hand, a soldier in the Royal Engineers remembers the committee's work as having a powerful effect in remote parts of the theatre. Transferring from Beirut, from a unit showing signs of disaffection, to Haifa, he found the troops there in a 'worse — or more advanced' condition. All were following the negotiations at Kantara, some two hundred and fifty miles away.

'Just as I arrived at Haifa, a committee was making its report of what had transpired between themselves and the officers upon whom they had been waiting to discuss the situation. Down at the Base Camp at Kantara a Sergt. Ratcliffe of the Royal Engineers had sought permission to arrange for a public meeting in the large concert hall. He had quoted the description of the army given by Mr Churchill on one occasion in the House of Commons that we were "citizen-soldiers". If we were, then (it was argued), we were within our rights in claiming to meet in public and discuss our grievances. Exactly who gave the necessary or desired permission was not stated but personally I felt it was General Allenby himself. Anyhow the meeting was held and the Concert Hall packed — and the RMP looked on and did nothing.

'Speeches were made and a series of demands framed. These were wholly and solely concerning demobilization. . . . General Allenby was given three days in which to pass these demands to London and get a reply. (Later the time was extended to five days.)

'At the conclusion of the meeting the crowd stood to attention and sang *God Save the King*.'[34]

The following extracts from the official records will illustrate the anxiety with which the eleventh day of May 1919 — six months to the day since the Armistice in France — was approached by those responsible for order in the theatre.

3 May	We gave WO full details of the morale of troops in EEF with special reference to the trouble which may arise on May 11th.
8 May	We give WO full reasons of discontent amongst NCOs & men in this force.
9 May	General Allenby asks Rt Hon W. Churchill that every pledge may be fulfilled by WO as there is a dangerous & growing unrest.
9 May	We ask WO to keep their promise & return all RAOC personnel who we have sent on leave, as their not being returned, & in some cases demobilized is causing great discontent, & disappointment to men who would have had leave had the others returned.
10 May	We inform WO that the reinforcements they are sending for Supply, HT & MT are absolutely inadequate & at the rate they are sending them it will take 1 year to demob them & a dangerous situation will arise.'[35]

In England, one historian has claimed, a campaign launched by the Soldiers', Sailors' and Airmen's Union, and supported by the *Daily Herald*, to press for demobilization on the 11 May, had negligible effect.[36] In Egypt and Palestine this day marked the high point of the soldiers' agitation, compelling the authorities to modify their plans. GHQ in Cairo now decided that 'owing to discontent we can only send home men for demob by length of service'; other considerations would have to be ignored.[37] This decision 'would reduce the efficiency of our communications . . . and involve risk' to the military position.[38] But the alternatives were worse. To keep the 1914 and 1915 men back while discharging late arrivals would give more fuel to the committee at Kantara and extend the support it was drawing on elsewhere. And that support was taking forms that neither army nor committee could contain. At 2.45 p.m. on 11 May, the stack of tibben at the Main Supply Depot, RASC, Kantara, was destroyed by fire — this being the principal supply point of animal foodstuffs for the entire theatre.[39] Next day the office of the Deputy Assistant Director, Ordnance Services, was burnt down and all his records destroyed; likewise the offices and stores of the camp commandant, Headquarters Camp, 10th Division.[40]

On balance, the staff at EEF headquarters responded more shrewdly to these problems than did their counterparts in France. As a committee member had suggested at Kantara, 'we looked upon our endeavours as a safety valve in a very explosive situation',[41] and the army evidently accepted this interpretation. Another man active in the agitation summed up official dealings, thus:

'There was real and justifiable discontent amongst all the men affected and the authorities had to take notice. But they acted with tact and restraint and when it was all over nobody was victimised and there were no recriminations.'[42]

An interesting footnote to the end of the campaign is to be found in the story of these soldiers as they journeyed home. An announcement in Sicily, for instance, that the homeward travel of one draft would be subject to delay, caused a flood of questions and complaints.

'Instead of replies our NCOs were arrested and court-martialled and the whole draft put under arrest and marched, (under observation from an armed machine-gun section) into a barbed wire enclosure. It was obvious that the story of our activities had lost nothing in the telling from Palestine to Italy.'[43]

Another soldier returning from this theatre recalls a chapter of disorder.

'Well, we arrived at Marseilles & were embarked with no one in charge there were hundreds of us so we found what I suppose was a Embarkation Camp I know there was a small staff with an officer in charge he kick up a row because there was no notification of us coming he said we would have to stop there while we fumigated that did it of course we had no Papers & there was all Rank & Regiments, but he gave a meal, then the Sailors nearly all with long beards said come on Boys we will go down the Station and get on a train for Boulogne. When we got to the station the Stationmaster said he hadn't any trains for us, so there was a whole row of cattle trucks with the horse manure still in them trucks all open at the side to let the Urine out, we brushed the manure out with our army caps and got in and stayed there till they found an engine.

'We were 2 or 3 days going across France. We were put in sidings for hours at a time, we never had any food or water all this time. At last we reached Boulogne and walked up a big hill to the Embarkation Camp there was a bit of trouble here the Officer in charge here said we would have to stop there till he heard more about us, he gave us some food and we all left for the docks. The cross-channel Boat Maid of Orleans was in dock, so the navy lad with us said come on Boys she goes to Dover so we all got on I thought it was going to sink with all us crowd it was awash, at last after it seemed hours trying to get us off the Boat they decided to sail.

'We reached Dover & England at last. We all got in a train what was going to Charing-Cross more trouble, the railway people would not move till we got off, so we had to sit it out again. At last they decided as there was so many of us they would have to take us to London.

'We got to Charing Cross early in the evening. Now what could we do the lads lived all over England, Scotland, Wales, & Ireland, and had no money or Railway Warrants to travel a few had some Egyptian Money that's all. Well . . . there were a good few of ASC men with us, and when we joined up at beginning of the War they sent us to what had been a Work-House at Grove-Park near Eltham Kent, so the whole lot of us get in a train going to Grove-Park. when we get to the old Work-House we find the Army has finished with it.

'We all trooped in hundreds of us. They gave us some tea, I take it had been handed back to the Work-House People.

'Well at last someone in the Government had found out we had arrived.

'They came to Grove-Park that evening with staff cars, one car dishing out some money another car dishing out Railway Warrants to the Home Town of everybody.

'They told us to go home for a month but we would have to come back to Crystal-Palace to be demobbed as all the other Demob Centres had been closed down.

'And when we did come back to Crystal-Palace a colonel there ask us to forget what had happened.

'I ask you . . . '[44]

12
Agitators and Discontented Men

On 20 December 1918, before the infantry had been touched by any serious unrest, and at a time when agitation among the service troops had only just begun, the Adjutant General, Fourth Army, BEF, distributed his instructions for the winter. They referred at length to discipline and, with some prescience, gave warning of attempts by malcontents to organize the men.

In the first place, he directed, the laxities which had followed the Armistice would not be permitted to remain. A certain slackness was pointed to in conduct and saluting: all ranks would pay more attention to the latter, and their bearing would be worked on and improved. There was no question of introducing a reform. 'It has been suggested that saluting be abolished, except on duty. The Army Commander cannot accept this suggestion.' In addition to provisions such as these, however, the headquarters of all units, down to the level of brigade, were warned about the likely disposition of the troops and the conduct of the miscreants among them.

'Agitators and discontented men are not to be allowed to address assemblies of soldiers. It will be the duty of every officer, NCO and Military policeman to report immediately, to the nearest Headquarters, any meetings at which men are being incited to discontent or acts of indiscipline, and the Headquarters concerned will be held responsible that the ring-leaders are at once arrested and the meeting dispersed.'[1]

The authorities were prepared, therefore, for a degree of disaffection, but were to be almost overwhelmed by the scale and anger of the disturbances which actually broke out. In a single week, according to the Secretary of State for War, more than thirty cases of 'insubordination' were reported from the different centres;[2] far from arresting ringleaders and dispersing gatherings of discontented men, officers were soon parleying with privates, and corporals and sergeants were to be found stiffening, not good discipline, but the organization of a meeting or a march.

For the government and informed opinion, the dangers seemed

quite plain. In January 1918, through strikes in vital cities, the German socialists had tried to paralyse the Imperial army and thus disrupt the war. Their moves had not succeeded; but, within months, the German revolution had engulfed those factories and streets. Was such an outcome likely in Great Britain? For the parallels were clear. Unlike the German workers, whose strikes had failed to shake the army or cut off military supplies,[3] John Pantling's companions had brought their army to a halt. In January 1919 they had cut its main supply line on the route through Calais docks. The army was im- perilled: and generals sat down with privates and conceded their demands. In Germany and Russia, revolutionary politics waxed strong as discipline declined. Did the strikes in British bases mark the first stage in a train of similar events?[4]

With hindsight, a comparison with Germany and Russia is not easy to sustain. Revolutionary politics had reached the German soldiers only after prolonged periods of hunger,[5] and at a time of setbacks in both diplomacy and war. In England, the position of the possessing classes, though shaken, was far from being broken. They could cope with industrial disputes. And, though disaffection in the army reduced the powers at the government's disposal, such dis- affection, when devoid of political expression, no more represented revolution than did strikes for higher wages in the mines and en- gineering shops. The real question, whether mutinies were taking place or not, remained: with what views did the troops regard the army and the State? Did they intend to destroy discipline and thence supplant their rulers? Or merely to graft on to the army the rights appropriated by the urban working class? Of course, reforms intro- duced at the behest, not of the officers, but of the rank and file, had shaken the Old Army; a fact sufficient, in that day and age, to convince some officers that their world was coming to an end.[6] But these reforms and the disruptions they induce may, ultimately, have small effect upon the modern State.

Karl Liebknecht, who had sought to undermine the Imperial army in order to build socialism in Germany itself (and whose death not long thereafter demonstrated how far distant lay his destination), wrote, in November 1918, of the outlook of his country's soldiers, the majority of whom 'are revolutionary against militarism, against war, and the open representatives of imperialism: in relation to socialism they are still divided, hesitant and immature.'[7] In the English streets and bases, in France, the Near and Middle East, British soldiers hesitated in relation not only to socialism, but also to the 'open representatives' of the old regime. How else to explain developments in, for instance, Folkestone: where thousands of British soldiers, bearing union jacks, marched out of camp to call on the local mayor; where, having failed to gain redress, they telegraphed to Horatio Bottomley (the vulgarian on whom Kenneth Grahame modelled Mr Toad) and asked him to come down;[8] and where, at a concert laid on to entertain them, the mutineers sang *God Save the King* 'with special heartiness' — a Methodist minister, indeed, had 'never heard the National Anthem sung with more enthusiasm'?[9]

The Folkestone concert party, the telegrams to Mr Toad, bore no relation to the spirit of disintegration sweeping through the German army at this time. But the disintegration of the German front-line forces, the chaos and disorder in the rear, flowed from something larger than the fact of Germany's defeat. It was linked to German politics as well. For Liebknecht and his colleagues had opposed the war outright. Their party, the Independent SPD, campaigned not only in the factories and streets, but also among Germany's armed forces. They received support, therefore, from discontented soldiers when, acting sagaciously or not, they rose against the State. The left in the United Kingdom sowed no such seeds for the British army's 'agitators and discontented men'[10] to reap. The labour movement had supported the war effort, and had long neglected the question of military reform. When, one day in 1917, Ramsay MacDonald and Philip Snowden seemed about to tamper with the army, in calling for 'Councils of Workmen's and Soldiers' Delegates' to be established in Great Britain, their audience was rapidly assured that this was 'not . . . subversive, not unconstitutional';[11] soldiers, in any case, were scarcely to be won by a single resolution passed at a single meeting miles from any depot or encampment. In essence, the Adjutant General was left in complete charge of the ranks, no more under pressure with an army of four million than he had been when it was a tiny fraction of that size. Of course, from time to time labour leaders voiced a wish to raise the soldiers' wages or to curb some disciplinary excess. Some queried the capital sentences handed out by field general courts-martial. But none raised the matter of reforms within the army: the introduction of those measures which would curtail the power of officers and give more rights to the men.

At the fringes of the labour movement and the intelligentsia, a small minority of socialists and pacifists opposed the war outright. Initially, this minority sought to counter the weight of warlike propaganda; later, as volunteering gave way to conscription, it strove to defend young men who refused orders to enlist. It lacked the strength, however, to alter the conditions met with by privates in the ranks, and lacked both strength and inclination to carry over to the trenches the kind of programme which, in Germany, Karl Liebknecht and Rosa Luxemburg embraced.

In Great Britain, no part of the Opposition challenged the Old Army traditions upon which discipline was based. It was left to foreigners to express surprise that the army of a democracy could be organized along such lines. Crown Prince Rupprecht of Bavaria, for instance, noted in December 1917 that one single German soldier had been shot on account of aggravated refusal of orders; scores of British soldiers, he had come to realise, had been executed for such crimes.[12] These executions surprised not only German generals but also Australian officers and men. The Australians fought as volunteers, without threat of firing squads if they chanced to disobey; week in week out, though, they attended military parades in which reports of British executions were solemnly read out. Such public warnings, judged necessary to keep British troops in line, 'aroused in the Australians, officers and men, only a sullen sympathy and a fierce pride that their own people was strong enough to refuse this instrument to its rulers.'[13]

The Australian people, too, kept social relations within their army more in tune with democratic sensibilities than was — or is — the case in the UK. Anzac troops were contemptuous of the narrow discipline to which British troops subscribed, and were led by officers who had first shown their qualities as privates in the ranks.[14] Social distinctions between officers and men, so characteristic of the British army, were therefore less pronounced; Australian-born soldiers could not, for instance, be induced to serve as officers' servants, while the British system of superior messing arrangements for officers, universal even in the trenches, was not found in Anzac front-line units.[15]

Given their inattention to reform, neither the socialists nor the Labour leadership were well placed, in the months after the Armistice, to influence the ranks when the army's discipline broke down. Indeed, they continued to shrink back from any action which might help indiscipline to spread. The *Herald*, the leading organ on the left, scarcely covered the scores of mutinies in which the army was engulfed. It reported the details of just one, that at Folkestone during January 1919. Labour's newspaper drew no comparisons between the demands of soldiers, and those of the workers' movement elsewhere in the land; it promoted no discussion of what might happen if discipline continued to wear thin; it gave no advice to other soldiers as to the channels, conventional and unconventional, through which they might forward their complaints.

George Lansbury, too, had a chance to talk to soldiers at the height of the unrest. Lansbury, 'the most prominent figure on the Left',[16] visited both Folkestone and Brighton at a time when soldiers were leaving their encampments and taking to the streets. These men seemed disenchanted with both government and war. Spurning all opportunity to address them, he continued with the programme for his talks. His subject? In Folkestone it was 'Labour and the Church'. He spoke of the dignity with which God had invested every human being, of the need for it to be made a reality on earth; hoped that the Church would not adhere to any one political party, for it should stand above all three; and stressed that the teachings of the Bible, as interpreted by him, could form the basis for a real revolution.[17]

During the winter of 1918–1919, the stability of British society was placed, for once, in doubt. In certain cities socialism made ground, and, in many units of the army, the officers lost their power to command. But the two phenomena never actually linked up. Pre-occupied with the wider questions thrown up by the war, the left had neglected the condition of the army. It had ignored, in short, the tensions which resulted when a nineteenth-century discipline pressed down on several million working men. Accordingly, when the soldiers acted, they did so without reference to developments in Great Britain as a whole. They asked for improvements in conditions, for a change in discipline, for a clear acceleration in the pace of their discharge. These claims were modest, but courageously expressed. To organize fellow-soldiers in convening meetings, demonstrations, strikes, to take part in such events oneself, or merely to stand back in the role of a spectator, is to commit grave military offences and ones which, in any army, are punished with the severest penalties of all. Nor, even after the Armistice, were the risks perceptibly decreased.[18] However, these actions were offset, if not actually negated, in their political effect, by the gulf which separated the striking soldiers from the workers' movement in Great Britain as a whole. This gulf ensured that, throughout those days, the soldiers' dramas formed but a sideshow to wider demonstrations of unrest.

Sideshow? This is to turn topsy-turvy the picture of what actually took place. For it was the soldiers who furnished the government's most determined opposition. In 1919 their strikes in France and Egypt outran, in their significance, the fluttering of the red flags on the Clyde. In Calais, a gathering of soldiers had brought the army to its knees. Their compass was narrow, but the mood was very firm.

'But how are we going to occupy Germany if you all want to go home?', the generals had asked. 'Our delegation's reply was that we neither knew nor cared, but it wasn't going to be us.'[19]

At Kantara, a general officer questioned the committee, over one of their demands, 'Suppose we do not grant it, what will you do?' The answer was gentleness itself. 'Our reply was that we looked upon our endeavours as a safety valve in a very explosive situation and if it was not granted we would resign as a committee and let things take their natural course.'[20] The military authorities picked up the velvet glove. This was not the streets of Glasgow. No mounted police, no raw battalions, could have stood against this crowd. For behind the troops and their committee, there stood an iron fist: a great network of communications up and down the coast; a close watch on the negotiations by disaffected men; a growing tension in the theatre, such that whole depots were beginning to burn down.

During the war itself, against strikers in Great Britain, the government had one card it could play. It could draft men for the front. And this card, often openly set down, had powerful effect. Men would accept 'dilution', long hours, and a retreat from solidarity itself, rather than risk a trip to France. The 'opposition' in the army was made of sterner stuff. In the Base camp at Etaples, each man had made that trip. Some had gone willingly, some had had to be dragged on to the boat. But, by 1917, each of them knew what his visit there entailed. At the beginning of the year, Wilfred Owen had visited Etaples. In camp, he had seen a strange look on men's faces, 'an incomprehensible look, which a man will never see in England, though wars should be in England; nor can it be seen in any battle. But only in Etaples. It was not despair, or terror, for it was a blindfold look, and without expression, like a dead rabbit's.'[21]

A blindfold look? Haig wrote of a 'spirit of devotion'.[22] In any case, on Monday, 10 September all this was swept away. That morning, a corporal was court-martialled, for his part in an affray; and no soldier in Etaples could doubt that the penalty was death. Nonetheless, at least fifteen hundred men broke out that afternoon;[23] decided that they, too, would face that same court-martial rather than respect the Old Army's regime. The 'manufacturing hands'[24] had found conditions in the Base camp at Etaples more 'brutalizing' than any other they had known. 'Like passing through hell for two weeks', as one Scotsman has described it.[25]

On that historic day, this Scotsman, together with some friends, chose the mud and slaughter of 3rd Ypres rather than the risk of capital court-martial. 'The whole lot of us were packed off up the line next day (less ammunition) for doing the right thing, it didn't make any difference as we were only passing through.'[26] No matter: there were hundreds more just as willing to face the wrath of GHQ. And there was little in the workers' movement in Great Britain to compare with attitudes like theirs.

Notes

Introduction

1. Hon. J.W. Fortescue, *A History of the British Army*, London 1920, vol. 10, p. 205n.
2. Ibid., pp. 205–6.
3. Lt-Gen. Sir William Bellairs, *The Military Career: A Guide to Young Officers, Army Candidates and Parents*, London 1899, pp. 63–64.
4. Fortescue, London 1923, vol. 11, pp. 8–9.
5. Fortescue, London 1930, vol. 13, p. 8.
6. *Annual Report of the Inspector-General of Recruiting for the Year 1900*, Cd 519, 1901, p. 14.
7. Fortescue, vol. 13, p. 563.
8. Ibid., p. 8.
9. *Report of the Committee appointed by the Secretary of State for War to consider the Terms and Conditions of Service in the Army*, C. 6582, 1892, p. 31.
10. Fortescue, vol. 13, p. 573.

Chapter 1

1. Samuel P. Huntington, *The Soldier and the State: The Theory and Politics of Civil-Military Relations*, Cambridge, Mass. 1957, p. 43. Officers of the artillery and engineers, however, did not obtain their commissions by purchase. Hon. J.W. Fortescue, *A History of the British Army*, London, 1923, vol. 11, p. 459.
2. Charles M. Clode, *The Military Forces of the Crown; Their Administration and Government*, London 1869, vol. 1, pp. 28, 68; vol. 2, pp. 62–63.
3. *Report from the Select Committee on Army and Navy Appointments*, 1833 (No. 650), appendix 1, p. 274.
4. A British Officer, *Social Life in the British Army*, London 1900, p. xvi.
5. Arvel B. Erickson, 'Abolition of Purchase in the British Army', in *Military Affairs*, Washington D.C. 1959, vol. 23.
6. The militia was the old 'Constitutional Force' of England, its officers owing their position to property qualification, its ranks being filled by agricultural labourers. It served principally as a source of recruits for the Regular army.
7. *Report of the Committee Appointed to Enquire into the Entrance Examinations (in Non-Military Subjects) of Candidates for Commissions in the Army*, C. 7373, 1894, appendix x.
8. Lt-Gen. Sir William Bellairs, *The Military Career: A Guide to Young Officers, Army Candidates and Parents*, London 1899, pp. 63–64.
9. Ibid. Bellairs also supplied the parentage of the gentlemen at Woolwich, where

cadets were studying for the artillery and engineers. Their social origins were very much the same.

10. Fortescue, vol. 10, pp. 205–6. The 'old stock' was, of course, the 'lesser or greater landed gentry', whose sons, as a rule, possessed a private income of their own. Ibid; Fortescue, vol. 11, p. 30. Fortescue admits that to gauge aristocratic membership of the officer corps by counting titles is to apply rude tests: ' . . . for in England a very large proportion of the true aristocracy is untitled, and a very large and increasing proportion of the titled families is not aristocratic.' Fortescue, vol. 10, p. 205.

11. P.E. Razzell, 'Social Origins of Officers in the Indian and British Home Army', *British Journal of Sociology*, London 1963, vol. 14, p. 253. Within the 'landed upper classes', Razzell distinguishes between the aristocracy, on top, and the landed gentry immediately beneath it. Ibid., p. 259.

12. Anonymous, *The Army From Within*, London 1901, pp. 137–8.

13. *Social Life in the British Army*, p. 36.

14. Ibid., pp. xviii-xix.

15. A British Officer, *An Absent-Minded War*, London 1900, pp. 21–22.

16. Maj.-Gen. J.F.C. Fuller, *The Army in My Time*, London 1935, p. 37.

17. *An Absent-Minded War*, pp. 36–37.

18. Ibid., pp. 54–56.

19. Razzell, p. 254.

20. *Annual Report of the Inspector-General of Recruiting for the Year 1900*, Cd 519, 1901, p. 14.

21. Alan Ramsay Skelley, *The Victorian Army at Home, The Recruitment and Terms and Conditions of the British Regular, 1859–1899*, London 1977, p. 298.

22. Of the many mischiefs resulting from Free Trade, Sir John Fortescue suggests, the most serious, from the military point of view, was 'the physical deterioration of the men bred in towns and the steady fall in the supply of rustic recruits'. Fortescue, vol. 13, p. 8.

23. Skelley, p. 298.

24. 25,900 out of a total of 40,701 in 1898, for instance. *General Annual Return of the British Army for the Year 1898*, C. 9426, 1899, p. 32.

25. A.F. Corbett, *Service Through Six Reigns: 1891 to 1953*, Norwich 1953, p. 4.

26. *Report of a Committee of General and Other Officers of the Army on Army Re-Organization*, C. 2791, 1881, p. 16.

27. As the Adjutant-General declared, ' . . . we get practically an almost unlimited supply of hobbledehoys, young men who can earn only about 5s. a-week, and who are kicked out by their parents . . . ' *Report of the Committee appointed by the Secretary of State for War to consider the Terms and Conditions of Service in the Army*, (Wantage Committee), C. 6582, 1892, Minutes of Evidence, p. 8.

28. Lt-Col. F. Maurice, *Sir Frederick Maurice, A Record of His Work and Opinions*, London 1913, p. 261.

29. A Late Staff Sergeant of the 13th Light Infantry, *Camp and Barrack-Room; or, the British Army as It Is*, London 1846, p. 13.

30. An appendix to the report of a government committee set out, for the years 1859 to 1888, the figures for recruiting for the army, pauperism, and exports and imports per head of population. There appeared no clear relationship between the first and the remaining sets of figures. *Report of the Committee appointed to inquire into certain Questions that have arisen with respect to the Militia*, C. 5922, 1890, appendix 2.

31. Fortescue, vol. 11, pp. 8–9; vol. 13, p. 8. The army rejected, on medical grounds, a greater proportion of city-dwellers, as compared with country-dwellers, amongst those trying to enlist. Thus, 41 per cent of 'General Casuals, Town' were

rejected, as compared with 29 per cent of 'Agricultural, i.e. Farm Servants' in the year 1903–04. *Annual Report of the Director of Recruiting and Organization for the year ended 30th September, 1904*, Cd 2265, 1905, appendix F(a).

32. Wantage Committee, *Report*, p. 6.

33. *Memorandum by the Inspector-General of Recruiting*, C. 57, 1870, p. 1.

34. *Life in the Ranks of the English Army*, 1883, quoted by J.K. Dunlop, *The Development of the British Army 1899–1914*, London 1938, p. 37.

35. Maurice, pp. 135–6.

36. *The Army From Within*, pp. 72–73.

37. *Social Life in the British Army*, pp. 152–3.

38. *An Absent-Minded War*, p. 6.

Chapter 2

1. Lt-Gen. Sir Brian Horrocks' Introduction, in Jock Haswell, *The Queen's Royal Regiment*, London 1967, pp. 7–8.

2. Baron de Jomini, *The Art of War*, Philadelphia 1862, p. 278.

3. Richard Price, *An Imperial War and the British Working Class, Working-Class Attitudes and Reactions to the Boer War 1899–1902*, London 1972, pp. 190, 194.

4. Ibid.; Rayne Kruger, *Good-bye Dolly Gray, The Story of the Boer War*, London 1959, pp. 150–1.

5. *Report of His Majesty's Commissioners Appointed to Inquire into the Military Preparations and other matters connected with the War in South Africa*, 1903, Cd 1789, 1904, p. 83.

6. Richard Burton Haldane, *An Autobiography*, London 1931, p. 187.

7. Brig.-Gen. J.E. Edmonds, *Military Operations: France and Belgium, 1914*, London 1922, vol. 1, p. 7.

8. The Volunteer Movement had sprung up in 1859, to oppose what some saw as a threat from France. It endured for half a century, 'maintaining always a very few choice corps which were creditably efficient, and a very great many which served no purpose . . . ' Hon. J.W. Fortescue, *A History of the British Army*, London 1930, vol. 13, pp. 527–8. The Yeomanry, on the other hand, were a force of part-time cavalry, 'troops and squadrons of tenant-farmers and their sons, acting under the command of their landlords and their landlords' sons for the preservation of internal order.' Fortescue, vol. 11, p. 43.

9. Edmonds, vol. 1, p. 8.

10. Ibid., p. 7.

11. Haldane, p. 188.

12. J.K. Dunlop, *The Development of the British Army 1899–1914*, London 1938, p. 299.

13. Ibid., p. 305.

Chapter 3

1. Field-Marshal Viscount French of Ypres, *1914*, London 1919, pp. 78, 286.

2. Brig. Gen. J.E. Edmonds, *Military Operations: France and Belgium, 1914*, London 1925, vol. 2, pp. 5–6.

3. Edmonds, *1914*, vol. 2, p. 3.

144

4. Ibid., p. 4.

5. Edmonds, *1915*, vol. 1, p. 52.

6. Lt-Col. Howard Green, *The British Army in the First World War*, London 1968, pp. 4–5.

7. Ibid., p. 1.

8. French, p. 42.

9. Alan Ramsay Skelley, *The Victorian Army at Home*, London 1977, p. 303.

10. French, p. 42.

11. In suburbs and small towns, 'the drill hall was as much part of the fabric as the non-conformist chapel'. John Keegan, *The Face of Battle*, London 1976, p. 224.

12. Richard Price, *An Imperial War and the British Working Class*, London 1972, p. 229.

13. Ibid., p. 13.

14. Green, p. 38.

15. Ibid.

16. French, p. 295.

17. Report of the Ministry of National Service, quoted in J.M. Winter, 'Britain's "Lost Generation" of the First World War', in *Population Studies*, London November 1977, vol. 31, p. 456.

18. Green, p. 40.

19. French, p. 293.

20. Ibid., p. 298; Hon. J.W. Fortescue, *A History of the British Army*, London, vol. 13, pp. 527–8.

21. Green, pp. 61–63.

22. Ibid.; Keegan, p. 220.

23. Edmonds, op. cit.

24. Edmonds, *1915*, vol. 1, p. 54.

25. Edmonds, *1916*, vol. 2, p. 571.

26. Ibid., p. 570.

27. Green, p. 3. On learning that he was to join a regular battalion, Lt Wilfred Owen felt that he had come off 'mighty well'. Such pleasure, in these circumstances, was apparently widespread.

> 'Those posted to the Regular battalions at once assumed an air of slight superiority over those of their contemporaries going up to Territorial or Kitchener's army units. This superiority was quite unjustified as the drafting warrant officer at the Base Depot knew the men not at all.'

Owen, in fact, like more than a million others, was sent to whichever unit in his regiment needed reinforcing at the time. Green; H. Owen and J. Bell, eds., *Wilfred Owen: Collected Letters*, London 1967, p. 421. Letter of 1 January 1917.

28. Edmonds, *1915*, vol. 1, p. 54.

29. French, p. 264.

30. Green, pp. 38–39, 64.

31. C.E.W. Bean, ed., *Official History of Australia in the War of 1914–1918*, Sydney 1921 onwards, vol. 5, p. 540.

32. Bean, vol. 6, p. 1087; Green, p. 70.

33. Edmonds, *1917*, vol. 1, p. 555.

34. Bean, vol. 6, p. 1085.

35. Bean, vol. 5, p. 2.

36. Edmonds, *1915*, vol. 2, p. vii.

37. Fortescue, vol. 13, p. 21.

38. Linesman, *Words by an Eyewitness: The Struggle in Natal*, Edinburgh 1901, pp. 22, 25.

39. French, p. 298.

40. Edmonds, *1917*, vol. 1, p. 554.

41. Bean, vol. 3, p. 53.

42. Ibid., p. 54.

43. Ibid.

44. J.M. Winter, working from literary sources, memoirs, and mortality statistics, suggests that subalterns were drawn 'almost exclusively' from that section of the population which had attended public school or university. Winter, p. 464.

45. Edmonds, *1915*, vol. 2, p. viii.

46. A.J.P. Taylor, *English History 1914–1945*, Oxford 1965, p. 62.

47. Despite the shortage, the officer selection boards did not lose their heads. Hundreds of thousands of miners volunteered, or were taken, from the pits. Not one of them appears to have been granted a commission. Winter, pp. 454, 457.

48. Fortescue, vol. 11, pp. 8–9.

Chapter 4

1. John Keegan, *The Face of Battle*, London 1976, p. 217; William Gallacher, *Revolt on the Clyde: An Autobiography*, London 1949, p. 18.

2. A.J.P. Taylor, *English History 1914–1945*, Oxford 1965, pp. 38–39.

3. Board of Trade and Ministry of National Service figures, cited in J.M. Winter, 'Britain's "Lost Generation" of the First World War', in *Population Studies*, London November 1977, vol. 31, pp. 452–4.

4. Major Desmond Chapman-Huston and Major Owen Rutter, *General Sir John Cowans GCB, GCMG, The Quartermaster-General of the Great War*, London 1924, vol. 2, p. 342.

5. Taylor, p. 59.

6. Winter, p. 451.

7. Taylor, p. 28, 53.

8. Edmonds, *1915*, vol. 1, pp. 51–52.

9. Taylor, p. 53.

10. Edmonds, *1915*, vol. 1, p. 52.

11. Edmonds, *1916*, vol. 1, p. 151.

12. Ibid.

13. Edmonds, *1918*, vol. 1, p. 51; Taylor, pp. 55, 97–8.

14. A.L. Morton and G. Tate, *The British Labour Movement 1770_1920*, London 1956, pp. 245–7.

15. C.E.W. Bean, ed., *Official History of Australia in the War of 1914–1918*, vol. 3, p.60.

16. Hon. J.W. Fortescue, *A History of the British Army*, London 1920, vol. 10, p. 201.

17. Alan Ramsay Skelley, *The Victorian Army at Home*, London 1977, p. 137.

18. Bean, vol., p. 25.

19. Ibid., vol. 3, p. 56; vol. 5, pp. 26–8; vol. 6, p. 485.

20. Ibid., vol. 6, pp. 875–6, 932–3, 937–9, 1083.

21. Ibid., vol. 6, p. 1083.

22. Ibid., vol. 4, p. 732n; Col. H. Stewart, *The New Zealand Division 1916–1919, A Popular History Based on Official Records*, Auckland 1921, p. 617.

23. Anthony Babington, *For the Sake of Example: Capital Courts-Martial 1914–1920*, London 1983, p. 120.

24. On at least two occasions, men were shot for simple insubordination — one of them for refusing to put on his cap. Ibid., pp. 42, 72.

25. On reading the recommendation of a court-martial, that a condemned private be shown mercy on account both of his previous good record and of the intense shelling he had undergone, Sir Douglas Haig is said to have written: 'How can we ever win if this plea is allowed?' Ibid., p. 81. Australia's official history records Haig's 'conviction' that his Australian force, by the example of misconduct which it set, 'constituted a danger to his army's discipline'. Vol. 6, p. 485.

26. Bean, vol. 3, p. 58.

27. Crown Prince Rupprecht von Bayern, *Mein Kriegstagebuch*, Munich 1929, vol. 2, pp. 303–4.

28. Bean, vol. 3, p. 58.

29. Ibid., vol. 3, p. 59, vol. 5, p. 31.

30. Fortescue, vol. 11, pp. 8–9.

31. Taylor, p. 28.

32. Ibid., p. 32.

33. Babington, p. 67.

34. R. Blake, ed., *The Private Papers of Douglas Haig 1914–1919*, London 1952, p. 95. Diary entry for 11 June 1915.

35. Babington, p. 189.

36. Ibid., p. 16.

37. Taylor, pp. 60–61.

38. Public Record Office, WO 95/26, Adjutant General, GHQ, 'General Routine Orders', September 1916.

39. Only two New Zealanders were shot, throughout the war, for military offences: Private Hughes, and one further offender who had taken part in a protest against conditions in the military prison at Blargies, France. Babington, p. 94.

40. Private Bennett, reports Anthony Babington, who has had some access to the records of courts-martial, joined the army six weeks before the outbreak of war. 'His company sergeant-major described him as a man who practically went off his head from sheer terror the moment he came under shellfire.' His corps commander, on reviewing sentence, felt that the penalty was just. ' "Cowards of this sort are a serious danger to the army," he wrote. "The death penalty is instituted to make such men fear running away more than they fear the enemy." ' Babington, p. 80. (Babington gives the date of execution, incorrectly, as being 'early in September'.)

John Bennett, whether cowardly or not, had good basis for his fears. The 1st Battalion, Hampshire Regiment, had been almost wiped out during a few brief hours on the first day of the Somme: it 'had suffered so severely that no one could be found at the end of the day to describe, reliably, what had happened'. Martin Middlebrook, *The First Day on the Somme, 1 July 1916*, London 1971, p. 269. Bennett was aged nineteen at the time of the execution. (Death certificate.)

41. Private Anderson had volunteered for service at the peak of Kitchener's recruiting campaign in the early autumn of 1914. He had walked away from the working party, telling the officer in charge: 'I am getting out. I can stick it no longer. My nerves are gone.' Anderson claimed in his defence that he had been treated in hospital for a nervous breakdown during the previous January after being buried in a dugout. He also said that two of his brothers had been killed in France and another had been wounded at Gallipoli. Babington, p. 80.

42. Ibid., pp. 29–30.

43. Bean, vol. 5, p. 31; Rupprecht von Bayern.

44. Babington, pp. 42, 72, 143.

45. Letter from William Edwards, 23 September 1965. Mr Edwards volunteered early in the war, and served with the 18th Battalion, Welch Regiment.

46. Ibid.

47. Ibid.

48. Letter from C.A. Saysell, 2 October 1965.

49. Cameron Hazlehurst, *Politicians at War, July 1914 to May 1915*, London 1971, pp. 198–9.

50. Col. R.H. Beadon, *The Royal Army Service Corps: A History of Transport and Supply in the British Army*, Cambridge 1931, vol. 2, p. 410.

51. Col. A. Fortescue Duguid, *Official History of the Canadian Forces in the Great War, 1914–1919*, General Series, Ottawa 1938, vol. 1, pp. 135–141.

52. Bean, vol. 1, p. 111. Within three months, a quarter of these first Canadian arrivals had gone down with venereal disease. Lord Kitchener delivered an admonition to each man, that he should be courteous to all women and intimate with none. Duguid, p. 141.

53. Arthur Crookenden, *The History of the Cheshire Regiment in the Great War*, Chester 1939, p. 345.

Chapter 5

1. H. von Kuhl, *Der deutsche Generalstab in Vorbereitung und Durchführung des Weltkrieges*, Berlin 1920, p. 103.

2. O. Jászi, *The Dissolution of the Habsburg Monarchy*, Chicago 1929, pp. 15–8.

3. Ibid.

4. U. von Cramon, *Unser Österreich-Ungarischer Bundesgenosse im Weltkriege*, Berlin 1920, p. 9.

5. Jászi.

6. General Ludendorff, *My War Memories 1914–1918*, London 1919, vol, 1, pp. 117–8; vol. 2, p. 642.

7. Maj.-Gen. Sir Alfred Knox, *With the Russian Army 1914–1917*, London 1921, pp. xvii-xix.

8. *Official History of the Canadian Forces*, vol. 1, p. 7; C.E.W. Bean, ed., *Official History of Australia in the War of 1914–1918*, Sydney 1921 onwards, vol. 1, pp. 20, 27.

9. Bean, vol. 1, p. 32.

10. Ibid., vol. 1, p. 43.

11. Ten out of a total of sixty-two divisions in January 1918. Brig. Gen. J.E. Edmonds, *Military Operations: France and Belgium, 1918*, London 1935, vol. 1, p. 48.

12. Bean, vol. 3, p. 892.

13. The New Zealand government, however, under British pressure, agreed to permit death sentences for military offences. Ibid., vol. 5, p. 28.

14. Ibid., vol. 4, p. 948.

15. For Haig's views, ibid., vol. 3, pp. 56–57; vol. 5, pp. 26–28; vol. 6, p. 485. For Rawlinson's views, ibid., vol. 5, p. 26. For the views of Macready, the Adjutant General, Sir Nevil Macready, *Annals of an Active Life*, London 1924, p. 278.

16. Bean, vol. 6, p. 6.

17. Of the rank and file of the first Canadian contingent, over 65 per cent had been

born in the British Isles. *Official History of the Canadian Forces*, vol. 1, p. 53.

18. Public Record Office, WO 95/43, Canadian Section, Third Echelon, GHQ, *War Diary*, 4 January and 16 February 1918.

19. Ibid., 20 March 1918.

20. Edmonds, *1915*, vol. 1, p. 52.

21. WO 163/21, Army Council Minutes 1915–1916, meeting of 28 July 1916. Cf. Wingate's unwillingness to accept a draft of Maoris. Sir George Arthur, *Life of General Sir John Maxwell*, London 1932, p. 180n.

22. The authorities in Ottawa pondered the wisdom of permitting Canadian Indians to enlist, 'on the ground that the Germans might not observe the usages of war towards them'. Some were in fact enrolled. 'Coloured volunteers were refused.' *Official History of the Canadian Forces*, vol. 1, p. 52.

23. WO 163/21, Army Council Minutes 1915–1916, meeting cited.

24. Sir George Arthur, p. 166.

25. Suzanne Brugger, *Australians and Egypt 1914–1919*, Melbourne 1980, p. 102.

26. 'There is no doubt,' the Foreign Office recorded, 'that we squeezed the country very hard.' Public Record Office, FO 371/3714, quoted Brugger, p. 93.

27. Bean, vol. 7, pp. 366, 678.

28. Lt Col. G.E. Badcock, *A History of the Transport Services of the Egyptian Expeditionary Force, 1916, 1917 and 1918*, London 1925, p. 14.

29. Edmonds, *1914*, vol. 1, p. 13.

30. A.J.P. Taylor, *English History 1914–1945*, Oxford 1965, p. 83.

31. Sir George Arthur, pp. 179, 181; WO 163/22, Army Council Minutes 1917–1918, meeting of 25 June 1917.

32. Memorandum, German General Staff to Foreign Ministry, 5 August 1914, quoted in Fritz Fischer, *Germany's Aims in the First World War*, London 1967, p. 126.

33. P.S. O'Hegarty, *A History of Ireland under the Union*, London 1952, pp. 447–51.

34. Stephen Gwynn, *Experiences of a Literary Man*, London 1926, p. 300–301. These soldiers, officers and other ranks alike, were perhaps breaching army regulations. 'Officers, non-commissioned officers, and private soldiers are forbidden to institute, or take part in, any meetings, demonstrations, or processions for party or political purposes in barracks, quarters, camp or elsewhere.' *The Queen's Regulations and Order for the Army* (1883), pp. 89–90, quoted Alan Ramsay Skelley, *The Victorian Army at Home*, London 1977, p. 138.

35. For the strength and preparedness of the Ulster Volunteers, see *Intelligence Notes 1913–1916*, B. MacGiolla Chiolle, ed., Dublin 1966, pp. 16–37, 94–102.

36. Ibid., pp. 104, 109–10; Dorothy Macardle, *The Irish Republic*, Dublin 1951.

37. The Earl of Oxford and Asquith, *Memories and Reflections 1852–1927*, vol. 2 London 1928, p. 5.

38. Denis Gwynn, *The Life of John Redmond*, London 1932, p. 361.

39. When the Volunteer movement split, about 160,000 of its members followed John Redmond; less than 10,000 remained. Colonel Moore, commanding the Irish Volunteers, had urged Redmond in the last days of July 1914 to advise army reservists to refuse orders unless the passage of the Home Rule Bill were guaranteed. Redmond declined to lay down this condition. B. MacGiolla Chiolle, p. 110. Denis Gwynn, pp. 357, 365–6, 392n.

40. Denis Gwynn, pp. 349–51, 365.

41. *Return of the Troops on Foreign and Home Service* (115), 1821; *General Annual Return of the British Army for the year 1898*, C.9426, 1899, p. 94; *General*

Annual Reports on the British Army for the Period from 1st October, 1913, to 30th September, 1919, Cmd 1193, 1921; *Report on Recruiting in Ireland*, Cd 8168, 1916, p.2.

42. Hervey de Montmorency, *Sword and Stirrup, Memories of an Adventurous Life*, London 1936, p. 245. Not all the protagonists of Ulster were opposed to the embodiment of the Irish Volunteers. General Sir Ian Hamilton and Lord Roberts both showed interest in such a scheme. James R. White, *Misfit, An Autobiography*, London 1930, pp. 327–38.

43. Montmorency; Denis Gwynn, pp. 389, 402.

44. Michael MacDonagh, *The Irish on the Somme*, London 1917, p. 122; Denis Gwynn, pp. 396–7.

45. Sir Francis Vane, *Agin the Governments*, London 1929, p. 248 et seq. William Martin Murphy, who had engineered the Dublin lock-out, suggested to a meeting of Dublin employers that they sack able-bodied men to stimulate recruiting. Dorothy Macardle, *The Irish Republic*, Dublin 1951, p. 139.

46. M. Lennon, 'A Retrospect', in *Banba*, Dublin, February 1922, vol. 2, p. 302.

47. Denis Gwynn, pp. 393–8.

48. Sir Francis Vane, pp. 251–3.

49. J. Keating, 'The Tyneside Irish Brigade', in Felix Lavery, ed., *Great Irishmen in War and Politics*, London 1920, pp. 125–7.

50. Denis Gwynn, p. 400.

51. Vane, p. 248. Most of the subalterns for the 16th Division were drawn from exclusive units of London Territorials; a few were Irish but all were Unionist.

52. Denis Gwynn, pp. 400–411.

53. WO 162/27, Memorandum of 3 June 1915, Table B; *Report on Recruiting in Ireland*, Cd 8168, 1916, p. 2.

54. B. MacGiolla Chiolle, p. 210.

55. WO 32/4307, Document 6, statement by the Assistant Commissioner of Police for Ireland.

56. The local inspectors reported small increase in anti-British activity during 1915. See B. MacGiolla Chiolle, pp. 112, 176.

57. Denis Gwynn, pp. 439–46. According to Gwynn, 'some inexplicable fatality had pursued the Irish regiments since the beginning of the War'. The 2nd Battalion, Royal Munster Fusiliers, at Etreux, the 1st Munsters and the 1st Royal Dublin Fusiliers at Gallipoli, and the 10th Division at Suvla Bay had all suffered great losses for which neither adequate official explanation nor, it was felt, sufficient recognition had been forthcoming. Rumours were current in Dublin of the kind that, of six hundred Connaught Rangers who left early in the war, only forty-two survived. Lennon, p. 302.

58. B. MacGiolla Chiolle, pp. 114–5.

59. The recruiting booth opened in Grafton Street to coincide with Asquith's heavily guarded visit received, according to one account, only six applicants that night. Lennon, p. 304.

60. B. MacGiolla Chiolle, pp. 116–7, 162–5.

61. Montmorency.

62. Monteith, p. 43.

63. G. de C. Parmiter, *Roger Casement*, London 1936, p. 189. Detailed accounts of Casement's failure are to be found in Monteith, and Denis Gwynn, *The Life and Death of Roger Casement*, London 1930.

64. WO 35/69, GHQ Home Forces, Operations Circular, 24 April 1916. WO 32/4307 deals with the military aspects of the Rising, but nothing of great significance

has been allowed to slip the 75 and 100 year rules. For a blow-by-blow account of the Rising, see Max Caulfield, *The Easter Rebellion*, London 1964.

65. *The Freeman's Journal*, Dublin, 26 April– 5 May 1916.

66. Frank Crozier, *Impressions and Recollections*, London 1930, p. 56.

67. On 28 April, officers were still arriving in Dublin on leave; HQ Dublin requested that this be stopped. (WO 32/4307, telegram of 28 April 1916.) Leave was again granted in the Guards Division after 3 May.

68. WO 95/4828, General Staff, 10th Division, *War Diary*; WO 95/4829 A and QMG 10th Division, *War Diary*.

69. WO 95/1971, 8th Battalion, Royal Munster Fusiliers, *War Diary*, 10 May 1916. This simple incident gave rise to a multitude of tales. Denis Gwynn, for instance, describes how a patrol brought the posters back from the German lines 'in triumph' (*Life of John Redmond*, pp. 494–5); others, that the Irish troops swept forward to punish the German affront.

The mood in other units of the 16th Division is harder to uncover, and some of the War Diaries for the Division are missing from the series.

70. WO 95/1975, 9th Battalion, Royal Munster Fusiliers, *War Diary*, 22 May 1916.

71. The Chief of the Imperial General Staff, leaving England, visited the headquarters of 16th Division on 6 May. The Commander-in-Chief, BEF, visited the 1st Battalion, Irish Guards, on 28 April, and on 5 May a company of the 8/9th Battalion, Royal Dublin Fusiliers, was paraded before him. WO 95/1957, Adjutant and Quartermaster General's Branch, 16th Division, *War Diary*, May 1916; WO 95/1197, A and QM's Branch, Guards Division, *War Diary*, 28 April 1916; WO 95/1974, 8th Battalion, Royal Dublin Fusiliers, *War Diary*, 5 May 1916.

72. WO 95/1216, 1st Battalion, Irish Guards, *War Diary*, 2 and 16 June 1916. No record of the conversation remains.

73. Letter from John Murphy, September 1965. Mr Murphy was a regular soldier serving with the Munsters. For the official account, see WO 95/2298, HQ, 86th Brigade, *War Diary*, 24 April 1916.

74. Letter from Walter James Pogue, 9 November 1965. Mr Pogue served with the Royal Dublin Fusiliers. See also Sir Nevil Macready, *Annals of an Active Life*, London 1924, vol. 1, p. 242.

75. J. Murphy, letter cited.

76. Interview with Charles Doran. Mr Doran joined the Leinsters in 1915.

77. WO 32/4307, letters of 3 and 6 May 1916. Macready thought it necessary 'to draw a distinction between rebels in arms and legitimate adversaries such as the Boers who were enlisted at the close of the South African war for service in East Africa'. Ibid.

78. Lavery, p. 185.

79. WO 163/21, Precis 838, p. 55.

80. WO 95/2301, 1st Battalion, Royal Dublin Fusiliers, *War Diary*, 21 July 1916.

81. Sir George Arthur, pp. 283–8.

82. WO 163/21, Precis 838.

83. State Paper Office, Dublin, Papers of the Chief Secretary's Office, 1916. Report compiled on 5 October 1916 for the Lord Lieutenant.

84. Sir George Arthur, p. 285.

85. WO 106/314, Document 33, 29 March 1918.

86. Denis Gwynn, p. 530. Lloyd George wrote to Redmond on 29 September 1916 proposing such a merger; Redmond replied that the move would prove disastrous for recruiting.

87. WO 95/26, Adjutant General, GHQ, *War Diary*, 26 October 1916.

88. WO 95/1970, 6th Battalion, Royal Irish Regiment, *War Diary*, 24 November 1916.

89. By March 1918 Englishmen contributed one-third of the Division's strength. Public Record Office, CAB 23/5/374 and 375.

90. 'Marlborough had early set his face against so vicious a system . . . he fully recognized the magnitude of its evil . . . the practice had been found ruinous to the service, prejudicial alike to the corps that furnished and that received the draft.' Hon. J.W. Fortescue, *A History of the British Army*, vol. 1, p. 557.

Chapter 6

1. Col. R.H. Beadon, *The Royal Army Service Corps, A History of Transport and Supply in the British Army*, Cambridge 1931, vol. 2, p. xxvi.

2. Ibid., p. 93.

3. Ibid., p. 97.

4. Ibid., p. 87.

5. Maj.-Gen. A. Forbes, *The Great War: A History of the Army Ordnance Services*, London 1929, vol. 3, p. 89; Major O.C. Guinness, OBE, 'Notes on the Mutiny at Etaples Base in 1917', MS written for the authors in 1965. Major Guinness was Camp Adjutant, Etaples Base, in 1917.

6. R.H. Mottram, 'Behind the Lines: First and Second Armies', in Maj.-Gen. Sir Ernest Swinton, ed., *Twenty Years After, The Battlefields of 1914–18: Then and Now*, London, n.d., pp. 204–5; Guinness.

7. Guinness.

8. Public Record Office, WO 95/4027, Base commandant, Etaples, *War Diary*, monthly summary of events for September 1917, p. 73.

9. H. Owen and J. Bell, eds., *Wilfred Owen: Collected Letters*, London 1967, pp. 13, 421.

10. In fact, 'they had already been passed in England as fully trained'. C.E.W. Bean, ed., *Official History of Australia in the War of 1914–1918*, Sydney 1921 onwards, vol. 3, p. 177.

11. Interview with J.A. Mitchell, 17 October 1965; Guinness; Lt.-Col. T.C. Loveday, MBE, letter to the authors, 30 September 1965. Mr Mitchell served with the Cameronians; together with the remnant of his battalion, he was sent to Etaples from Arras. The Australian government's historian confirms their information about the operation of the base. Bean, vol. 3, pp. 176–8.

12. Loveday.

13. Anonymous letter to the authors, 29 September 1965.

14. J. Hays, letter to *The Observer* (London), 16 February 1964.

15. For the official ration scale, see p. 166, below.

16. Interview with J.A. Mitchell.

17. Sir Nevil Macready, *Annals of an Active Life*, London 1924, pp. 225–6.

18. 'The Bull Ring at Etaples', in Sir Ernest Swinton, ed., p. 553.

19. H. Owen and J. Bell, eds., p. 421.

20. Ibid., p. 13.

21. Ibid., p. 521.

22. 'The Bull Ring at Etaples', in Sir Ernest Swinton, ed. p. 554–5.

23. Interview with J.A. Mitchell; 'The Bull Ring at Etaples', in Sir Ernest Swinton, ed., p. 553.

24. Ibid., p. 556.

25. WO 95/4027, Base commandant, *War Diary*, 9 September 1917.

26. Ibid.

27. Ibid.

28. Anonymous letter of 29 September 1965. The policeman concerned, Private H. Reeve, stated after the event that he had no revolver, but, being threatened by the crowd, snatched one from an Australian or New Zealander. He fired two or three shots before the weapon was snatched from him in turn. Corporal W.B. Wood, 4th Battalion Gordon Highlanders, was hit in the head and died that evening; a French-woman, standing in the road on the far side of the bridge, was also wounded. Reeve was convicted of manslaughter and received a sentence of one year's hard labour. WO 95/4027, Base commandant, *War Diary*, 9 September 1917.

Military policemen in France commonly carried pistols; there would be no reason why a soldier should be carrying one, least of all on a Sunday afternoon in a base camp. A.V. Lovell Knight, *The History of the Office of the Provost Marshal and the Corps of Military Police*, Aldershot 1943, p. 74.

29. Anon. letter of 29 September 1965.

30. WO 95/4027, Base commandant, *War Diary*, 9 September 1917.

31. Interview with J.A. Mitchell.

32. Anon. letter of 29 September 1965.

33. WO 95/4027, Base commandant, *War Diary*, 9 September 1917.

34. Ibid.

35. Guinness, *Notes on the Mutiny*. Some weight is added to Major Guinness's recollections, as compared to the Base commandant's diary written at the time, by the fictionalised account of the mutiny given in Henry Williamson's novel, *Love and the Loveless*, London 1958, pp. 251–66. Charles Carrington, in *Soldier from the Wars Returning*, London 1965, pp. 244–5, an autobiography displaying the licence of a novel, remembers being told, on arriving in Etaples in mid-September 1917, that for twenty-four hours 'the town and the base were in the hands of a mob of soldiers who had thrown the commandant into the river'.

36. Guinness.

37. WO 95/4027, Base commandant, *War Diary*, 9 September 1917.

38. Lady Angela Forbes, *Memories and Base Details*, London 1922, p. 267.

39. Anthony Babington, *For the Sake of Example: Capital Courts-Martial 1914–1920*, London 1983, p. 135.

40. William Allison and John Fairley, *The Monocled Mutineer*, London 1978, p. 91. Allison and Fairley give no source which could substantiate their claim.

41. WO 95/4027, Base commandant, *War Diary*, 10 September 1917.

42. Babington, pp. 132–3.

43. Ibid. Babington, who has had privileged access to the records of capital courts martial, identifies him only as Corporal S—, a thirty-year-old married man with two young children, serving with a Northumberland regiment.

44. WO 95/4027, Base commandant, *War Diary*, 10 September 1917.

45. Interview with J.A. Mitchell. It is possible, of course, that after nearly fifty years, Mr Mitchell confused the speakers at this meeting with the corporal who had been sentenced to be shot.

46. WO 95/4027, Base commandant, *War Diary*, 10 September 1917.

47. Forbes, p. 267.

48. WO 95/4027, Base commandant, *War Diary*, 11 September 1917.

49. Ibid.

50. Ibid.; G. Goold Walker, ed., *The Honourable Artillery Company in the Great War 1914–1919*, London 1930, p. 99.

51. WO 95/4027, Base commandant, *War Diary*, 11 September 1917.

52. Ibid., 12 September 1917.

53. Ibid.

54. Ibid.

55. Ibid., 13 September 1917.

56. Ibid.

57. Ibid., 14 September 1917.

58. WO 95/1665, 1st Battalion, Royal Welch Fusiliers, *War Diary*, 14 September 1917; WO95/4027, Base Commandant, *War Diary*, 14 September 1917; WO 95/1669, 22nd Battalion, Manchester Regiment, *War Diary*, 14 September 1917.

59. WO 95/574, General Staff, Cavalry Corps, *War Diary*, 14 September 1917.

60. WO 95/4027, Base commandant, *War Diary*, 14 September 1917.

61. Ibid., 15, 17 and 18 September 1917; WO 95/1669, 22nd Battalion, Manchester Regiment, *War Diary*, 15–17 September 1917. Curiously, Charles Carrington 'saw' a battalion of the Manchesters, which had been 'plucked out of Passchendaele', 'patrolling the streets of Etaples in fighting order, on 17th September . . . most cheerfully engaged in restoring order': Carrington, p. 245. The 22nd Manchesters had not been plucked out of Passchendaele; with the rest of 7th Division, the battalion had been withdrawn into GHQ reserve at the beginning of August, and was not due to return to the front until the end of September. Nor was it to be seen patrolling the streets of Etaples, cheerfully or otherwise, on 17 September or indeed on any other day. On the basis of his observations, Carrington concludes: 'While not grudging the rioters their bit of fun, the joke had gone far enough and it was time to get on with the war.' See WO 95/1669, 22nd Battalion, Manchester Regiment, *War Diary*, September 1917, and WO 95/1633, General Staff, HQ, 7th Division, *War Diary*, August and September 1917.

62. Guinness. C.E.W. Bean in the *Official History of Australia* (vol. 3, p. 177) agrees that the delays imposed on trained men by the requirements for further training at the base were 'often exasperating'.

63. Guinness.

64. Transport and supply activities, for instance, were carried out 'under the handicap of a personnel continuously in a state of flux, and continuously lower in bodily efficiency by the transfer of the most able-bodied categories to the fighting arms.' Beadon, p. 514.

65. Though she clearly did not know him, Lady Forbes describes Corporal Wood as 'a gallant Scotsman'. He had 'quite unwarrantably' been killed. *Memories and Base Details*, p. 267.

66. G. Goold Walker, ed., pp. 99–100.

67. WO 95/4027, Base commandant, *War Diary*, 10 September 1917.

68. Interview with J.A. Mitchell. During that interview, Mr Mitchell made no mention of the corporal who had been arrested and court-martialled. Nonetheless, perhaps some of the soldiers were hoping to release this man.

69. WO 95/4027, Base commandant, *War Diary*, 10 September 1917.

70. Allison and Fairley maintain that Private Percy Toplis, a deserter from the Royal Army Medical Corps, was brought in to chair a mutineers' committee. Their assertions, made in some detail but without citation of authority or source, remain unproven.

71. Public Record Office, War Cabinet Papers, CAB 24/79, GT 6874, Haig to Lord Derby, 3 October 1917, quoted by S.R. Ward 'Intelligence Surveillance of British Ex-Servicemen, 1918–1920', *Historical Journal*, vol. 16, Cambridge 1973, p. 180.

72. Ibid.

73. 'Extreme indiscipline' and 'inordinate vanity' were the kind of terms he was accustomed to employ. *Official History of Australia*, vol. 3, pp. 56–57.

74. CAB 24/79, GT 6874, Haig to Lord Derby, letter cited.

75. Babington, pp. 132–3.

76. H. Owen and J. Bell, eds., p. 521.

77. 'The Bull Ring at Etaples', p. 556.

78. Haig to Lord Derby, letter cited.

79. Hon. J.W. Fortescue, *A History of the British Army*, London 1923, vol. 11, pp. 8–9.

80. Haig to Lord Derby, letter cited.

81. Ibid.

82. Babington.

83. WO 95/4027, Base commandant, *War Diary*, 10 September 1917.

84. Ibid., 11 September 1917.

85. As Richard Cobb points out: 'Sunday is always a likely day for any form of crude popular protest, especially of course, a Sunday in camp.' Letter of 8 July 1969.

86. R. H. Mottram, 'A Personal Record', in R.H. Mottram, John Easton & Eric Partridge, *Three Personal Records of the War*, London 1929, p. 127.

Chapter 7

1. Report by General Smuts to a committee of Prime Ministers from the Dominions, June 1918. Public Record Office, CAB 1/26/20.

2. Public Record Office, WO 1971/33, letter from Lt Col. Commanding Chinese Labour Corps to Director of Labour, GHQ, 25 December 1917.

3. Robert Graves, *Goodbye to All That*, London 1957, p. 220.

4. G.L. Campbell, *The Manchesters*, London 1916, pp. 73–4; Graves, pp. 161–2.

5. WO 95/1633, General Staff, 7th Division, *War Diary*, August–September 1917.

6. G. Goold Walker ed., *The Honourable Artillery Company in the Great War 1914–1919*, p. 99.

7. Not long before being called on for duty at Etaples, the colonel commanding the 1st Battalion, HAC, had been asked if he could find two hundred candidates worthy of commissions. He promptly guaranteed five hundred. Ibid.

8. Hon. J.W. Fortescue, *A History of the British Army*, London 1930, vol. 13, p. 573.

9. *Official History of Australia*, vol. 3, p. 754; vol. 4, p. 760.

10. Major O.C. Guinness, letter to the authors, 11 August 1965.

11. WO 158/24, No. 273, Commander in Chief, France, to Chief of the Imperial General Staff (CIGS), 29 September 1917. Four days later, Haig was writing to Lord Derby to admit the existence of a 'spirit . . . of unrest'. (CAB 24/79, GT 6874, 3 October 1917). The contradiction is more apparent than real. His letter to Lord Derby was private, and informed him of the truth; that of 29 September was designed for wide dissemination, perhaps even newspaper publication, and was a piece of pure propaganda. Cf. copy of the same letter in WO 106/407.

12. WO 95/4027, Base commandant, Etaples, *War Diary*, 19 and 25 September 1917.

13. Ibid., monthly summary of events for September 1917, p. 73.

14. J.A. Mitchell, letter of 30 September 1965.

15. WO 106/401, No 6, *The British Armies in France as gathered from Censorship*, and accompanying letter from the CIGS to the Secretary, War Cabinet, 18 December

1917. In the German army, the field censorship also reported directly to OHL on the findings of such examination. Fritz Fischer, *Griff Nach der Weltmacht, Die Kriegszielpolitik des kaiserlichen Deutschland 1914–18*, Dusseldorf 1961, p. 832.

16. WO 158/45, f. 14, memorandum of 27 January 1918.

17. Sir H. de la P. Gough, *The March Retreat*, London 1934, p. 42.

18. WO 106/308, No. 15, Field Marshal Sir Douglas Haig to the CIGS, 8 October 1917, p. 9.

19. WO 158/45, memorandum cited.

20. WO 106/416/16, Meeting of the War Cabinet, 7 February 1918.

21. 'The bulk of the labour had to be provided by the fighting troops, and this interfered with the short period which was available for proper training and rest.' Brig. Gen. J.E. Edmonds, *Military Operations: France and Belgium, 1918*, London 1937, vol. 2, p. 478.

22. WO/416/1, Haig to the War Cabinet, 9 January 1918. 500,000 men were, according to this estimate, required by April; the CIGS had at most 225,000 'in sight'. WO 158/24, memorandum of 19 November 1917.

23. WO 106/407/27, letter from the CIGS to Sir Douglas Haig, 21 September 1917. In such fashion, too, did losses in Hungarian regiments during Austrian defeats lead to allegations that the Austrian leadership was principally to blame — though Austrians were in a minority amongst the general officers concerned. E. von Glaise Horstenau, *Die Katastrophe*, Zurich 1929, p. 267.

24. WO 158/24/273, letter from Sir Douglas Haig to the CIGS, 29 September 1917.

25. The war diaries of the 16th Division and its constituent units during this period are extremely difficult to follow. Many are missing for the month of March; others were compiled years after the event. There were allegations that units of the division retreated prematurely, but this has been denied. Within a week of the German onslaught, however, the fighting qualities of the 16th Division were the subject of Cabinet inquiry, 'with a view to throwing light on the probable fighting value of conscripted Irishmen, on which expert opinion is divided'. CAB 23/5/374. See also WO 95/1956, HQ, 16th Division, *War Diary*, letter of Maj.-Gen. C.P. Hull, 5 April 1918.

26. For the collapse and dispersal of the 16th Division, see WO 95/1956, HQ, 16th Division, *War Diary*; WO 95/1957, A and QMG's Branch, 16th Division, *War Diary*; and the individual battalion diaries for the period in question.

27. Edmonds, *1916*, vol. 2, p. 549n.

28. R.H. Beadon, *The Royal Army Service Corps*, vol. 2, Cambridge 1931, p. 93.

29. Ibid.; Edmonds, *1916*, vol. 2, p. 549n.

30. Edmonds, *1918*, vol. 1, p. 99.

31. Edmonds, *1918*, vol. 2, p. 478.

32. Edmonds, *1917*, vol. 1, p. 16.

33. Ibid., p. 17; Edmonds, *1916*, vol. 2, p. 549n.

34. Edmonds, *1918*, vol. 1, p. 99.

35. Edmonds, *1917*, vol. 1, p. 17.

36. C.S. Jarvis, *Desert and Delta*, London 1938, p. 160; Suzanne Brugger, *Australians and Egypt, 1914–1919*, Melbourne 1980, pp. 92–93.

37. Letter from Lt Col. T.C. Loveday, MBE, 11 October 1965.

38. Two strikes by men of the Egyptian Labour Corps in a large camp at Marseilles, the first during the summer of 1917 and the second that September, had centred on the terms of the contract by which they were engaged. Some men believed that their contracts had expired and that they were due for passage home. One man was court-martialled and shot. (Anthony Babington, *For the Sake of Example: Capital*

156

Courts-Martial 1914–1920, London 1983, p. 175.) The air raid must have proved unsettling for the Egyptians at Boulogne: they had understood, of course, that they were not to work within the zone of hostilities itself.

39. WO 95/83, Director of Labour, GHQ, *War Diary*, September 1917, Annexure F.

40. WO 95/4018, commandant, Calais Base, *War Diary*, 10–12 September 1917.

41. WO 95/83, Director of Labour, GHQ, *War Diary*, October 1917.

42. Ibid. Lt Col. Loveday remembers his brother arriving one morning at 15th Ordnance Depot, Rouxmesnil, near Dieppe. 'He had been travelling through the night from the North with a convoy of lorries conveying armed troops to augment our garrison. He had heard that there was some trouble with native labour corps men — he thought that there had been trouble elsewhere . . .

'Although our Depot was huge it was like a village but nothing leaked out. I have an idea that the negroes had staged some form of civil disobedience campaign but it was evidently a serious problem. A few days later all the SANLC details were moved away and I saw them no more. It seems to me that it was a protest against segregation . . .' Letter of 11 October 1965.

43. WO 95/83, Director of Labour, GHQ, *War Diary*, October 1917; WO 95/4018, commandant, Calais Base, *War Diary*, 16 December 1917.

44. Ibid., 25 February and 12 March 1918. In July 1917 a strike had taken place amongst Cypriot muleteers with the 10th Division in Salonica. Fifteen were arrested. The military authorities, however, under conditions less favourable to shootings out of hand, released them from their contracts. WO 154/89, HQ, 10th Division, *War Diary*, 19 July 1917.

45. WO 1971/33, letter from Lt Col., Commanding Chinese Labour Corps, to Director of Labour, GHQ, 25 December 1917.

46. WO 95/83, Director of Labour, GHQ, *War Diary*, September 1917, Annexure G2.

47. WO 106/327, Director of Military Operations, Situation Report No. 41, 'British Military Policy 1918–1919', 25 July 1918, p. 9.

48. WO 95/4018, Base commandant, Calais, *War Diary*, 21 July 1918. Comparing these disorders with those at Etaples the previous September, Richard Cobb notes that this is 'again a Sunday riot'. Letter of 8 July 1969.

49. WO 95/4018, commandant, Calais Base, *War Diary*, and accompanying MS diary, 22 July 1918.

50. WO 95/4018, Base commandant, Calais, *War Diary*, 22 July 1918.

51. Ibid., 23 July 1918.

52. Ibid., 23, 24, 27 July 1918; WO 95/3061, 1st Battalion, East Lancs Regiment, *War Diary*, 24 July 1918.

53. WO 95/4018, Base commandant, Calais, *War Diary*, 24–27 July 1918.

54. W.J. Pogue, letter to the authors, 14 November 1965. Mr Pogue, a warrant officer, was serving with the Royal Dublin Fusiliers.

55. WO 95/4018, commandant, Calais Base, *War Diary* and accompanying MS. diary, 6 and 14 September 1918.

56. WO 95/4185, General Base Depot, Royal Army Medical Corps, *War Diary*, 24 August 1918.

Chapter 8

1. Maj.-Gen. A. Forbes, *A History of the Army Ordnance Services*, vol. 3, London 1929, pp. v, 89–90.

2. Ibid., p. 111.

3. Col. R.H. Beadon, *The Royal Army Service Corps, A History of Transport and Supply in the British Army*, Cambridge 1931, vol. 2, pp. 94–97.

4. Forbes, p. 59.

5. One of the depots at Calais, for instance, comprised 'specially enlisted tradesmen of all sorts: gunsmiths, tinsmiths, carpenters, saddlers and shoemakers, etc.' Another army workshop was notifying the following vacancies at the end of 1918: 'Black-smiths; Boilermakers; Platers; Coppersmiths; Fitters:- Loco, Pipe, Tool, Westing-house Brake; Machine Men:- Turners Ord. and Screw-cutting; Welders Oxy-acetylene and Quasi Arc; Plumbers and White Metallers; Springsmiths; Tubers (Boiler).' A. Killick, *Mutiny! The Story of the Calais Mutiny, 1918*, Brighton n.d., p. 8; WO 95/861, A & QMG, X Corps HQ, *X Corps Routine Order No. 3039*, 9 December 1918.

6. Forbes, p. 177.

7. Public Record Office, WO 95/59, Director of Ordnance Services (DOS), *War Diary*, 26 November 1918.

8. Ibid.

9. WO 95/3994, DDOS (North), *War Diary*, 1 December 1918.

10. WO 95/59, DOS, GHQ, *War Diary*, 5 December 1918.

11. Ibid., 21 December 1918.

12. Ibid.

13. Ibid., 21 and 22 December 1918.

14. Ibid., 21 December 1918.

15. Ibid., 22 December 1918.

16. Ibid., 23 and 27 December 1918.

17. Ibid., 4 January 1919.

18. WO 95/3992, DDT (North), *War Diary*, 3 and 4 January 1919.

19. Ibid. Inspecting the ASC units at Boulogne, the DDT (North) came across a Horse Transport company, many of whose members had been court-martialled in December for 'Stealing Government property'. The deterioration in morale was attributed to excessive hours and lack of supervision. Ibid., 7 January 1919.

20. Ibid., 8 January 1919.

21. Ibid., 9 & 11 January 1919.

22. Ibid., 8 January 1919; WO 95/4005, Deputy Director of Transport (South), *War Diary*, 9, 10 and 12 January 1919.

23. Forbes, p. 175.

24. WO 95/3992, DDT (North), *War Diary*, 8 January 1919; WO 95/4005, DDT (South), *War Diary*, 9, 10 and 12 January 1919.

25. WO 95/60, DOS, GHQ, *War Diary*, 5 January 1919. The Army Ordnance Corps and the Army Service Corps had been granted the 'Royal' epithet at the beginning of the year.

26. Ibid., 12 January 1919.

27. Ibid., 25 January 1919. Even so, the Director of Ordnance Services believed that the storehouse and clerical staff had shown little disaffection, but were 'intimidated into joining the movement'. Ibid., 1 February 1919.

28. WO 95/3992, DDT (North), *War Diary*, 20 January 1919.

29. WO 95/3994, DDOS (North), *War Diary*, 16 January 1919.

30. WO 95/4019, Commander, Royal Engineers, Calais Base, *War Diary*, 17 December 1918, and 15–16 January 1919.

31. WO 95/4025, AD Supplies, Dunkirk Area, *War Diary*, 24–27 January 1919.

32. Valdelievre was the BEF's Returned Store Depot. Its function was 'the saving of

every scrap of material not absolutely worthless. . . .what was serviceable was passed on to the group, what could easily be made fit for further use was mended, what needed skill to repair went to the workshop.' It was staffed by about one thousand officers and men. Forbes, p. 100; Killick, p. 8.

33. WO 95/3994, DDOS (North), *War Diary*, 28 January 1919.

34. Ibid.

35. 'A participant' in the Calais strikes, quoted in T.H. Wintringham, *Mutiny*, London 1936, pp. 316–7.

36. WO 95/3994, DDOS (North), *War Diary*, 28 January 1919.

37. Ibid., 24 November 1918.

38. 'Leader of an early mutiny in the Valdelievre workshops', quoted in Wintringham, p. 311.

39. Forbes, p. 178.

40. Ibid., p. 177.

41. A. Killick, letters to *Tribune*, London, 9 December 1966 and 1 September 1967.

42. WO 95/3994, DDOS (North), *War Diary*, 28 January 1919. Apparently, Pantling was arrested 'whilst leaving an R.E. camp, where he had been organizing'. Wintringham, pp. 316–7.

43. WO 95/3994, DDOS (North), *War Diary*, 28 January 1919.

44. Ibid.

45. Ibid. The Depot at Vendroux received and stored all ordnance supplies reaching Calais by sea. Forbes, p. 97.

46. B.G.A. Cannell, *From Monk to Busman, An Autobiography*, London 1935, p. 80.

47. WO 95/3994, DDOS (North), *War Diary*, 28 January 1919. There had already been some trouble among the QMAAC at Boulogne. On 9 January 1919 the authorities had tried to tighten up on policing. 'The QMAAC personnel employed by the APD greatly resented the introduction of female Police, considering it an asperation [sic] on their character and good name. They stated that if the patrols were put on the whole of the APD women would cease work.' This threat was sufficient to get these police withdrawn. WO 95/26, Adjutant General, GHQ, *War Diary*, January 1919, 'Summary of Events and Information', sheet 9.

48. Quoted in Wintringham, pp. 317–8. The men were unarmed: 'The thought of using guns never entered our heads . . . the majority of our men had been up the line. There were plenty of new guns in the Ordnance Depot, and millions of rounds of ammunition, but we had seen enough of that nonsense to last us a lifetime.' Cannell, pp. 80–81. Cannell put the number of men involved at between three and four thousand.

49. WO 95/26, Adjutant General, GHQ, *War Diary*, 27 and 28 January 1919.

50. WO 95/60, DOS, GHQ *War Diary*, 27 and 28 January 1919.

51. WO 95/71, Director of Transport, GHQ, *War Diary*, 31 January 1919. Eventually, two officers got the NCOs and men together. Did they have grievances? 'They stated that they had not but that the strike was purely a sympathetic one.' WO 95/3992, DDT (North), *War Diary*, 27 January 1919.

52. 'The Ordnance were picketing the railway, preventing the running of supply, leave, and demobilisation trains.' WO 95/522, General Staff, Fifth Army HQ, *War Diary*, 28 January 1919.

53. WO 95/26, AG, GHQ, *War Diary*, 27 January 1919; Wintringham, p. 319.

54. WO 95/60, DOS, GHQ, *War Diary*, 27 January 1919.

55. Quoted in Wintringham, pp. 318–9.

56. Beadon, p. 87.

57. Ibid., p. 443. Several thousand hands were required for this job, the majority of them women.

58. Forbes, p. 90; About one hundred trucks a day were despatched in January 1919 from Calais Ordnance alone; during the period of the strike, however, no trucks at all were leaving for the front. WO 95/4021, Chief Ordnance Officer, Calais Base, *War Diary*, 'Schedule of Trucks Depatched from Calais (Including Docks and Les Attaques)', January 1919.

59. Beadon, pp. 91–92.

60. Forbes, p. 179.

61. WO 95/3994, DDOS (North), *War Diary*, 27 January 1919; WO 95/522, General Staff, Fifth Army HQ, *War Diary*, 28 January 1919; WO 95/4021, Chief Ordnance Officer, Calais Base, *War Diary*, January 1919.

62. Killick, letter to *Tribune*, London, 9 December 1966; Wintringham, pp. 316–24. This rank and file control led to better rations, a soldier has maintained. 'There was *plenty of food for everybody*. This only went to prove our surmise was right. Our food was being "flogged" to the French people. In fact, I saw baskets full of bully, cheese and bacon going out of the Camps at night. After the officers and NCOs had had their share, there were some bits of fat floating on hot water for the private's dinner!' Cannell, p. 81.

63. WO 95/26, Adjutant General, GHQ, *War Diary*, 28 January 1919; Wintringham, p. 319.

64. WO 95/3992, DDT (North), *War Diary*, 28 January 1919.

65. WO 95/60, DOS, GHQ, *War Diary*, 28–29 January 1919.

66. WO 95/23, General Staff (Operations), GHQ, 'Order No. O.A.35', 28 January 1919.

67. WO 95/522, General Staff, Fifth Army, *War Diary*, 28 January 1919; WO 95/2486, HQ, 105th Infantry Brigade, *War Diary*, 28 January 1919, Appendix 1, 'Brigade Order No. 1'. The Brigade comprised the 4th Battalion, North Staffordshire Regiment, the 15th Battalion, Cheshire Regiment and the 15th Battalion, Sherwood Foresters.

68. WO 95/23, General Staff (Operations) GHQ, 'Order No. O.A. 138', 28 January 1919.

69. WO 95/2486, HQ, 105th Infantry Brigade, *War Diary*, 28 January 1919.

Chapter 9

1. R. Higham, *Armed Forces in Peacetime*, London 1962, pp. 7–9.

2. Ibid., pp. 10–11.

3. C.E. Callwell, *Field-Marshal Sir Henry Wilson, His Life and Diaries*, London 1927, vol. 2, p. 160.

4. WO 95/2301, 1st Battalion, Royal Dublin Fusiliers, *War Diary*, 10–2 January 1919.

5. Letter from the Adjutant General, No. A.G. 554/1/F2(M) of 13 November 1918, sent to all units, cited in WO 95/966, A and QMG's Staff, XIX Corps HQ, *War Diary*, Routine Order No. 1452, 17 November 1918; WO 95/59, Director of Ordnance Services, GHQ, *War Diary*, 5 December 1918.

6. Higham.

7. Interview with A. Charman, 26 January 1966. Mr Charman, a regular soldier, was serving with the Royal Horse Artillery at Le Havre Base.

8. Ibid. The military records suggest that miners were arriving at the Base ports

without having had sufficient food *en route*. A & QMG's Staff, XIX Corps, HQ, *War Diary*, Routine Order No. 1475, 23 November 1918.

9. Charman, interview cited. The date and scale of the conflagration are confirmed by the diaries of the Queen Mary's Army Auxiliary Corps, whose personnel were charged with cooking in the camps. On the morning of 10 December 1918 the Deputy Controller, Havre Area, QMAAC, visited the cookhouses which had survived the fire, and found her cooks to be 'showing an excellent example to the Troops. Special praise was given to Worker Sargent for her cool behaviour when a number of men entered her office'. The diary speaks of several camps being burned down the night before. The officer commanding, Royal Engineers, Le Havre, drew up a list of 'buildings destroyed and damaged' on the night of 9 December; the list is not appended. WO 95/85, Area Controller, Havre, QMAAC, *War Diary*, 10 December 1918; WO 95/4034, Officer Commanding, RE, Le Havre, *War Diary*, 9, 13, and 15 December 1918.

10. WO 95/4031, Base commandant, Havre, *War Diary*, 15 December *et seq*. 1918.

11. Interview with A. Charman; *Folkestone Express*, Folkestone, 21 December 1918.

12. WO 95/4185, General Base Depot, RAMC, *War Diary*, 13–15 December 1918.

13. General Routine Order No. 6239, quoted in WO 95/380, A and QMG's Branch, Third Army, *War Diary*, 17 February 1919.

14. Letter from Lt-Col. T.C. Loveday, 30 September 1965.

15. *Folkestone Express*, 11 January 1919.

16. Ibid.

17. Ibid.

18. Ibid.

19. War Office communiqué of 5 January 1919, quoted in the *Folkestone Express*, 11 January 1919.

20. *Folkestone, Hythe, Sandgate and Cheriton Herald*, Folkestone 11 January 1919.

21. *The Herald*, London 11 January 1919.

22. *Folkestone Express*, 11 January 1919; *Sussex Daily News*, Brighton 6 January 1919; Callwell, pp. 160–1.

23. *Folkestone Express*, 11 January 1919.

24. *Folkestone, Hythe, Sandgate and Cheriton Herald*, 11 January 1919.

25. *Folkestone Express*, 11 January 1919.

26. Ibid., quoting a War Office communiqué on 5 January 1919.

27. Ibid.

28. *Sussex Daily News*, 7 January 1919.

29. Ibid., 8 January 1919.

30. Ibid.

31. Ibid.

32. Ibid., 9 January 1919; Callwell, p. 162. General Robertson, in command in the Home Counties, was uncertain whether loyal units could be used against these men. 'He doubted if they would in the last resort fire on comrades who marched on London.' David Lloyd George, *The Truth About the Peace Treaties*, London 1938, vol. 1, p. 151.

33. *Sussex Daily News*, 9 January 1919; letter from Harold V. Gane, 4 October 1965. Mr Gane was serving as a boy soldier with the 3rd Battalion, Wiltshire Regiment.

34. L. Laurence, *The Shoreham Mutiny*, MS. written for the authors in 1965, pp. 1–2. Mr Laurence was invalided home from France in 1918; after hospital, convalescence, and a period of leave, he was posted to the camp at Shoreham.

35. Letter from L. Laurence, 13 October 1965.
36. Laurence, p. 2.
37. *Sussex Daily News*, 7 January 1919.
38. Ibid.
39. Ibid.
40. Ibid.
41. Laurence, p. 5; *Sussex Daily News*, 8 January 1919.
42. Laurence, p. 3.
43. Ibid., pp. 4–5.
44. *Sussex Daily News*, 8 January 1919.
45. Ibid., 9 and 10 January 1919.
46. Laurence, p. 6.
47. Ibid.
48. Letter from E.S. Wiggins, 1 October 1965.
49. Callwell.
50. WO 95/26, Adjutant General, GHQ *Summary of Events and Information, January 1919*, War Office letter of 4 January 1919.
51. For an account of how cavalry was used to quash a demonstration in London in February 1919, see E.B. Ashmore, *Air Defence*, London 1929, pp. 115–6.
52. WO 95/2486, 105th Infantry Brigade HQ, 35th Division, *War Diary*, 28 January 1919.

Chapter 10

1. WO 95/522, General Staff, Fifth Army, *War Diary*, 28 January 1919.
2. WO 95/26, Adjutant General, GHQ, *War Diary*, 28 January 1919. In the event, no one succeeded in reaching England, the army ordering the turning back, in mid-Channel, of the boats then heading for Calais.
3. Ibid. An incident during the opening stages of the German Revolution provides an interesting parallel to these events. Early in November 1918 the Berlin garrison commander halted the operation of the trains. 'The stopping of railway transportation led, on November 8, to a demonstration of furloughed soldiers who were thus detained in Berlin.' R.H. Lutz, 'The German Revolution, 1918–1919', Stanford University Publications, University Series, *History, Economics, and Political Science*, California 1926, vol. 1, p. 48.
4. WO 95/2486, HQ, 105th Infantry Brigade, *War Diary*, 28–29 January 1919.
5. WO 95/23, General Staff (Operations), GHQ, *Order No. O.A. 35/2*, 28 January 1919. Both divisions arrived next day, Wednesday, though not without confusion. Part of 35th Division, including its machine-gunners, was sent to Dunkirk by mistake. WO 95/2470, General Staff, 35th Division, *War Diary*, 29 January 1919.
6. WO 95/23, General Staff (Operations), GHQ, *Order No. O.A. 236*, 24 December 1918.
7. WO 95/41, QMG's Branch, GHQ, *Explanatory Review*, December 1918, p. 8.
8. WO 95/3011, General Staff, 59th Division, *War Diary*, 1, 29 and 31 December 1918.
9. WO 95/41, QMG's Branch, GHQ, *Explanatory Review*, December 1918, p. 8.
10. WO 95/3011, General Staff, 59th Division, *War Diary*, 6 January 1919.
11. Graves, p. 162.
12. The use of this division in such capacity was not good for its morale. Early in the

162

Second World War it had to be disbanded.

13. WO 95/966, A and QMG, XIX Corps HQ, *XIX Corps Routine Order No. 1516*, 12 December 1918.

14. Cannell, p. 81.

15. WO 95/2486, HQ, 105th Infantry Brigade, *War Diary*, 29 January 1919. The diary speaks of more than a thousand men leaving in the course of the day; the Adjutant General, however, mentions only a few hundred. WO 95/26, AG, GHQ, *War Diary*, 29 January 1919.

16. Ibid.; WO 95/2470, General Staff, 35th Division, *Order B/1*, 29 January 1919; ibid., *War Diary*, 30 January 1919, and appendix 'Calais Operations', 29 January 1919.

17. WO 95/60, Director of Ordnance Services, GHQ, *War Diary*, 29 January 1919.

18. WO 95/2486, HQ, 105th Infantry Brigade, *War Diary*, 29 January 1919.

19. WO 95/26, AG, GHQ, *War Diary*, 29 January 1919; WO 95/60, DOS, GHQ, *War Diary*, 29 January 1919; WO 95/2470, General Staff, 35th Division, *War Diary*, 29 January 1919.

20. Ibid., Order B/1, 29 January 1919. This order was communicated by a staff officer, in person: it called for verbal acknowledgement alone, and forbade the use of the telephone in connection with the operation. Ibid., Order No. G.A. 615, 30 January 1919.

21. WO 95/2470, General Staff, 35th Division, *War Diary*, 30 January 1919.

22. Ibid., January 1919, Appendix 'Summary from Advanced Divisional Head-quarters at 105th Brigade'.

23. WO 95/2486, HQ, 105th Infantry Brigade, *War Diary*, 30 January 1919. The four delegates were subsequently tried by court-martial. WO 95/26, AG, GHQ, *War Diary*, 31 January 1919. Haig, apparently, was in favour of a death sentence but Churchill was against it, fearing domestic repercussion. Martin Gilbert, *Winston S. Churchill*, London 1975, vol. 4, pp. 192–3.

24. WO 95/26, AG, GHQ, *War Diary*, 30 January 1919; WO 95/71, Director of Transport, GHQ, *War Diary*, 30 January 1919. One source gives as thirteen the number of delegates provided by each side; another source mentions the same number, and writes of the soldiers' delegation being presided over by a Scots VC. T.H. Wintringham, *Mutiny:* London 1936, p. 320; A. Killick, *Mutiny! The Story of the Calais Mutiny 1918*, Brighton, Sussex, n.d., p. 15.

25. WO 95/3994, DDOS (North), *War Diary*, 29–30 January 1919.

26. WO 95/60, DOS, GHQ, *War Diary*, 29 January 1919.

27. Ibid., 1 February 1919.

28. Wintringham, pp. 320–1. This incident is not mentioned in the official diaries. Pantling died on 13 February 1919 from influenza, whose fatal consequences, thousands of his fellow soldiers thought, were directly linked with his physical condition after periods in custody. John Pantling's death certificate, *q.v.*; Wintringham, p. 324; Cannell, p. 82.

29. WO 95/26, AG, GHQ, *War Diary*, 30 January 1919.

30. WO 95/71, Director of Transport, GHQ, *War Diary*, 30 January 1919.

31. Ibid.

32. WO 95/26, AG, GHQ, *War Diary*, 30 January 1919.

33. Ibid.

34. WO 95/60, DOS, GHQ, *War Diary*, 30 January 1919.

35. Anonymous participant, quoted in Wintringham, pp. 321–2.

36. E.S. Holland, 'Demobilization', in *Army Quarterly*, vol. 3, No. 2, London January 1922, pp. 343–4. Sir John Fortescue thought it 'noteworthy' that, at a critical

moment during the mutinies at Spithead and the Nore, 'the Government suddenly granted to the Army the solid increase of pay for which the military authorities had entreated in vain from 1784 to 1792'. Hon. J.W. Fortescue, *A History of the British Army*, vol. 4, London 1906, p. 531.

37. One small mystery remains. Was the timing of the conference designed to deprive the one strike of all aid from the organizers of the other? On this, there is no official answer to be found.

38. WO 95/4019, Commander, Royal Engineers, Calais Base, *War Diary*, 3 February 1919.

39. WO 95/3992, DDT (North), *War Diary*, 29 and 31 January 1919; WO 95/71, Director of Transport, GHQ, *War Diary*, 31 January 1919.

40. WO 95/3994, DDOS (North), *War Diary*, 1 February 1919.

41. WO 95/23, General Staff (Operations), GHQ, *Order No. O.A. 61*, 29 and 30 January 1919; *Order No. 241*, 31 January; *Order No. O.A. 241*, 2, 3, 6 and 10 February; *Order No. O.A. 35*, 8 February 1919. A month later, the greatest threat came not from those sections of the working class still serving in the army, but from their compatriots at home. Accordingly, the 30th and 59th Divisions were moved from France to England. This move supplemented the return of the cavalry regiments for garrison duty, planned by the War Office at the beginning of the year. Ibid., *Order No. O.A. 243* and *Order No. O.A. 243/1*, 22 March 1919; *Order No. O.A. 238*, 15 February 1919; *Order No. O.A. 109/1*, 17 January 1919. See also WO 95/26, AG, GHQ, *War Diary*, 'Summary of Events and Information', January 1919, and letter from the War Office of 4 January 1919 cited there.

The Motor Drivers of the Women's Legion also played a part. They had been sent to France after the Armistice, and enabled the demobilization of male drivers in the RASC to proceed. In mid-February 1919 the Quartermaster General appealed strongly to them not to ask for a release. In his mind, perhaps, was an idea that these women would prove loyal if the RASC men went on strike again. Certainly, they helped the government during the rail strike later in the year. Major D. Chapman-Huston and Major O. Rutter, *General Sir John Cowans*, GCB, GCMG, vol. 2, London 1924, pp. 135–7.

Chapter 11

1. Public Record Office, WO 95/4470, Egyptian Expeditionary Force, Kantara Area Reception Station, *War Diary*; Col. R.H. Beadon, *The Royal Army Service Corps, A History of Transport and Supply in the British Army*, Cambridge 1931, vol. 2, p. 227.

2. V.W. Garratt, *A Man in the Street*, London 1939, pp. 203–4.

3. WO 95/4377, EEF, GHQ, Deputy Adjutant General, *War Diary*, 22 November 1918; WO 95/4401, Administrative Commandant, Port Said, *War Diary*, 11–12 November 1918.

4. WO 95/4732, 19th Battalion, Rifle Brigade, *War Diary*, 13 November 1918.

5. Garratt, p. 247. The official record notes 'a certain amount of damage' and a demonstration. WO 95/4725, Palestine Lines of Communication, Adjutant and Quartermaster General's Branch, *War Diary*, Monthly Report, November 1918.

Pianos had played a part in an earlier affray. During the so-called Battle of the Wassa, in Cairo's red-light district (2 April 1915) 'Australian and New Zealand troops were sacking a brothel in the Haret el Wassa as a reprisal for the infection spread among soldiers by diseased prostitutes working in the area. They heard a rumour that other soldiers had been stabbed in a neighbouring house, and rioted, throwing the women and their bullies out into the street, and tossing their possessions, notably the pianos, after them.' Suzanne Brugger, *Australians and Egypt, 1914–1919*, Melbourne 1980, p. 145.

6. Letter from H. Williams, 18 October 1965. Mr Williams was serving in the 24th Stationary Hospital, Kantara, in the period after the Armistice.

7. Letter from Edward Pointon, July 1965. Mr Pointon served with the Royal Engineers in the Near East.

8. Williams.

9. WO 95/4378, GHQ, 3rd Echelon, Deputy Adjutant General, *War Diary*, 31 December 1918.

10. W.S. Mead, *The Mutiny of Kantara 1919, By one who took part*, MS. 1965. Mr Mead, who served as a private in the Royal Army Medical Corps, wrote, for the authors, this account of events at Kantara.

11. Lt Col. A.P. Wavell, 'The Strategy of the Campaigns of the Egyptian Expeditionary Force', in *Army Quarterly*, vol. 3, No. 2, London 1922, pp. 246, 249.

12. Beadon, pp. 245–6.

13. WO 95/4725, Palestine L. of C., A & QMG's Branch, *Monthly Report*, December 1918, p. 11; *Official History of Australia*, vol. 7, pp. 788–9, *The Times*, London, 19 May 1964. The Australian Official History maintains that this action by the Anzacs was partly intended to 'work off their old feeling against the bias of the disciplinary branch of General Headquarters'. vol. 7). The Commander-in-Chief, EEF, took up the gauntlet, thus: 'Lord Allenby had the Anzacs paraded at Gaza and addressed them. He told them he had been proud of them, once, but was ashamed of them now; he had withdrawn his recommendations for decorations and hoped to get the Anzacs out of Palestine as soon as possible. Then the incredible happened. As if rehearsed, the assembled Australian troops counted, in unison, slowly from one to 10 and ended with a roar of "out".' A.F. Nayton, letter to *The Times*, London, 29 May 1964. Mr Nayton was military governor of Beersheba in 1918.

14. WO 95/4725, Palestine L. of C., A & QMG's Branch, *Monthly Report*, December 1918, p. 11.

15. WO 95/4377, GHQ, Deputy Adjutant General, *War Diary*, 28 January 1919.

16. Ibid., 2, 14, 18, 20 and 26 February 1919.

17. WO 95/4725, A & QMG's Branch, *Monthly Report*, February 1919, p. 10.

18. WO 95/4483, XX Corps, HQ, Deputy Adjutant & Quartermaster, *War Diary*, March 1919; Lt Col. P.G. Elgood, *Egypt and the Army*, Oxford 1924, pp. 348–9.

19. WO 95/4470, Kantara Area, HQ, *War Diary*; WO 95/4725, A & QMG's Branch, *Monthly Report*, March 1919, p. 18; Williams.

20. Letter from P. McCormack, June 1965. Mr McCormack served with the Royal Field Artillery in Mesopotamia and Northern Palestine. Another informant recalls, however, that there was trouble at the Demobilization Camp after the parade. Mead.

21. In Mesopotamia, too, men awaiting demobilization were ordered up country, for duty against the local population. 'We refused saying that we had not enlisted for this purpose, & as there was always trouble there, we should have had difficulty in getting back. We stood our ground & gained the day . . . ' Letter from Herbert G. Stone, 30 September 1965. Mr Stone, a volunteer, was a sergeant in the Royal Army Service Corps.

22. WO 95/4732, 19th Battalion, Rifle Brigade, *War Diary*, April 1919.

23. Ibid., 29 April 1919.

24. Mead. Mr Mead specifically mentions participation by Australian and New Zealand troops. Viewing the situation as a whole, however, Suzanne Brugger suggests

that: 'Against the increasingly mutinous behaviour of some British units in Egypt who were thoroughly impatient of the extension of their service, the Australian troops stand out as being singularly uninvolved in agitations and as the most reliable section of the force. Their sense of frustration at the delay in their repatriation was turned not against the Army authorities but against the Egyptians.' Brugger, p. 98.

25. McCormack.

26. WO 95/4732, 19th Battalion, Rifle Brigade, *War Diary*, 29 April 1919.

27. Williams. Mr Williams has set out the names of the committee members, together with their units:

L.T. Rabley, RE Signals (Chairman); J. MacDougall Grant, RAOC (Vice-Chairman); J.M. Brown, RE Signals; F. Sumner, RAOC; J. Wintrop, RODRE; A. Henson, RODRE; D. Shearson, BHTD; T.H. Simkiss, BHTD; H.D. Webster, AHTD; T. Lamb, AHTD; H. Bloomfield, Adv. MT Sub Depot, Kantara; S.T. Pugh, Adv. MT Sub Depot, Kantara; G. Rees, RASC Kantara; F. Cutler, RASC Kantara; J.H. Reeves, RAMC; J. Vaughan, RAMC; H. Williams; H. Scholfield, 24th Stationary Hospital, Kantara; T. Brodrick, RAF; E.K. Bacon, RAF; C. Watkins, Alexandra Unit, RAOC Dump, Kantara; A.B. Hall, 114th Sanitary Sect.; F.E. Horns, RODRE, Ludd.

H. Williams, letter of 27 September 1965.

28. WO 95/4377, Deputy AG, GHQ, *War Diary*, 1 April 1919.

29. Ibid., 14 March 1919.

30. H. Williams, letter of 18 October 1965.

31. Ibid. What kind of men are elected to rank and file committees on occasions such as these? The *Official History of Australia* describes an incident in France in September 1918, when an Australian infantry battalion refused orders. 'Being left to themselves they at once re-established strict military form in the battalion, choosing from their own number commanders to carry on temporarily the absent officers' duties. It was noticeable that those selected were not the 'bad hats' or of the demagogue type, but the men most fitted to lead in action, and strict discipline was maintained.' vol. 6, p. 938.

32. WO 95/4737, 347th MT Company, L. of C., *War Diary*, 6, 10, 12 and 13 May 1919.

33. WO 95/4401, Administrative Commandant, Port Said, *War Diary*, 12 May 1919.

34. E. Pointon, letter cited. It was Sergeant Rabley, not Ratcliffe, who was chairman of the committee; but of course Mr Pointon had not been present at Kantara, and had learnt the details only when the news passed up the coast.

35. WO 95/4377, Deputy AG, GHQ, *War Diary*.

36. S. R. Ward, 'Intelligence Surveillance of British Ex-Servicemen, 1918–1920', in *Historical Journal*, Cambridge 1973, vol. 16, pp. 184–5.

37. WO 95/4377, Deputy AG, GHQ, *War Diary*, 14 May 1919.

38. Ibid., 22 May 1919.

39. WO 95/4470, 19th L. of C. Supply Company, ASC, Kantara Area, *War Diary*, 11 May 1919. The extent of the loss is not recorded, but the depots contained up to 120,000 tons of hay stuffs and 100,000 tons of grain stuffs, quite apart from food stocks for the men. Beadon, p. 227.

40. WO 95/4570, A & Q Branch, 10th (Irish) Division, *War Diary*, 12 May 1919.

41. H. Williams, letter of 18 October 1965.

42. Pointon.

43. Ibid.

44. Letter from J.E. Crouch, 18 October 1965. Mr Crouch, a lorry driver, enlisted in the Army Service Corps in 1915 and served in the Middle East throughout the war.

Chapter 12

1. Public Record Office, WO 95/445, Adjutant & Quartermaster's Branch, Fourth Army, *War Diary*, December 1918, Appendix C, 'Fourth Army Administrative Instructions for Winter 1918–1919', Section III, 'Discipline & Provost Duties'. Russian influence was particularly feared. 'All possible steps' were taken after the Armistice 'to prevent Russian Prisoners of War entering our lines', and to halt the spread of 'Russian Bolschevist [sic] Revolutionary Literature'. WO 95/42, DA & QMG (South), *War Diary*, 15 Dec. 1918; WO 95/755, V Corps HQ, A & QMG, 'Summary of Correspondence Passing through "A" Office', 18 November 1918; ibid, *War Diary*, 14 January 1919.

2. W.S. Churchill, *The World Crisis, The Aftermath*, London 1929, p. 61.

3. Fritz Fischer, *Griff nach der Weltmacht, Die Kriegszielpolitik des kaiserlichen Deutschland 1914–18*, Dusseldorf 1961, p. 832.

4. A generation later, Hitler — or rather, von Guderian — strove to reach and hold those self-same Channel bases. Had he succeeded, the British army would never have escaped. In 1919 men of the Army Ordnance and Army Service Corps held tight the noose which, in 1940, the German High Command strove unsuccessfully to grasp.

5. Rations for the British and German armies may be straightforwardly compared. By mid-1917, the German soldier was down to 500g of bread and 250g of meat per day; his allowances fell further as the war went on. Rations for the BEF in France changed little throughout the entire period of war.

'Two rations were established: one for the troops on the fighting front and another and slightly lower for those on the lines of communication . . . . The normal daily higher scale ration was as under:

Meat, fresh or frozen	1 lb
Bacon	4 oz
Bread	1 lb or 10 oz biscuit
Butter	2 oz (3 times a week)
Jam	3 oz
Tea	$5/8$ oz
Sugar	3 oz
Condensed milk	1 oz
Cheese	2 oz
Oatmeal	2 oz (3 times a week)
Potatoes	2 oz
Fresh vegetables	8 oz (or 2 oz dried vegetables)
Tobacco or cigarettes	2 oz (once a week)
Matches	1 box (3 times a fortnight)

With salt, pepper and mustard: also rum at the discretion of the GOC.'

Military Operations: France and Belgium, 1916, vol. 1, p. 105; Col. R.H. Beadon, *The Royal Army Service Corps*, vol. 2, p. 95.

6. J.F.C. Fuller, *The Army in My Time*, London 1935, p. 157.

7. Karl Liebknecht, *Ausgewählte Reden, Briefe und Aufsätze*, Berlin 1953, p. 469.

8. *Folkestone Express*, Folkestone, 11 January 1919; Peter Green, *Kenneth Grahame 1859–1932, A Study of His Life, Work and Times*, London 1959, p. 242.

9. *Folkestone, Hythe, Sandgate & Cheriton Herald*, Folkestone, 11 January 1919.

10. WO 95/445, Fourth Army, A & QMG's Branch, *War Diary, loc. cit.*

11. Sir Nevil Macready, *Annals of an Active Life*, London 1924, pp. 297, 301; Walter Kendall, *The Revolutionary Movement in Britain 1900–21*, London 1969, pp. 174–5.

12. Crown Prince Rupprecht, *Mein Kriegstagebuch*, vol. 2, pp. 303–4, diary entry for 21 December 1917.

13. *Official History of Australia*, vol. 5, p. 31.

14. *Official History of Australia*, vol. 3, pp. 53–4, 892; vol. 6, pp. 19–21.

15. *Official History of Australia*, vol. 3, pp. 53–4, 125; vol. 6, pp. 6, 21.

16. A.J.P. Taylor, *English History 1914–1945*, p. 614.

17. *Folkestone Express*, January 1919.

18. Two sergeants organized a protest in North Russia: they were sentenced to be shot. Twenty-five men of the Machine Gun Corps struck work in France against excessive working hours: they received up to five years penal servitude apiece. Edmund Ironside, *Archangel 1918–1919*, London 1953, p. 113; V.V. Marushevsky, 'God na Sever', *Beloye Delo, Letopis' Beloy Bor'by*, (Ed. A.A. Von-Lampe), Berlin 1927, vol. 2, pp. 43–44; WO 95/1334, 2nd Bn, Machine Gun Corps, *War Diary*, 10 & 11 June 1919.

19. A. Killick, *Mutiny! The Story of the Calais Mutiny 1918*, Brighton, Sussex, n.d. p. 15.

20. H. Williams, letter of 18 October 1965.

21. *Wilfred Owen: Collected Letters*, p. 521.

22. Haig to Lord Derby, 3 Oct. 1917, letter cited.

23. WO 95/4027, Base Commandant, Etaples, *War Diary*, 10 September 1917.

24. Fortescue, *A History of the British Army*, vol. 11, pp. 8–9.

25. Anonymous letter to the authors, 29 September 1965.

26. Ibid.

Index

Agitators, in working class, 34; absence
of (1914), 39; blamed for unrest, 74–
5, 107; presence of (1918), 134, 136
Alexandretta, unrest at, 123
Alexandria, during nationalist uprising,
125
Allenby, Sir E., reports unrest, 130–1;
angry with Anzacs, 164
Alsatians, in German army, 47
Anderson, J., executed, 42; army service,
146
Anonymous Scotsman, describes Etaples
mutiny, 67; refuses to take part, 139–
40
Aristocracy *see* Landed Classes
Armenians, in Russian army, 47
Armistice, army's new duties under, 101,
124, 126, 139; affects soldiers'
minds, 101; as focus of unrest, 122–3
Army Council, discusses coloured
troops, 49; discusses Irish troops, 61;
discusses pay, 91
Arson, at Le Havre, 102–3, 160; in EEF,
123, 131, 139, 165
Asquith, H.H., administration of, 24–5;
pre-occupied with Ireland, 52; his
relations with Redmond, 52, 55;
visits Dublin, 55, 149
Asser, Lt-Gen., visits Etaples, 68, 71
Attestation, 36
Australian Defence Act, 38
Australian forces, quality of, 31, 48;
formation of, 48; composition of, 48;
officer selection in, 33, 137; lack
social distinctions, 137; exempt from
death penalty, 38–9; appalled by
executions, 43, 137; contemptuous
of British discipline, 137; their
indiscipline in BEF, 38, 80, 146 153–
4; indiscipline in EEF, 124, 127, 163–
5; their behaviour at Etaples, 67, 74,
152; their links with Scots, 80;

officers' messing in, 137
Australian Government, aids UK, 48;
resists conscription, 48, 74; resists
Haig, 38; relations with UK, 78
Austro-Hungarian Empire, strain of war
on, 46, 77; composition of army of,
47; occupation duties of, 60;
leadership blamed, 155

Babington, Judge A., on Labour MPs, 39
Bachelor's Walk, affray at, 52; recalled
by Connolly, 57; recalled by soldiers,
88
Bacon, E.K., at Kantara, 165
Battalion system, 22–4, 29
Bean, C.E.W., on inexperience of
soldiers, 32; on independent outlook
of Australians, 38; on English
politics, 39; on Scottish-Australian
friendship, 80; criticizes Etaples
administration, 64, 153
Bedfordshire Regiment, unrest in, 107
Beirut, unrest at, 122–3, 130
Bellairs, Sir W., on open competition, 15
Bennett, John, execution of, 41;
cowardice of, 146
Black, P., execution of, 43
Bloomfield, H., at Kantara, 165
Boer War, 23–4; lessons of, 24, 32; Irish
regiments in, 51; Fenians during, 51
Bolsheviks, influence on BEF, 48, 81, 99,
117–8, 166; and Winter Palace, 80
Bottomley, H., 136
Boulogne Base, role of, 98, 101; strikes
at, 85–6, 155–6; threat of strike at,
158; incident at, 132; lecture given
at, 121; policing precautions at, 121
Brighton, unrest in, 108, 138
British Expeditionary Force, mooted,
24; mobilized, 25; leaves England,
26; organization of (1917), 63;
threatened by Calais mutiny, 98,

112, 120, 135, 138, 158–9; reduced in size, 121 *see also* Strength
Brodrick, T., at Kantara, 165
Brothels, 85, 163–4
Brown, J.M., at Kantara, 165
Bull Ring *see* Etaples Base
Byng, Sir J., in Calais, 99, 114–7

Cairo, unrest in, 123, 128, 163–4; during nationalist uprising, 125
Calais Base, role of, 63–4, 89, 95–6, 98, 112–3; unrest amongst front-line soldiers at, 87–8, 113–6; amongst labour companies at, 86; amongst QMAAC personnel, 96, 117–20; amongst ordnance men, 90, 93–7, 117–21, 125; amongst army service men, 91, 97, 117–21, 125; effect of strikes at, 98, 138, 166
Cameronians (Scottish Rifles), 117, 151
Cadets *see* Officer Cadets
Canadian forces, composition of, 48, 147–8; quality of, 31, 48; enthusiasm amongst, 45; discontent amongst, 45; 'defeatism' in, 48; their bad characters removed, 49
Canadian Government, aids UK, 48; refuses conscription, 48; debates Canadian Indians, 148; refuses coloured volunteers, 148
Canche, River, incidents at, 69–70, 75
Cape Coloured Labour Battalion, 84
Card, E., executed, 43
Cardwell, E., reforms army, 13–14
Carey, J., executed, 42
Carrington, C., imperfect recollections of, 76, 152–3
Carson, Sir E., Ulster's leader, 52; his recruiting role, 61
Casement, Sir R., on Irish soldiers, 58; hung in effigy, 59
Casualties *see* Losses
Catering *see* Rations
Cavalry, its role at Etaples, 70–2, 76, 78–9; its use against unrest in UK, 111–2, 143, 161, 163
Cavalry Corps, 70
Censorship, of press, 57–8, 81; of mail, 58, 81; *see also* Military Censor
Charman, A., witnesses riots, 102; war service of, 159
Cheshire Regiment, 159

China, contribution of, 85
Chinese Labour Companies, conditions for, 85; shootings in, 78
Churchill, W.S., informed of unrest, 130–1, 134; opposes death penalty, 162; his words quoted, 130
Cinemas, 67, 118–9
Cities, as source of recruits, 18–9, 28, 34–5, 55, 142
'Citizen-Soldiers', 121, 130
Class *see* Landed Classes, Middle Classes, Working Class
Clydeside, unrest on, 35, 119, 138–9
Coalminers, recruiting of, 19, 35, 145; military qualities of, 28; independent outlook of, 44–5; and Military Service Act, 37; refused commissions, 145; in 50th Division, 28; in 10th Division, 54; demobilization of, 101–3, 114; riots amongst, 102–3; 160; in EEF, 123
Cobb, Prof. R., on significance of Sundays, 154, 156
Coloured labourers, in BEF, 84–6, 156
Committees of soldiers, at Etaples, 69, 73, 153; at Calais, 98–9, 113, 115, 117–8; at Kantara, 126–31, 139, 165; at Shoreham, 108; type of men joining, 165
Competition, for commissions, 13–6
Connaught Rangers, support Irish Nationalist Party, 51–2; praised, 55; losses amongst, 149
Connolly, J., opposes war, 57
Conscientious objectors, 84, 136
Conscription, introduced, 36; extended, 36–7; limited effect of, 37; as consequence of war with Germany, 46; blamed for Etaples mutiny, 74–5; at end of war, 115, 121; used to control working class, 139; in Australia, 48; in Austria-Hungary, 47, 62; in Canada, 48; in France, 23; in Germany, 23, 47, 60; in Ireland, 61–2, 155; in Russia, 47
Continental Daily Mail, 58, 82
Contracts, for coloured labourers, 84–5, 155–6; for Cypriots, 156; in demobilization scheme, 104–6
Convalescence camps, 65
Councils of Workmen's and Soldiers' Delegates, 136

Councils, Soldiers', at Calais, 98, 118–9; in Folkestone, 105; *see also* Committees

County Associations, Territorial, 26–7

Courts martial, role of, 38, 136, 146; sentences of (1916), 41–3, 146; at Etaples, 69, 139, 152; in Labour Corps, 155; at Calais, 118, 162; in North Russia, 167; in Sicily, 132

Cowans, Sir J., and Women's Legion, 163

Cowardice, on Somme, 40–1; deterred, 43, 146

Crimins, H., executed, 41–2

Croats, in Austro-Hungarian army, 47

Crouch, J.E., recalls disorders, 132–3; war service 166

Crozier, F.P., on Easter Rising, 58

Cutler, F., at Kantara, 165

Czechs, in Austro-Hungarian army, 47; disloyalty of, 47; oppose Bolsheviks, 47; comparison with Irish, 60, 62

Dallas, Gen., 105–6

Damascus, discontent in, 128

Danes, in German army, 47

Dardanelles campaign, 50, 58, 123, 149

de Montmorency, H., 54

Death penalty, role of, 38, 40–3, 136–8; imposition of (1914–19), 40; examples of, 41–43, 146; widely publicized, 43; limited utility of, 75; Haig insists on, 38, 146, 162; Churchill opposes, 162; deters cowards, 146; at Etaples, 69, 74–5, 139–40; at Marseilles, 155; in North Russia, 167; in Australian units, 38–9; in New Zealand units, 146–7; in German army, 38, 137

'Defeatism', in BEF, 48–9, 86

Delegates *see* Deputations

Demobilization, as issue in unrest, 92–3, 95, 104–13, 116, 118, 120–1, 123–9, 131, 138, 164

Demobilization Centres, in England, 100, 111, 133

Demobilization Scheme, drawn up, 100; details of, 100, 101, 104–5; operation of, in France, 114–5, 117; in Egypt, 123; reform of, 111, 119–21, 125, 129, 131

Demobilization Staging Camps, in France, 114–5; at Kantara, 123, 125–9

'Demobilizers', role of, 100, 123

Depper, C., executed, 42

Deputations, soldiers', at Le Havre, 92: at Calais, 93–4, 113, 116–20. 162; at Folkestone, 105–6; at Shoreham, 109; at Kantara, 126–8

Derby, Lord, 36, 154

Desertion, in BEF, 40–3, 75; in Austro-Hungarian army, 47

Detention camps *see* Prisons

Dieppe, native labour at, 85, 156; policing precuations at, 121

Director of Labour, BEF, duties of, 84; shootings policy of, 78; denies shootings, 78

Director of Ordnance Services, BEF, role of, 89; visits Calais, 116–7; discusses reforms, 90–1, 93; denounces strikers, 99, 157

Director of Transport, BEF, role of, 89; visits disaffected units, 91–2, 97, 116, 118–20; discusses reforms, 91–2, 118–20

Discipline, nature of, 27; role of gentlemen in, 14; tested by losses, 30, 40; instilled via duties, 20; via suppression, 31; via humiliations, 37–8; via persuasion, 72; via fear, 72; via shootings, 111; is brutalizing, 139; impossible strains on, 76; deterioration in, 66, 74–6, 79, 103, 123–4, 135, 138; curtails men's rights, 38; tightened up, 134; in Australian units, 38, 74, 80, 146, 165; in Scottish units, 80; in Welsh units, 44–5; Prince Rupprecht on, 38

Division, Anzac Mounted, indiscipline of, 124

Division, Guards, quality of, 31

Division, 7th, at Etaples, 71, 153; 'top notch', 79

Division, 10th, formed, 54; composition, 54; during Easter Rising, 58–9; in Egypt, 131; in Salonica, 58–9, 156

Division, 16th, formation of, 54; rural emphasis of, 55; officers of, 55–6, 149; Irish features suppressed, 55; quality of, 31, 155; during Easter Rising, 59, 150; at Etaples, 81;

during 3rd Ypres, 83; altered composition of, 61–2, 84, 151; decline of, 61–2, 84, 155

Division, 18th, quality of, 31

Division, 29th, at Messines Ridge, 59

Division, 30th, polices demobilization scheme, 114–5, 121; duties in England, 163

Division, 31st, polices demobilization scheme, 114–5; duties in Calais, 114, 121, 161; alleged barbarity of, 115

Division, 33rd, polices demobilization scheme, 114–5, 121

Division, 35th, failure of, 31; polices demobilization scheme, 114–5; duties at Calais, 99, 114–7, 121, 159, 161; alleged barbarity of, 115

Division, 36th, embodies Ulster Volunteers, 54; ignres Easter Rising, 58; fate of, 61–22

Division, 50th, composition of, 28

Division, 51st, quality of, 31; indiscipline in, 88

Division, 59th, serves in Dublin, 58, 115; polices demobilization scheme, 114–5, 121; duties in England, 163; reputation of, 115, 162

Divisional system, established, 24; extended, 27, 29; creates loyalties, 40; at Etaples, 64; in French army, 22–3; in German army, 22–3

Dock strike, in Liverpool, 37; in Dunkirk, 93

Dominions *see* Australia, Canada, New Zealand, South Africa

Donoughmore, Lord, 23

Doran, C., moves to England, 60; war services of, 150

Dover, incidents at, 106, 132

Drill, importance of, 19–20; resentment over, 103, 107

Duffy, G., refused commission, 56

Duke of Cambridge's Own, 23

Dunkirk Base, unrest at, 93, 97, 120

East Africa, campaign in, 49; contribution spurned, 49

East Lancashire Regiment, 87–8

Easter Rising, Royal Commission on, 56–7; effect on army, 58–9, 150; suppression of, 58, 149–50

Edmonds, Sir J., on New Army divisions, 32; on coloured labour, 85

Education, of officers, 14, 16

Edwards, W., describes Welsh attitudes, 44; recalls unrest, 44; war service of, 147

Egypt, nationalism in, 46–7, 49–50, 125–6; contribution to war, 49, 84, 148

Egypt, Palestine, and Syria, campaign in, 49, 50, 122

Egyptian army, help spurned, 49–50, 124

Egyptian Expeditionary Force, strength of, 122; composition of, 124; unrest in, 122–33

Egyptian Labour Companies, BEF, strikes among, 85–6, 155–6

Egyptian Labour Corps, EEF, 50

Egyptian Transport Corps, EEF, 50

Empire, British, army's duties in, 22, 27; impact of war on, 46; composition of, 47; expansion of, 124

Estonians, in Russian army, 47

Etaples Base, role of, 30, 64, 95, 144; training at, 64–6; Bull Ring, 64–6, 81; disturbances at (1917), 66–81, 95, 139–40, 152–3; disturbances at (1918), 88, 103; reform of, 76, 81; precautions at, 121

Executions *see Death Penalty*

Expansion, army, during Boer War, 23–4; inquiry into, 24

Expeditionary Force *see* British Expeditionary Force, Egyptian Expeditionary Force

Expletives, used by NCOs, 66; addressed to NCOs, 44, 98; addressed to officers, 69, 109, 127, 164; addressed to fellow-soldiers, 119

Field Punishment *see* Punishment

Fifth Army, retreat of, 32; at Calais, 99

Fiji, contribution of, 84

Finns, not conscripted by Tsar, 47

Firing Squad *see* Death Penalty, Shootings

Folkestone, coalminers arrive at, 103; vandalism in, 104; demonstrations at, 104–6, 136–7; Lansbury visits, 138

Forbes, Lady A., witnesses Etaples mutiny, 68–9, 153

Fortescue, Sir J., on antipathy to army, 10; on landed classes, 9–10, 15, 142; on working class life, 34; on agitators, 34, 39; on Free Trade, 142; on Volunteer Movement, 143; on Yeomanry, 143; on pay and discontent, 163

Fourth Army, disciplinary instructions for, 134

France, army of, 22–3, 77, 82; socialism in, 46

Free Trade, mischief of, 142

French, Sir J., commands BEF , 26; his worries, 27, 32; asks for reinforcements, 29; describes Territorials, 28, 30; receives help, 50

Games see *Sports*

Gane, H., recalls demonstrations, 107; war service of, 160

General Election (1906), 51–2; (1918), 101

General Headquarters, BEF, deals with bad characters, 49; organizes training, 64; deals with Etaples mutiny, 70–1, 76, 79–81; modifies policy, 76–7, 81; permits shootings, 78, 85–6; prepares for German offensive, 83; reflects on hours and pay, 90–2; sends miners home, 101; operates demobilization scheme, 114–5; handles Calais strikes, 99, 113–4, 116–8, 120; takes precautions, 121; *see also* Director of Labour, Director of Ordnance Services, Director of Transport, French, Haig, Macready, Quartermaster General, Wroughton

General Headquarters, EEF, deals with discontent, 122–33; *see also* Allenby

Gentlemen, role of, 14, 16, 23; temporary gentlemen, 33

Gentry *see* Landed Classes

George, D. Lloyd, election campaign (1918), 101–2; messages to troops, 110–11; writes to Redmond, 150

George V, expresses thanks, 59

Georgians, in Russian army, 47

German army, organization of, 22–3; contains non-German soldiers, 47; contains socialists, 60; does not rely on death penalty, 38, 137; taunts

Irishmen, 59, 150; is free of discontent, 77, 135; succumbs to discontent, 135–6, 161; is not well-fed, 135, 166

German Government, its hopes for Ireland, 52; its policy on socialists, 60

German High Command, pins hopes on revolution, 50–1; monitors morale, 154–5; aims for Calais (1940), 166

German Revolution, 135–6, 161

Giles, P., executed, 41

Gladstone, W.E., ministry (1868), 13–4

Gloucestershire Regiment, 107

Gough, Sir H., 82

Grant, J., at Kantara, 165

Graves, R., his overconfidence, 76, 80; assesses different units, 79

Guard duties, importance of, 19–20; men refuse, 127; organized by soldiers, 126, 128

Guards units, unreliable, 111

Guinness, O., witnesses disturbances, 68; his views on Etaples mutiny, 72; his war service, 151

Gwynn, S., stands for parliament, 51; serves in ranks, 56; describes estrangement of soldiers, 60–61

Haddock, A., executed, 42–3

Haifa, unrest at, 130

Haig, Sir D., commands BEF, 32–33; favours death penalty; dares not shoot Australians, 78; criticises Australians, 48, 74, 146–7, 153–4; deals with Etaples mutiny, 73–6, 81, 139, 154; stresses need for rest, 82; refutes MPs' criticism, 83; visits Irish units, 150; denies discontent exists, 81, 86, 154

Haldane, R., reforms army, 24–5; plans expeditionary force, 24

Hall, A., at Kantara, 165

Hamilton, Sir I., on Irish Volunteers, 149

Hampshire Regiment, its losses on Somme, 146

Health, of other ranks, 18–19, 31; link with Free Trade, 142; link with unrest, 44–5; *see also* Venereal Disease

Henson, A., at Kantara, 165

Herald, 95, 131, 137

Higgins, J., executed, 41

Home Rule, as political issue, 52–53, 61, 148

Honourable Artillery Company, composition of, 76, 80, 154; does duty at Etaples, 70–73, 79–80

Horns, F., at Kantara, 165

Horse Transport *see* Royal Army Service Corps

Hours of work, as factor in unrest, 89–94, 96, 112, 118–20, 157

Hughes, F., executed, 41, 146

Hussars, 10th, officer's income in, 16

Hussars, 15th, at Etaples, 70–71

Hussars, 19th, at Etaples, 71

India, at war's outbreak, 46; her contribution, 50, 84–85, 122, 124; her losses, 50; her soldiers slighted, 50; her soldiers loyal, 127; *see also* Muslims

Indian nationalism, 46–7, 50

Inexperience, of officers, 31–2; of new soldiers, 29–32

Infantry Base Depots, at Etaples, 64, 65, 72, 81, 144; at Calais, 87–88

Intimidation, 116, 118, 157

Ireland, welcomes war, 47; supplies recruits, 53, 56, 61; withdraws moral support, 61

Irish Citizen Army, 57

Irish Guards, formed, 51; during Easter Rising, 59, 150

Irish nationalism, in nineteenth century, 51; (1906), 51–2; during war, 56–62, 149; undermines 16th Division, 83–84

Irish Nationalist Party, before war, 51–52; supports war, 52, 61; criticizes Haig, 83

Irish Republican Brotherhood, 57

Irish soldiers, support Nationalist Party, 51–2; deeds of, 58, 149; disloyalty of, 57–8; not fully trusted, 53, 54, 60, 155; isolated from public, 61; distrust Scots, 80–81, 88; at Etaples, 80–81; lack recognition, 149; at 3rd Ypres, 83–4

Irish Volunteers, formed, 52; strength of, 52, 148; split in, 52, 148; spurned, 53, 55; praised, 58; not welcomed into army, 55, 149

Ismailia, unrest at, 124

Jews, in Russian army, 47

Kantara Base, role of, 122; unrest at, 122–3, 125–30, 164–5

Kettle, T., refused commission, 56

King's Liverpool Regiment, 28

King's Own Scottish Borderers, fire on crowd, 52; applauded, 52

'King's Regulations', 38, 129, 148

Kitchener, Lord, appeals to nation, 27; offers slight to Welsh, 45; dislikes Irish, 53, 55; spurns Irish Volunteers, 53; safeguards women, 147

Kitchener division *see* New Armies

Labour, Director of *see* Director of Labour

Labour Corps, BEF, formation of, 84; duties of, 84–5; unrest in, 78, 85–6, 93

Labour leaders, accept war, 37, 39, 46, 136; support Derby scheme, 36; neglect army, 136–8

Lamb, T., at Kantara, 165

Landed Classes, military obligations of, 9, 13–14, 23; their role in Militia, 141; in Yeomanry, 143; supply officers, 14–15, 22, 28, 141; monopolize leading ranks, 17; subdivide into aristocracy and gentry, 142; titled and untitled, 142

Lansbury, G., 138

Laurence, L., describes Shoreham mutiny, 108–11; his war service, 160–1

Le Cateau, battle of, 26

Le Havre Base, role of, 63–4, 89; unrest at, 90, 92, 102–3; precautions at, 121

Leave, during Easter Rising, 58, 150; as factor in unrest, 91, 104–5, 111–13, 116, 123, 125, 131

Leave men, on strike in England, 104–7, 111–12; on strike in France, 113–17, 161–2; in German army, 161

Leinster Regiment, moves to England, 60

Letts, in Russian army, 47

Liebknecht, K., 135–7

Lines of Communication, BEF, organisation of, 63, 89, 98

Lines of Communication, EEF, organisation of, 49–50, 122, 130–1

Lloyd, Gen., 126

Lorrainers, in German army, 47

Losses, scale of, 26, 29, 30, 40, 50; effect on efficiency, 29, 30, 32, 33; effect on LOC , 72; effect on Irish divisions, 61, 83–4; controversy over, 57, 149; link with morale, 77

Loveday, T., on coloured labour, 85, 156; on vandalism, 103–4; on training methods, 65; his war service, 85

Luxemburg, R., 137

McCormack, P., on strike in Sudan, 127; his war service, 164

MacDonald, J.R., 136

Macready, Sir N., on Irish problem, 60–1, 150; on convalescence camps, 65; on Australians, 147

Machine Gun Corps, unrest in, 167

Machine guns, use of, to curtail unrest, 71, 99, 132

Mahon, Sir B., 54

Maidstone, demonstration in, 107

Manchester Regiment, territorial units of, 28; W. Owen joins, 64; its duties at Etaples, 71–2, 76, 79, 153; not plucked out of Passchendaele, 153

Maoris, not wanted by Gen. Wingate, 148

Markiewicz, countess, 60

Marlborough, duke of, 20, 90, 151

Marseilles, incidents at, 132, 155

Mathew, Sir C. *see* Director of Ordnance Services

Maxwell, Sir J., in Egypt, 49–50; in Ireland, 60–1

Mead, W., describes strike, 127; his war service, 164

Meetings, soldiers', in BEF, 69, 73, 75, 96, 102, 104–5; in England, 106–10, in EEF , 129–30; illegality of, 138, 148; headquarters warned against, 134

Mesopotamia, campaign in, 50, 59, 164; unrest in, 164

Messing, officers', 65, 102, 137

Middle Classes, excluded from officer corps, 13, 16; admitted to officer corps, 33

Military Censor, assesses morale, 81–2, 154–5

Military Police, at Etaples, 66–8, 70–73,

78, 152; at Calais, 87–8; at Kantara, 128, 130; weaponry of, 152; relations with Anzacs, 38; are reminded of duties, 134; *see also* Women's Police

Military Prisons *see* Prisons

Military Service Act, 36–7

Militia, supplies officers, 13–15; abolished, 24; role of, 141

Miners *see* Coalminers

Mitchell, J., witnesses Etaples mutiny, 69; criticises conditions, 65; war service of, 151

Mons, battle of, 26

Moore, Col., 148

Morale, an elusive notion, 77; in (1917), 77, 81–2; of Labour Corps, 85; of Irish units, 84–5

Motor Transport *see* Royal Army Service Corps

Muleteers, strike among, 156

Mottram, R.H., on Etaples mutiny, 76

Munition workers, 37, 79, 90

Murphy, A., executed, 41

Murphy, J., recalls strike, 60; war record of, 150

Murphy, W., aids recruiting, 149

Muslims, in Russian army, 47; in Indian army, 50

Mutiny, a complex notion, 10–11

National Anthem *see* Singing

New Armies, formation of, 27, 29; quality of, 32; tested in battle, 40, 146; Irish component of, 55; regulars look down on, 144

New Zealand Government, aids UK, 48; permits death penalty, 147

New Zealand forces, quality of, 31, 48; indiscipline of, in BEF, 66–67, 74 146, 152; indiscipline of, in EEF, 124, 127, 163–5; their relations with Scots, 78; *see also* Maoris

Newspapers, 86, 118, 120, 154; see also *Continental Daily Mail, Herald*

Nore, the, mutiny at, 80, 163

North Staffordshire Regiment, 114, 159

Northumberland Fusiliers, 69

Officer Cadets, 80; *see also* Honourable Artillery Company

Officers, social origins of, 9, 13–15, 29,

33, 145, 149; relations with other ranks, 20–1, 72, 76, 80, 137; religious qualifications of, 55–6, 149; *see also* Regimental officers, Australian forces, Messing

Open competition *see* Competition

Ordnance Services, Director of *see* Director of Ordnance Sevices

Other ranks, social origins of, 9, 17–18, 33; their trust in officers, 32–3, 40; *see also* Territorial army

Owen, W., background of, 33; visits Etaples, 64–5, 72; describes faces, 139; joins Manchesters, 144

Palestine, conquest of, 122

Pantling, J., joins delegation, 94; arrested and released, 95–8; court-martialled, 118; death of, 162

Paris Plage, 69–70

Parsons, Sir L., 54–5

Pay, officers', 16; other ranks', 89–90, 109, 111, 118–21, 124–5, 163

Pearless, Gen., 126

Pearse, Padraic, 58

Petrol, supply of, 98, 159

Picquets, official army, stand firm, 71–2, 80, 116; do not stand firm, 67–70, 75, 87–8, 116

Picquets, mutineers', 97–8, 105, 113, 158

'Pivotals', 100, 102, 123

Pogue, W., in Ireland, 60; at Calais, 88; war service of, 60, 156

Pointon, E., in Haifa, 130, 165; in Sicily, 132; war service of, 164

Poles, in German and Russian armies, 47

Police *see* Military Police, Women's Police

Port Said, 124, 130

Portuguese, in BEF, 62 84

Prisoners of war, Irish, 58; German, 84; Turkish, 126; Russian, 166

Prisons, military, and detention camps, at Etaples, 69, 72–3; at Blargies, 146; at Calais, 162

Private Income, officers' need for, 16, 33

Promotion, officers', 13–14, 17

Propaganda, Turkish, 49; German, 59, 150; British, 81, 86, 154

Provost Marshal *see* Military Police

Public Schools, 29, 33, 76, 145

Pugh, S., at Kantara, 165

Punishment, field, 44, 66–9, 87–8

Purchase system, 9, 13–14, 141

Purfleet, strike at, 111

Quartermaster General, BEF, examines hours and pay, 90–1, on vandalism, 103

Queen Mary's Army Auxiliary Corps, discontent in, 96–8, 117–8, 158; at Le Havre, 160

Queen's Royal Regiment, 107

Rabley, L., at Kantara, 129–30, 165

Racism, 49–50, 85, 148, 156

Railways, role of, in war, 50, 63, 84, 122, 125; in demobilization scheme, 115; importance of, at Etaples, 64, 66–71, 73; halted by soldiers, 97–8, 113, 158; unrest on, 124; incidents on, 132–3; vandalism on, 103, 105

Ramleh, 124, 130

Ration scale, in BEF, 166; in German army, 166; discontent over, in BEF, 65, 90, 93, 102, 107, 159–60; discontent over, in EEF, 123, 129, 132; *see also* Messing

Rations, supply of, in BEF, 63, 89, 98, 160; supply of, in EEF, 122, 165

Rawlinson, Sir H., 147

Recruiting Methods, 54–5, 149; *see also* Contracts

Recruitment, officer, *see* Purchase, Competition, Universities, Public Schools, Militia, Australian forces

Recruitment, other ranks, during Boer War, 23; from cities, 9, 10, 18–19, 33–4; from Ireland, 53, 56, 61, 149; rural emphasis in, 9, 10, 17; of young men, 18, 31, 115, 121, 142, 146; economic factors governing, 18– 19, 57, 142

Redmond, J., supports England, 52, 148; rebuffed by army, 55–6; helps recruiting, 55–6, 61, 148, 150

Rees, G., at Kantara, 165

Reeve, H., fires at crowd, 67; court-martial of, 152

Reeves, J., at Kantara, 165

Reform, army, (1871), 13; (1881), 22; (1906–09), 24, 25, 27; impelled by unrest, 76, 81, 135; Labour movement's attitude to, 136; *see also* Demobilization scheme, Hours of work

Regimental officers, background of, 9; importance of, 32–3, 72; Protestants preferred, 56

Regimental system, 9–10, 22–4, 28, 39, 64, 72

Reservists, supply of, 27, 30; in Ireland, 19, 53, 148

Rickman, A., executed, 42

Rifle Brigade, 123, 126–7

Roberts, Lord, 149

Robertson, Sir W., 107, 160

Rouen Base, 63, 98

Royal Army Medical Corps, discontent in, 103, 128–30, 165

Royal Army Ordnance Corps, role of, 85, 89, 98; composition of, 89, 95, 157; unrest in, BEF, 89–90, 92–8, 112–13, 115–21, 125, 128, 131, 158–9, 166; unrest in, EEF, 125, 128–9, 131, 165

Royal Army Service Corps, role of, 89, 92, 98; composition of, 89, 95, 124, 153; discontent of, in BEF, 91–3, 97–9, 112, 115–18, 120, 157, 166; discontent of, in EEF, 124–5, 128–31; 165; discontent of, in England, 106–7; discontent of, in Mesopotamia, 164

Royal Artillery, officer entry to, 140–1; unrest in, 102–3, 110, 159–60

Royal Dublin Fusiliers, deeds of, 58; composition of, 61; losses of, 149; during Easter Rising, 150; incidents in, 57, 60

Royal Engineers, officer entry to, 140–1; unrest in, in BEF, 93, 97–9, 120, 158; unrest in, in EEF, 124, 128–30, 165

Royal Irish Fusiliers, 84

Royal Irish Rifles, 58

Royal Irish Regiment, 55, 62

Royal Munster Fusiliers, 55, 59, 149

Royal Welch Fusiliers, at Etaples, 71–2, 76; R. Graves' confidence in, 79–80

Rumanians, in Austro-Hungarian army, 47

Rupprecht, crown prince, on discipline, 38, 43, 137

Rural areas, recruits from, 9–10, 18, 55, 142; army's link with, 22;

Yeomanry's link with, 28, 143; *see also* Landed Classes

Russia, welcomes war, 46; as theatre for British operations, 128, 167

Russian army, contains non-Russians, 47; collapses, 77, 81–2, 135

Russians, serve in BEF, 48–9; influence of, feared, 166

S., Corporal, arrest and trial of, 69, 74, 139, 153; army service of, 74, 152

Salisbury Plain, 45

Sandhurst, 14–16

Sargent, Worker, cool behaviour of, 160

Scotland, as source of recruits, 35–6; *see also* Scottish soldiers

Sassoon, S., 33

Saysell, C., recalls unrest, 44–5

Scholfield, H., at Kantara

Scottish soldiers, at Etaples, 65, 67, 80, 139–40; link with Anzacs, 78, 80; in Calais, 87–8, 117

Second Army, BEF, morale of, 81–2

Shearson, D., at Kantara, 165

Sherwood Foresters, 159

Shirkers, 36

Shootings out of hand, policy of, 78; practised, 85–6; sometimes inexpedient, 78, 111, 156, 160

Shoreham, mutiny at 107–11

Sicily, 132

Sikhs, 50

Simkiss, T., at Kantara, 165

Singing, 104, 108, 129, 130, 136

Sinn Fein, 51, 56–7, 60

Slovaks, in Austro-Hungarian army, 47

Smuts, J.C., reports on East Africa, 49; on morale, 77, 82–3

Snowden, P., 39, 136

Socialism, in UK, 46, 135–8; in army, 95, 135; in Germany, 46, 60, 77, 135–7; in France, 46

Soldiers' committees *see* Committees

Soldiers' Councils *see* Councils

Soldiers' meetings *see* Meetings

Soldiers', Sailors', and Airmen's Union, 131

Somme, battle of, 29, 32, 40, 146

Songs *see* Singing

South Africa, at outbreak of war, 46, 49; contribution of, 49, 84; *see also* Boer War

South African Native Labour
  Contingent, 85–6, 156
South-West Africa, 49
Sports and games, 16, 20, 28, 55, 65, 72
Special Reserve, role of, 24–5; (1914),
  26, 54, 57
Spithead, mutiny at, 80, 163
Stone, H., refuses duty, 164; war service
  of, 164
Strength, of a battalion, 22; of a division,
  24; of British army (1914), 36, 53;
  (1916), 36; of New Armies, 29; of
  Territorials, 26; of BEF (1914), 24–7;
  (1917), 63; (1918), 83, 155; of EEF,
  122
Suez Canal, 49–50, 122
Sumner, F., at Kantara
Sunday, as day of unrest, 73, 75, 96, 154,
  156
Supplies, scale and organisation of, for
  BEF, 63, 98; for EEF, 122, 131, 165
Swearing *see* Expletives
Syria, 122–3

Territorial army, established, 24–5, 27;
  social background of, 28, 144;
  loyalties of, 28; officers in, 28, 32–3;
  as source of officers, 33, 149; role
  (1914), 26–9, 122; second-line
  divisions of, 26, 29; quality of, 29–
  31; looked down on by regulars, 144
Tipperary, 60
Thomson, A.G., commandant at
  Etaples, 67–9, 78; removed
  therefrom, 76, 81
Tillett, B., 40
Titles, hereditary and courtesy, 9, 15,
  142
Toplis, P., alleged role of, 153
Trade unions, members of, 10, 35, 37;
  leaders of, 39, 46; spirit of, in army,
  95
Traditions, of Old Army, 10, 80, 102,
  137; of Old Contemptibles, 95
Training, in Wellington's time, 20;
  during war, 30, 31, 44, 45, 64–5, 72,
  155
Transport, Director of, *see* Director of
  Transport
Transylvanians, in Austro-Hungarian
  army, 47
Tyneside Irish Brigade, 55

Ulster, 56
Ulster Volunteers, 52–4, 148
Unions *see* Trade Unions, Councils
Universities, 13, 29, 33, 145
'Usages of War', 148

Valdelievre Returned Store Depot, BEF,
  functions of, 157–8; discontent at,
  93–6, 113, 119
Vandalism, 96, 103–4, 110, 123, 163–4
Vane, Sir F., 55
Vaughan, J., at Kantara, 165
Vendroux depot, BEF, role of, 158; unrest
  at 96, 113, 157–8
Venereal disease, 147, 164
Victimization, 94, 96, 106, 110–11, 127,
  132
Volunteer Movement, nature and
  efficiency of, 143; superseded, 24
Volunteering, as basis of British army,
  23; during war, 27, 29, 35–7; 56; in
  Ireland, 54, 56; Haig laments decline
  of, 74

Wales, as source of recruits, 35, 44–5,
  54; as scene of civil unrest, 37;
  slighted by Kitchener, 45
War Office, during Boer War, 23; under
  Haldane, 24; at outbreak of war, 26;
  does not control conscription, 37;
  wants Ulster Volunteers, 53; does not
  want Irish Volunteers, 53, 55;
  distrusts Irish, 56, 60; dilutes Irish
  regiments, 62; handles Easter Rising,
  59, 150; role of, in demobilization,
  100, 111; deals with unrest in
  England, 105–6, 109, 111, 163;
  learns of unrest in EEF, 122–5, 128–
  31
Ward, S., on discontent in army, 131
Wassa, battle of the, 163–4
Watkins, C., at Kantara, 165
'War weariness', 77, 82
Webster, H., at Kantara, 165
Welch Regiment, 44
Wellington, duke of, 14, 20
West Indies, contribution of, 84
Whitehall, demonstrations in, 106–7,
  112; *see also* War Office
Wild, A., executed, 41–2
Williams, H., witnesses strike, 128–9,
  165; war service of, 164

Williamson, Lt Col., 59
Williamson, H., fictionalizes Etaples mutiny, 152
Williamson, O., 129
Wilson, Sir H., 62, 87, 101, 111
Wiltshire Regiment, 107
Wintrop, J., at Kantara, 165
Wolseley, Lord, 54
Women, with BEF, 159; men doing work of, 109; see also Kitchener, Queen Mary's Army Auxiliary Corps
Women's Legion, 163
Women's Police, 158
Wood, W., death of, 67, 73; reputation of, 67, 73, 153

Woolwich, 141
Working class, antipathy of, to army, 9–10, 19, 37, 103; army's distrust of, 9–10, 19, 33–5, 39, 55, 75; brutalizing life of, 34–5, 139; welcomes war, 46; enters army, 34–7; is blamed for Etaples mutiny, 74–5, 80
Wroughton, J., visits Etaples, 70; visits Calais, 88, 97, 113–14, 117

Yeomanry, composition and role of, 28, 143; reformed, 24
Ypres, first battle of, 26; third battle of, 75, 83, 139–40, 153